GARFIELD

BACON ME DROOL

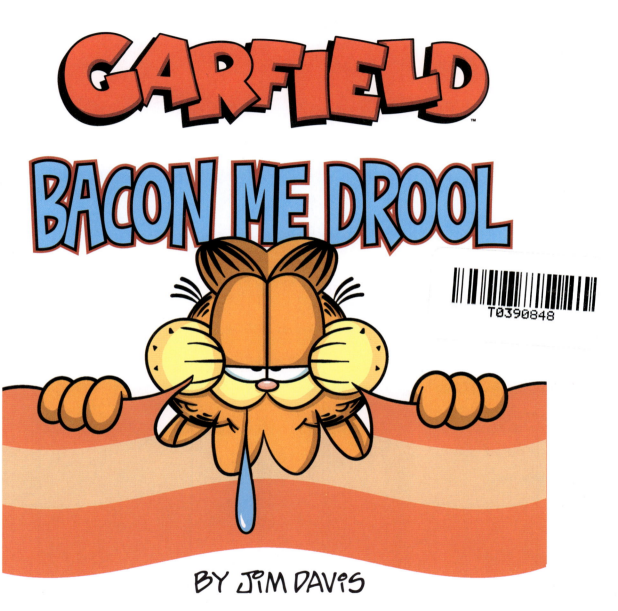

BY JIM DAVIS

Random House Worlds • New York

A Random House Worlds Trade Paperback Original

Copyright © 2025 by PAWS, Inc. All Rights Reserved. "GARFIELD" and the GARFIELD characters are trademarks of PAWS, Inc.
NICKELODEON is a Trademark of Viacom International, Inc.

Based on the Garfield® characters created by Jim Davis

Published in the United States by Random House Worlds, an imprint of Random House,
a division of Penguin Random House LLC, New York.

RANDOM HOUSE is a registered trademark, and RANDOM HOUSE WORLDS and colophon are trademarks of Penguin Random House LLC.

All of the comics in this work have been previously published.

ISBN 978-0-593-87350-2
Ebook ISBN 978-0-593-87351-9

Printed in China on acid-free paper

randomhousebooks.com

T#1317546

9 8 7 6 5 4 3 2 1

GARFIELD'S MORSELS OF WISDOM
Amusing musings from America's furriest philosopher

The gut wants what the gut wants.

Good things come to those who bake.

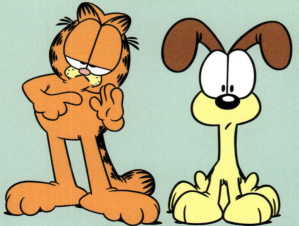

It's not whether you win or lose, it's how you place the blame.

Yawning should count as exercise.

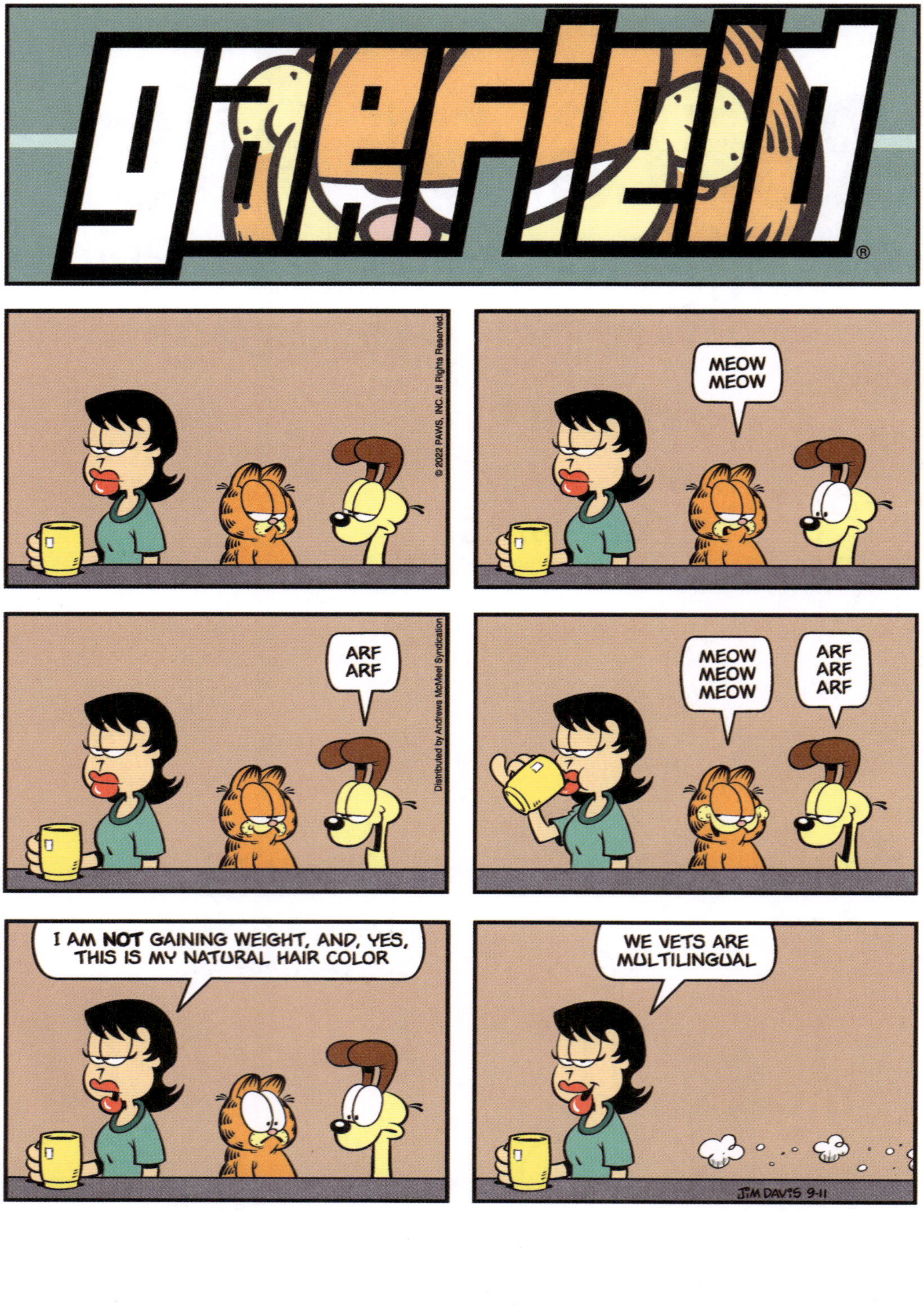
© 2022 PAWS, INC. All Rights Reserved.
MEOW MEOW
ARF ARF
Distributed by Andrews McMeel Syndication
MEOW MEOW MEOW
ARF ARF ARF
I AM **NOT** GAINING WEIGHT, AND, YES, THIS IS MY NATURAL HAIR COLOR
WE VETS ARE MULTILINGUAL
JIM DAVIS 9-11

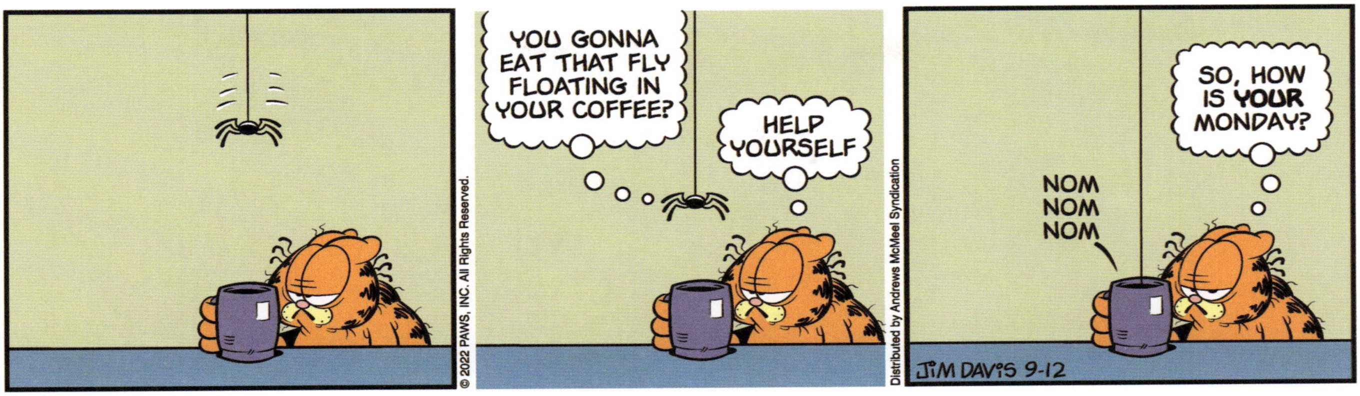
YOU GONNA EAT THAT FLY FLOATING IN YOUR COFFEE?
HELP YOURSELF
NOM NOM NOM
SO, HOW IS **YOUR** MONDAY?
JIM DAVIS 9-12
© 2022 PAWS, INC. All Rights Reserved.
Distributed by Andrews McMeel Syndication

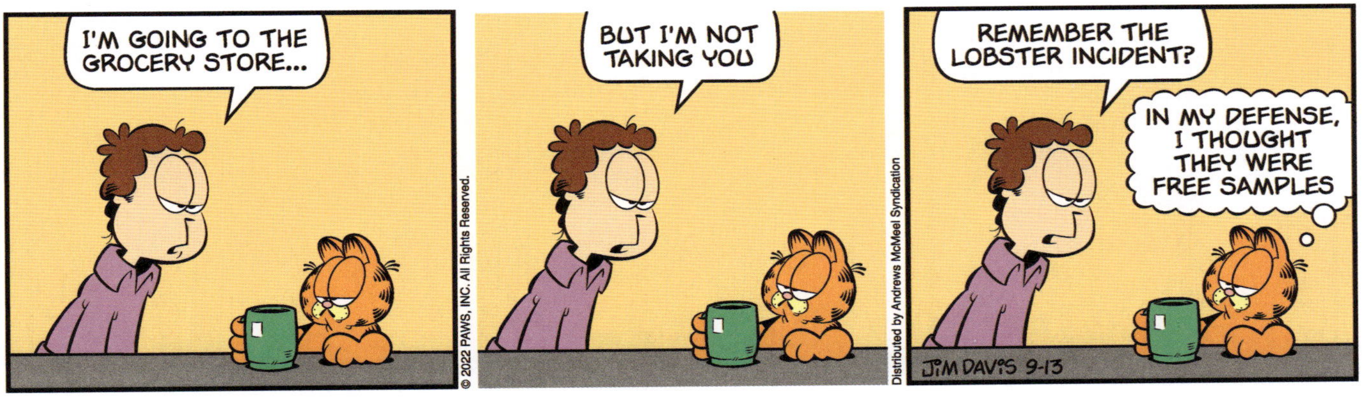
I'M GOING TO THE GROCERY STORE...
BUT I'M NOT TAKING YOU
REMEMBER THE LOBSTER INCIDENT?
IN MY DEFENSE, I THOUGHT THEY WERE FREE SAMPLES
JIM DAVIS 9-13
© 2022 PAWS, INC. All Rights Reserved.
Distributed by Andrews McMeel Syndication

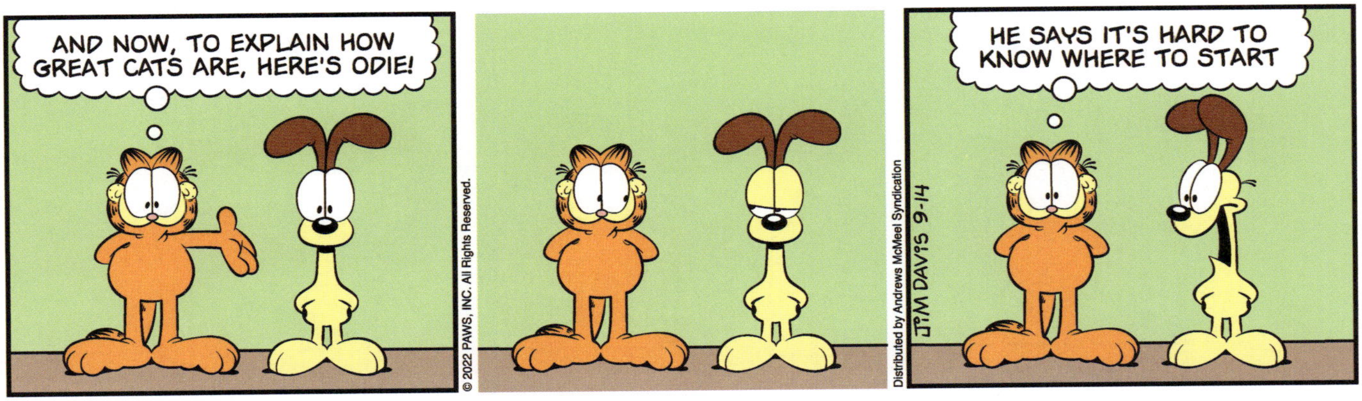
AND NOW, TO EXPLAIN HOW GREAT CATS ARE, HERE'S ODIE!
HE SAYS IT'S HARD TO KNOW WHERE TO START
JIM DAVIS 9-14
© 2022 PAWS, INC. All Rights Reserved.
Distributed by Andrews McMeel Syndication

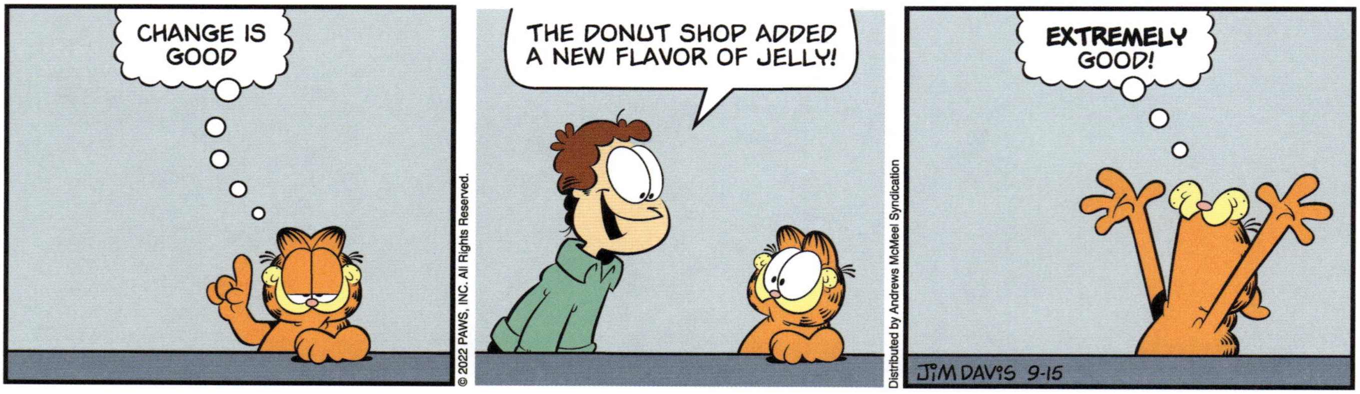
CHANGE IS GOOD
© 2022 PAWS, INC. All Rights Reserved.
THE DONUT SHOP ADDED A NEW FLAVOR OF JELLY!
Distributed by Andrews McMeel Syndication
EXTREMELY GOOD!
JIM DAVIS 9-15

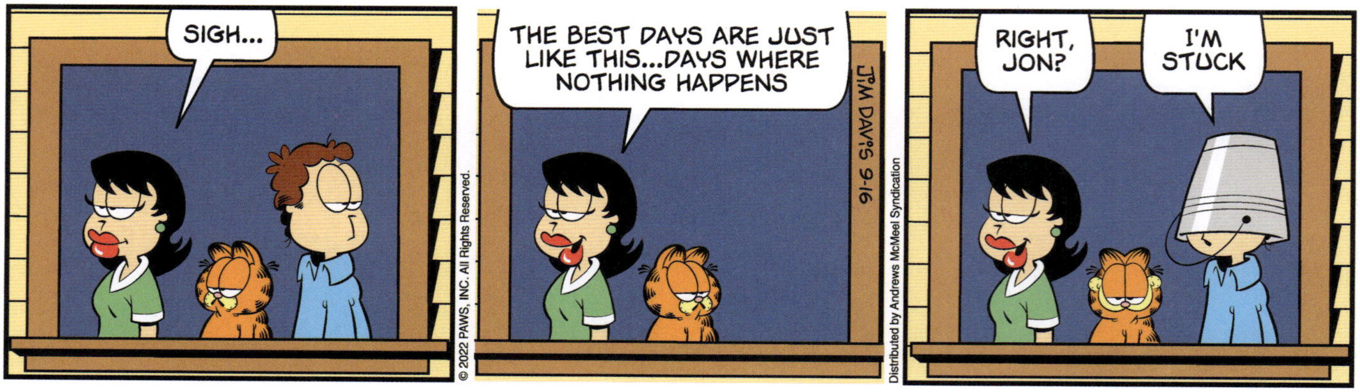
SIGH...
© 2022 PAWS, INC. All Rights Reserved.
THE BEST DAYS ARE JUST LIKE THIS...DAYS WHERE NOTHING HAPPENS
JIM DAVIS 9-16
Distributed by Andrews McMeel Syndication
RIGHT, JON?
I'M STUCK

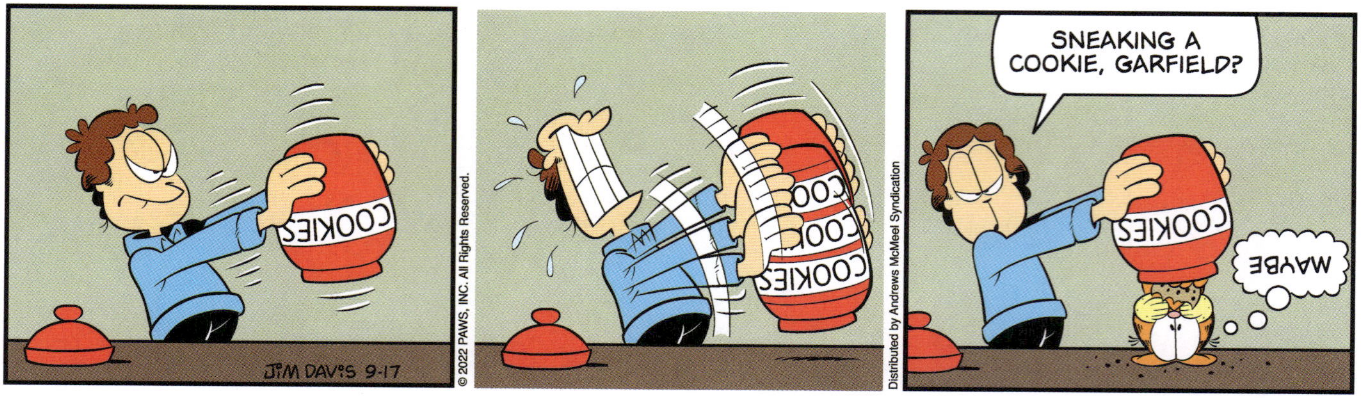
COOKIES
JIM DAVIS 9-17
© 2022 PAWS, INC. All Rights Reserved.
COOKIES
Distributed by Andrews McMeel Syndication
SNEAKING A COOKIE, GARFIELD?
COOKIES
MAYBE

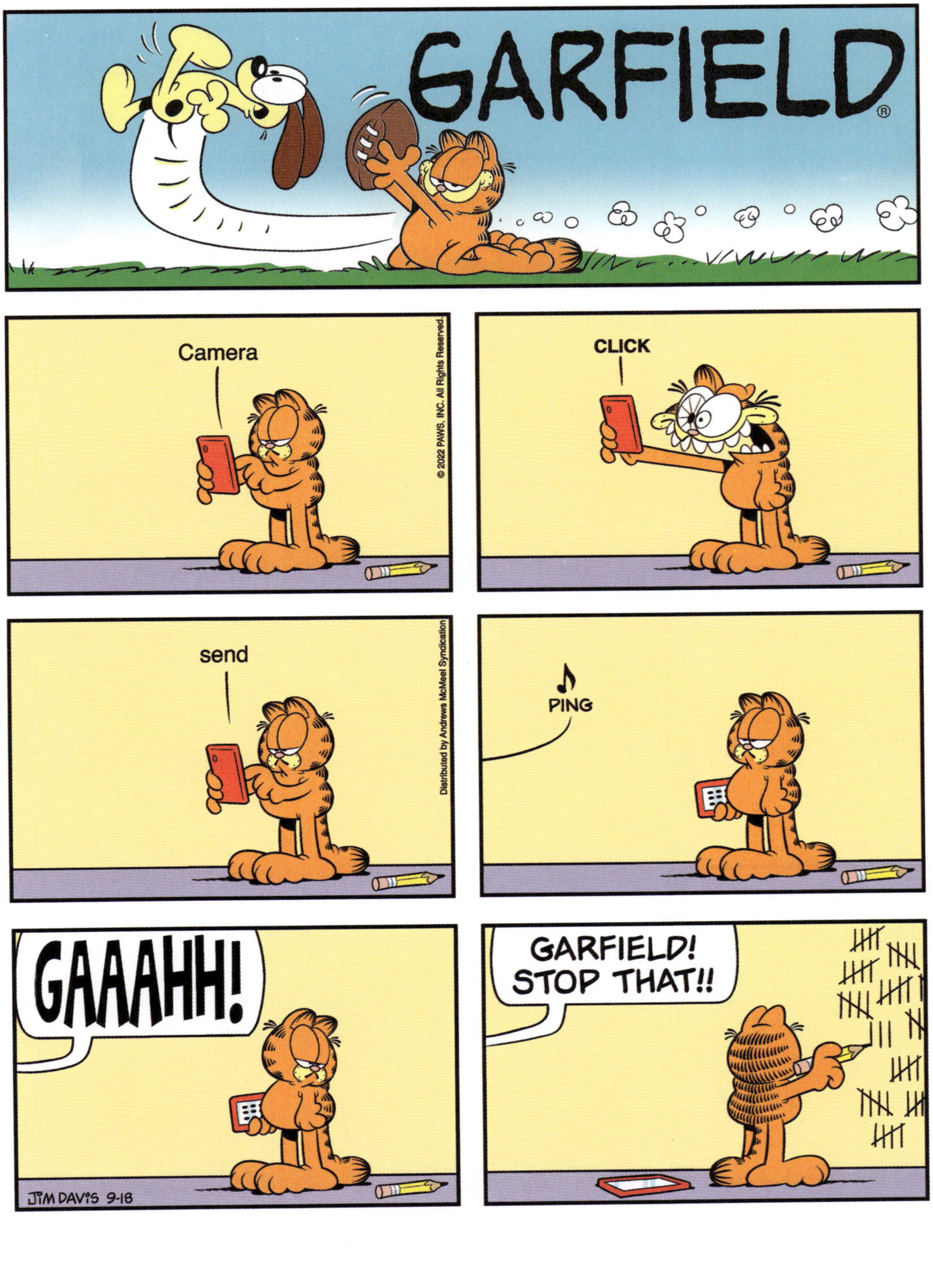
GARFIELD
© 2022 PAWS, INC. All Rights Reserved.
Distributed by Andrews McMeel Syndication
Camera
CLICK
send
PING
GAAAHH!
GARFIELD! STOP THAT!!
JIM DAVIS 9-18

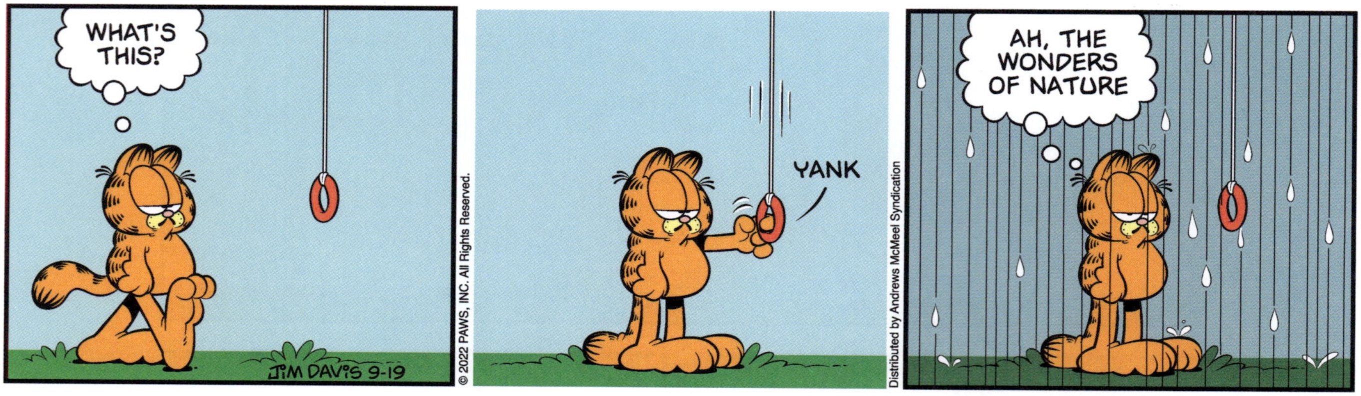
WHAT'S THIS?
YANK
AH, THE WONDERS OF NATURE
JIM DAVIS 9-19
© 2022 PAWS, INC. All Rights Reserved.
Distributed by Andrews McMeel Syndication

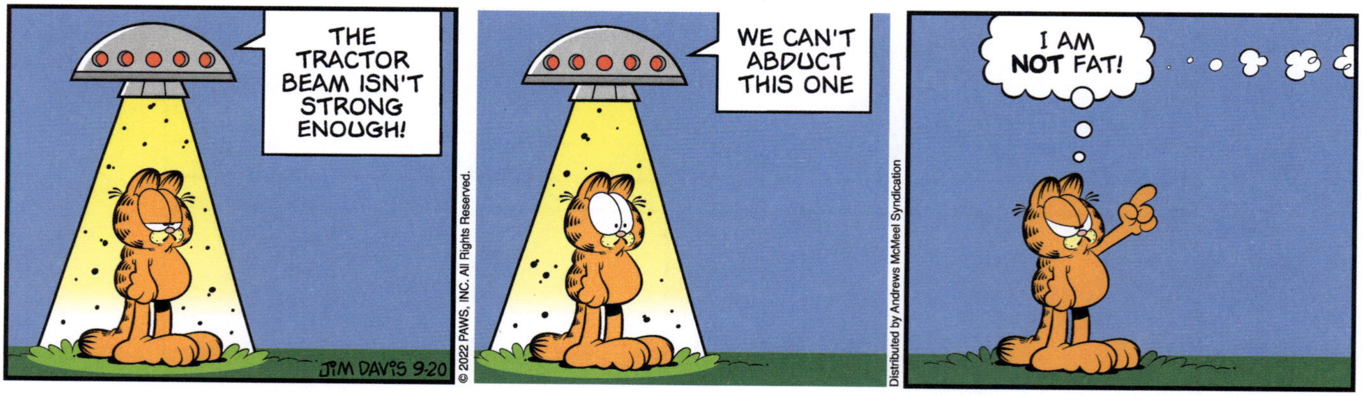
THE TRACTOR BEAM ISN'T STRONG ENOUGH!
WE CAN'T ABDUCT THIS ONE
I AM **NOT** FAT!
JIM DAVIS 9-20
© 2022 PAWS, INC. All Rights Reserved.
Distributed by Andrews McMeel Syndication

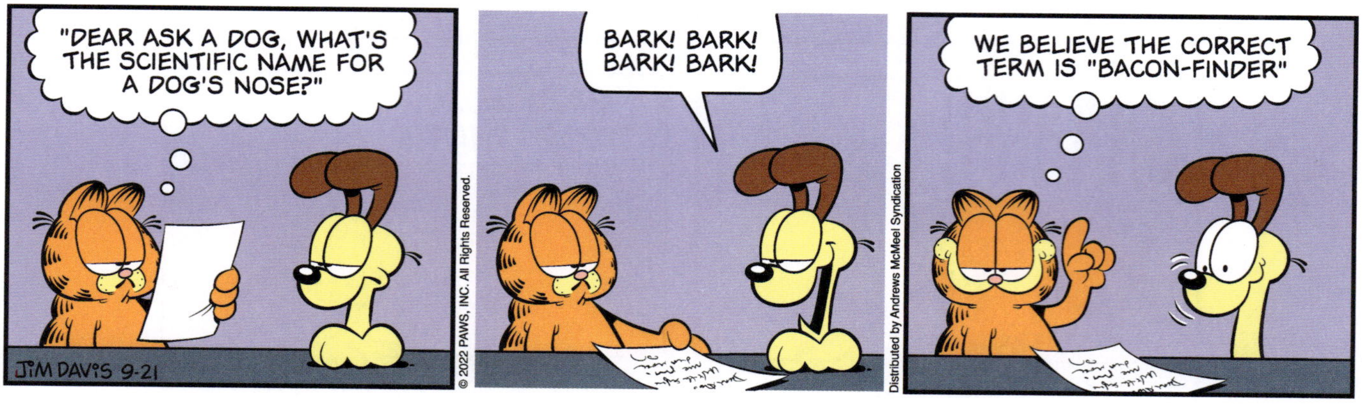
"DEAR ASK A DOG, WHAT'S THE SCIENTIFIC NAME FOR A DOG'S NOSE?"
BARK! BARK! BARK! BARK!
WE BELIEVE THE CORRECT TERM IS "BACON-FINDER"
JIM DAVIS 9-21
© 2022 PAWS, INC. All Rights Reserved.
Distributed by Andrews McMeel Syndication

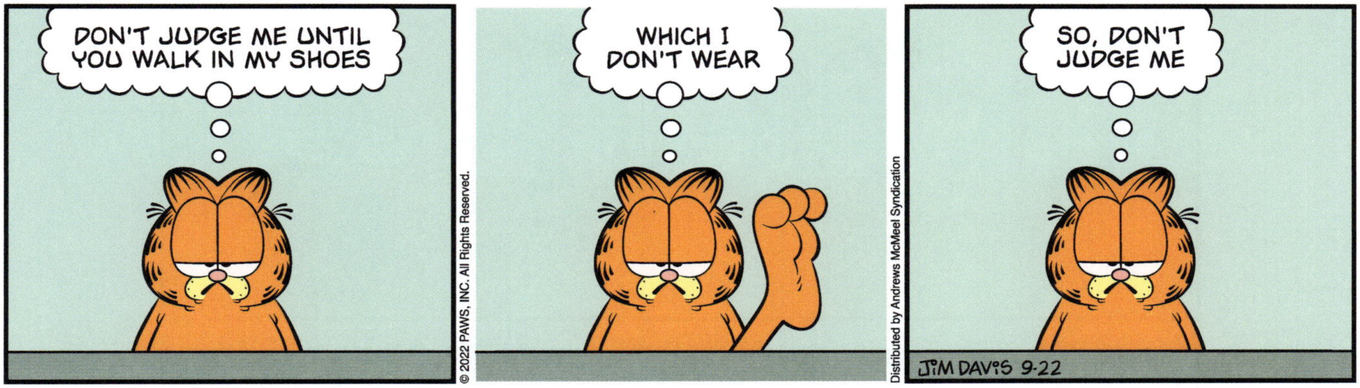
DON'T JUDGE ME UNTIL YOU WALK IN MY SHOES
WHICH I DON'T WEAR
SO, DON'T JUDGE ME
© 2022 PAWS, INC. All Rights Reserved.
Distributed by Andrews McMeel Syndication
JIM DAVIS 9-22

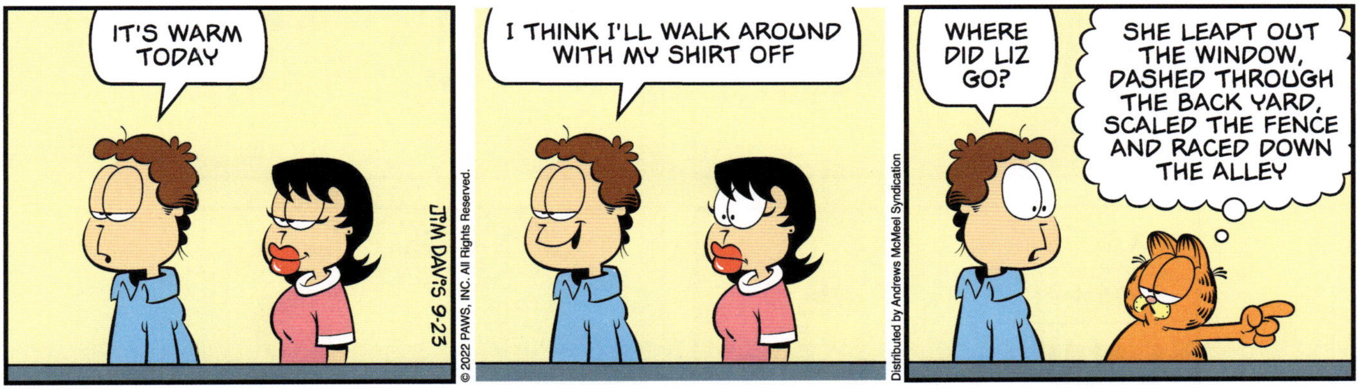
IT'S WARM TODAY
I THINK I'LL WALK AROUND WITH MY SHIRT OFF
WHERE DID LIZ GO?
SHE LEAPT OUT THE WINDOW, DASHED THROUGH THE BACK YARD, SCALED THE FENCE AND RACED DOWN THE ALLEY
JIM DAVIS 9-23
© 2022 PAWS, INC. All Rights Reserved.
Distributed by Andrews McMeel Syndication

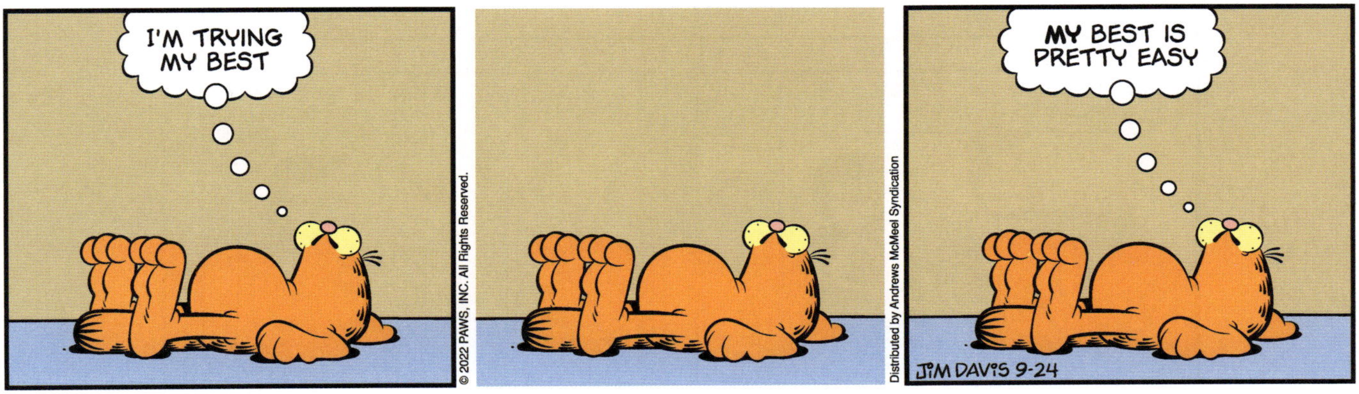
I'M TRYING MY BEST
MY BEST IS PRETTY EASY
© 2022 PAWS, INC. All Rights Reserved.
Distributed by Andrews McMeel Syndication
JIM DAVIS 9-24

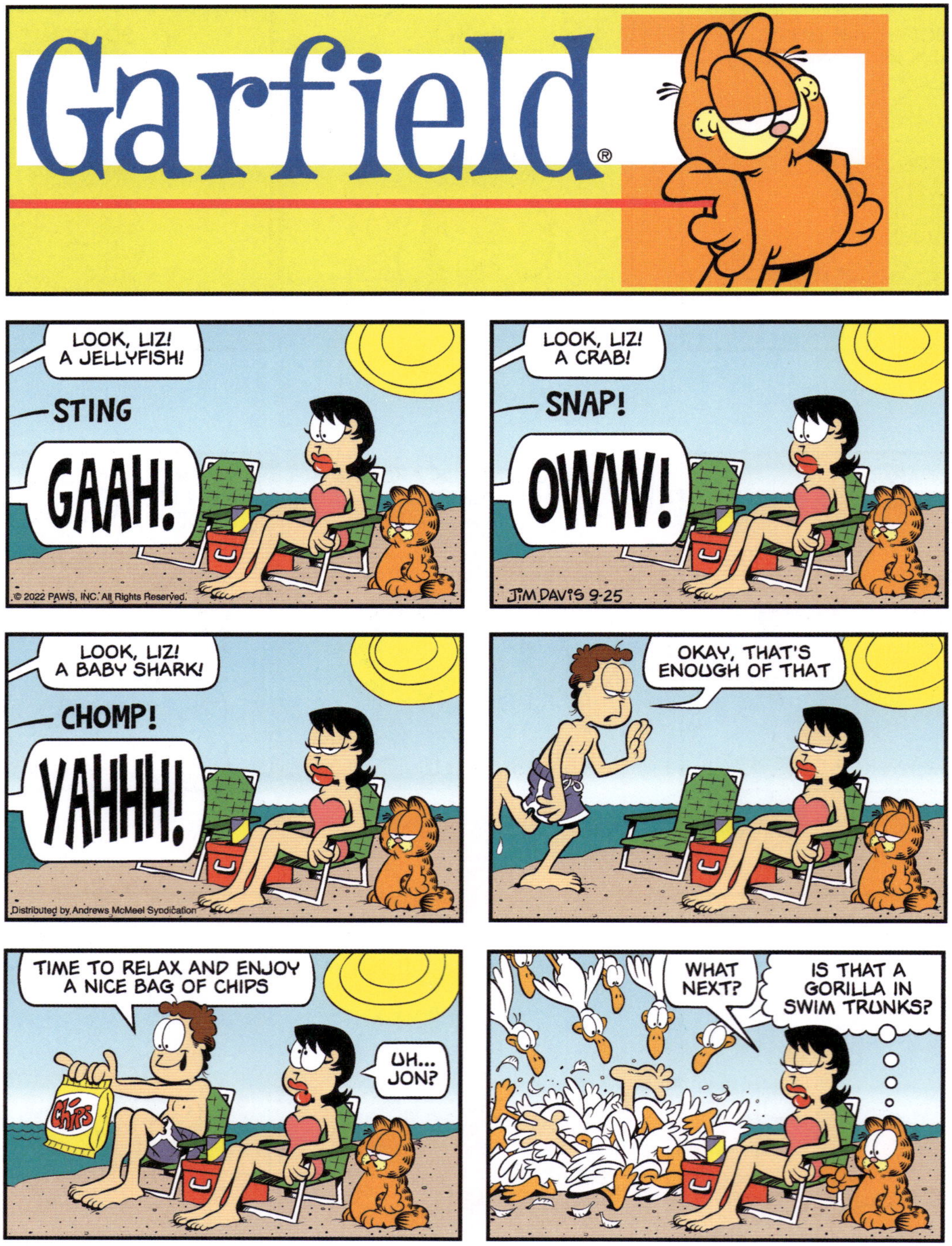
Garfield®
LOOK, LIZ! A JELLYFISH!
STING
GAAH!
© 2022 PAWS, INC. All Rights Reserved.
LOOK, LIZ! A CRAB!
SNAP!
OWW!
JIM DAVIS 9-25
LOOK, LIZ! A BABY SHARK!
CHOMP!
YAHHH!
Distributed by Andrews McMeel Syndication
OKAY, THAT'S ENOUGH OF THAT
TIME TO RELAX AND ENJOY A NICE BAG OF CHIPS
CHIPS
UH... JON?
WHAT NEXT?
IS THAT A GORILLA IN SWIM TRUNKS?

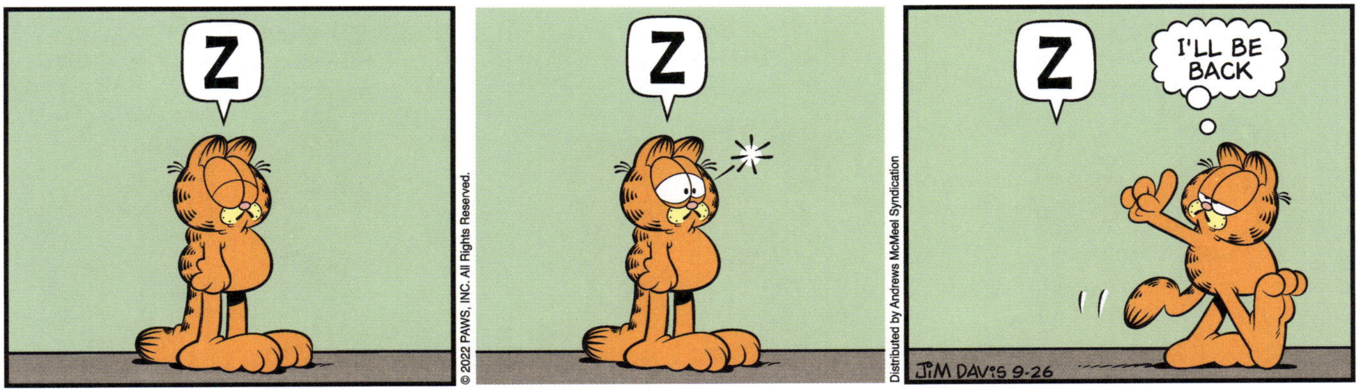
Z
Z
Z
I'LL BE BACK
© 2022 PAWS, INC. All Rights Reserved.
Distributed by Andrews McMeel Syndication
JIM DAVIS 9-26

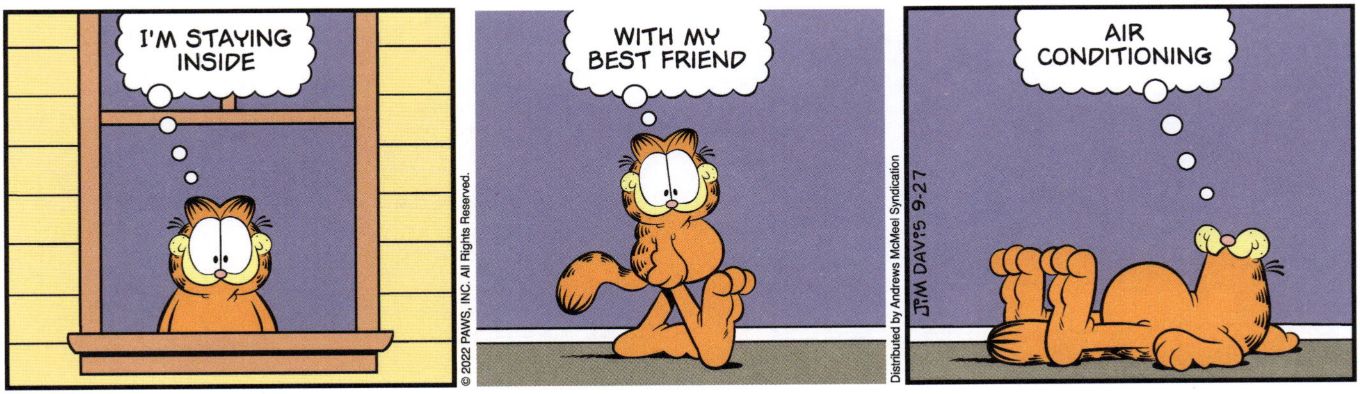
I'M STAYING INSIDE
WITH MY BEST FRIEND
AIR CONDITIONING
© 2022 PAWS, INC. All Rights Reserved.
Distributed by Andrews McMeel Syndication
JIM DAVIS 9-27

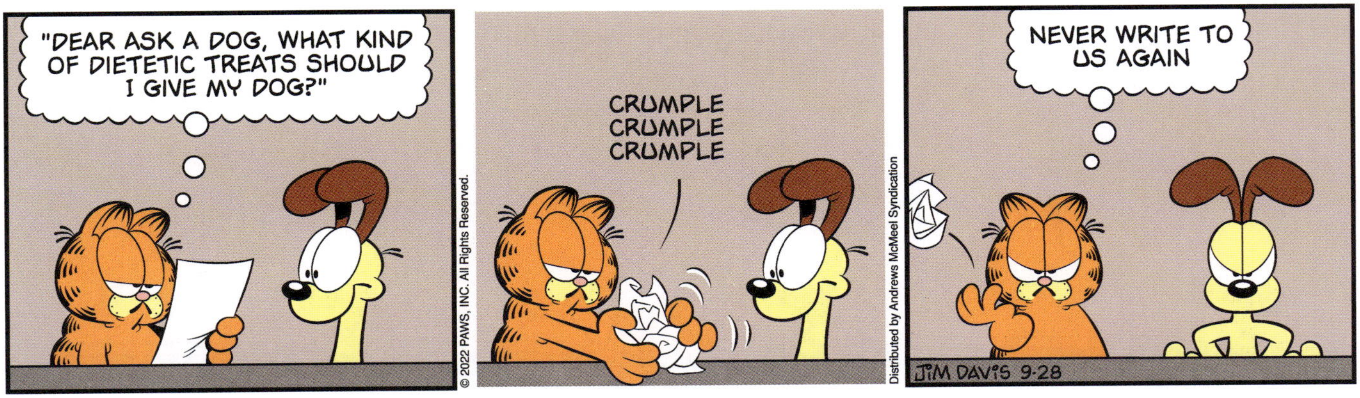
"DEAR ASK A DOG, WHAT KIND OF DIETETIC TREATS SHOULD I GIVE MY DOG?"
CRUMPLE
CRUMPLE
CRUMPLE
NEVER WRITE TO US AGAIN
© 2022 PAWS, INC. All Rights Reserved.
Distributed by Andrews McMeel Syndication
JIM DAVIS 9-28

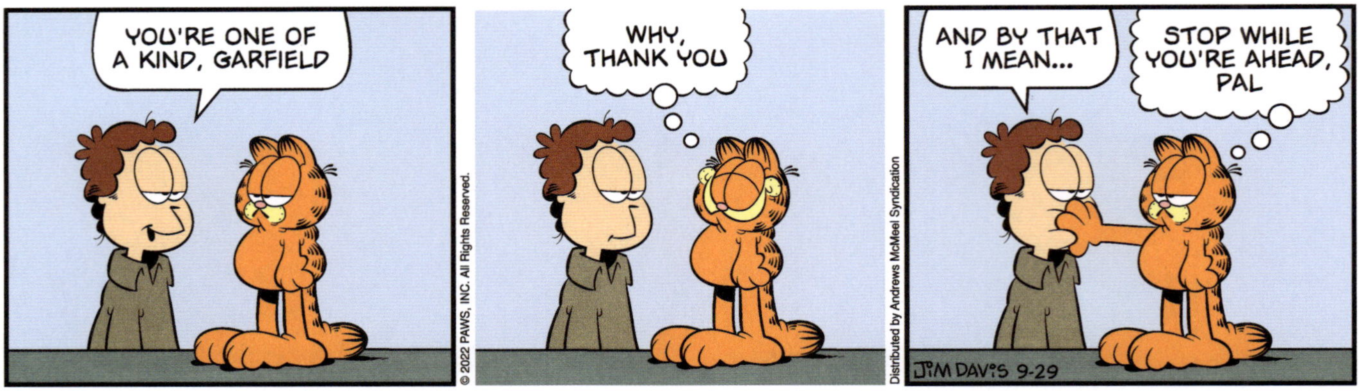
YOU'RE ONE OF A KIND, GARFIELD
WHY, THANK YOU
AND BY THAT I MEAN...
STOP WHILE YOU'RE AHEAD, PAL
© 2022 PAWS, INC. All Rights Reserved.
Distributed by Andrews McMeel Syndication
JIM DAVIS 9-29

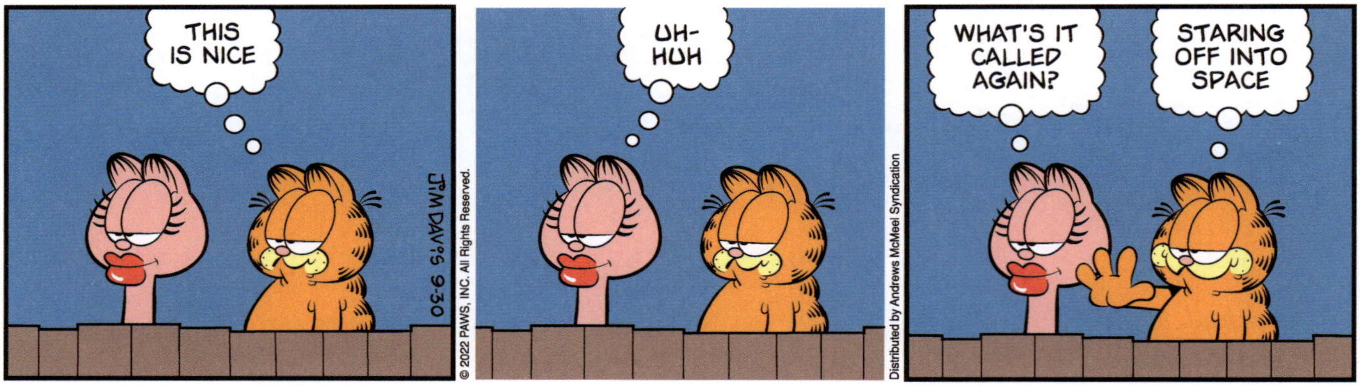
THIS IS NICE
JIM DAVIS 9-30
UH-HUH
WHAT'S IT CALLED AGAIN?
STARING OFF INTO SPACE
© 2022 PAWS, INC. All Rights Reserved.
Distributed by Andrews McMeel Syndication

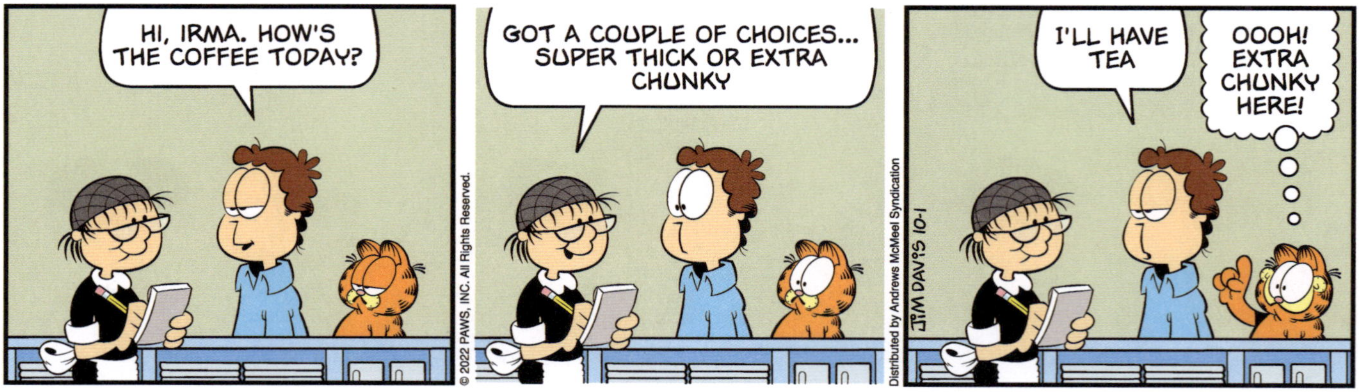
HI, IRMA. HOW'S THE COFFEE TODAY?
GOT A COUPLE OF CHOICES... SUPER THICK OR EXTRA CHUNKY
I'LL HAVE TEA
OOOH! EXTRA CHUNKY HERE!
JIM DAVIS 10-1
© 2022 PAWS, INC. All Rights Reserved.
Distributed by Andrews McMeel Syndication

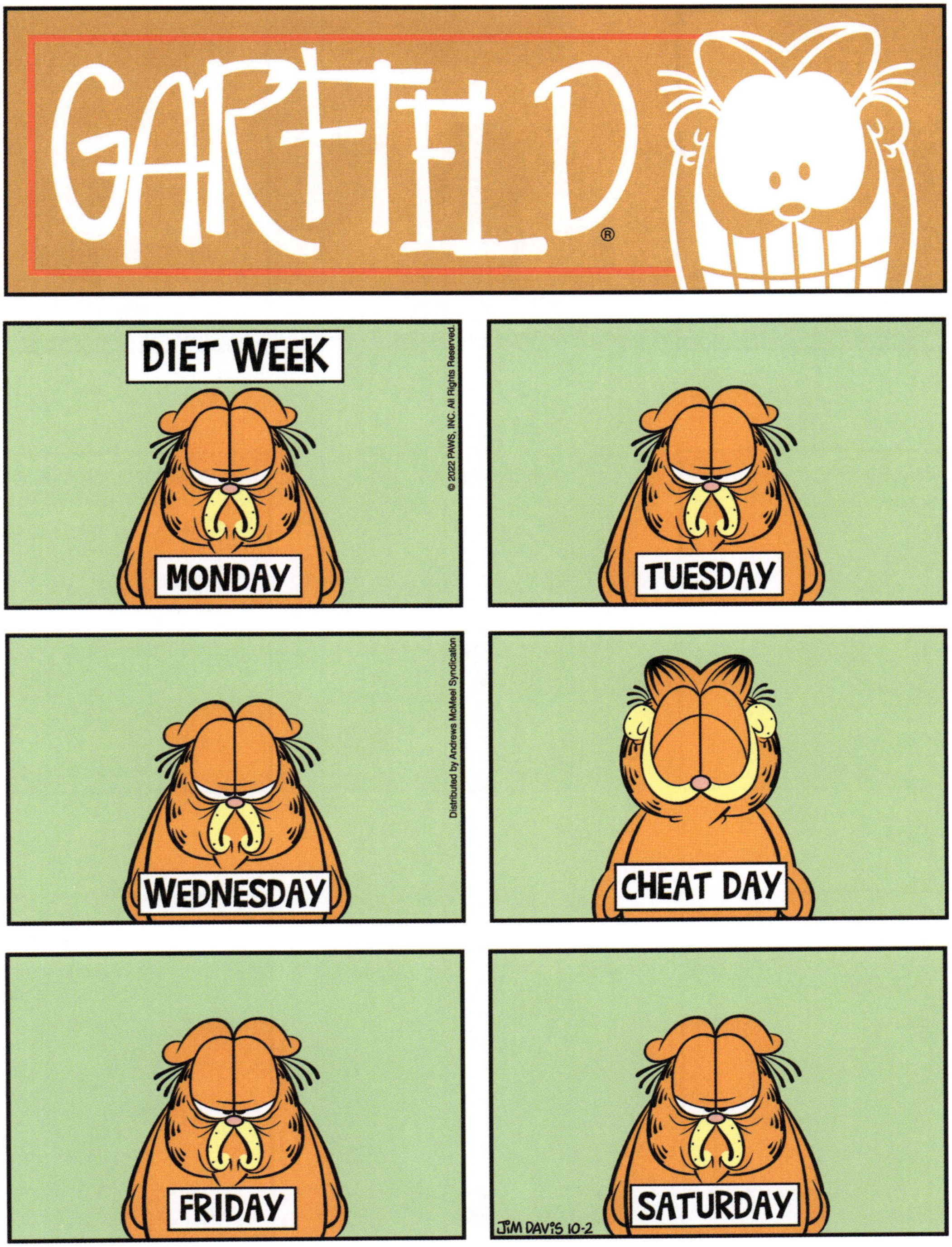
GARFIELD®
DIET WEEK
© 2022 PAWS, INC. All Rights Reserved.
MONDAY
TUESDAY
Distributed by Andrews McMeel Syndication
WEDNESDAY
CHEAT DAY
FRIDAY
JIM DAVIS 10-2
SATURDAY

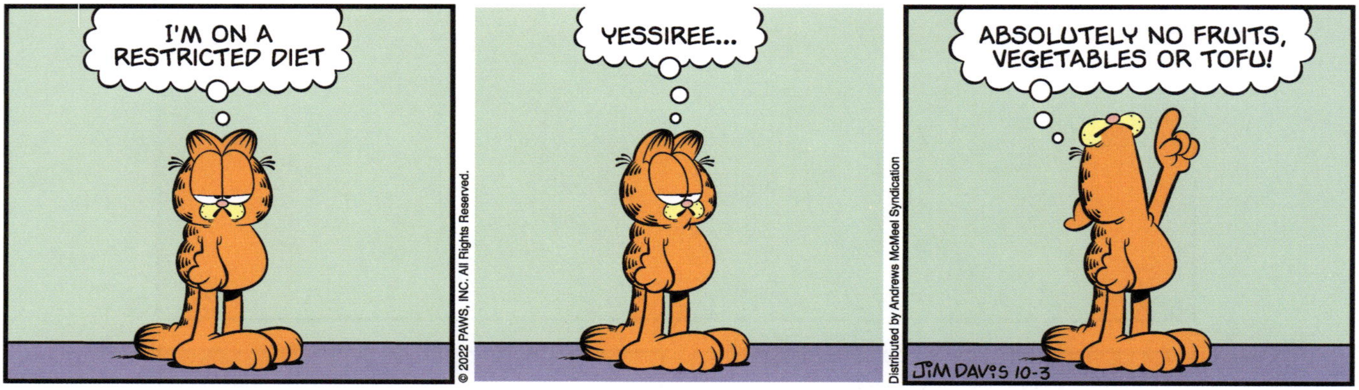
I'M ON A RESTRICTED DIET
YESSIREE...
ABSOLUTELY NO FRUITS, VEGETABLES OR TOFU!
© 2022 PAWS, INC. All Rights Reserved.
Distributed by Andrews McMeel Syndication
JIM DAVIS 10-3

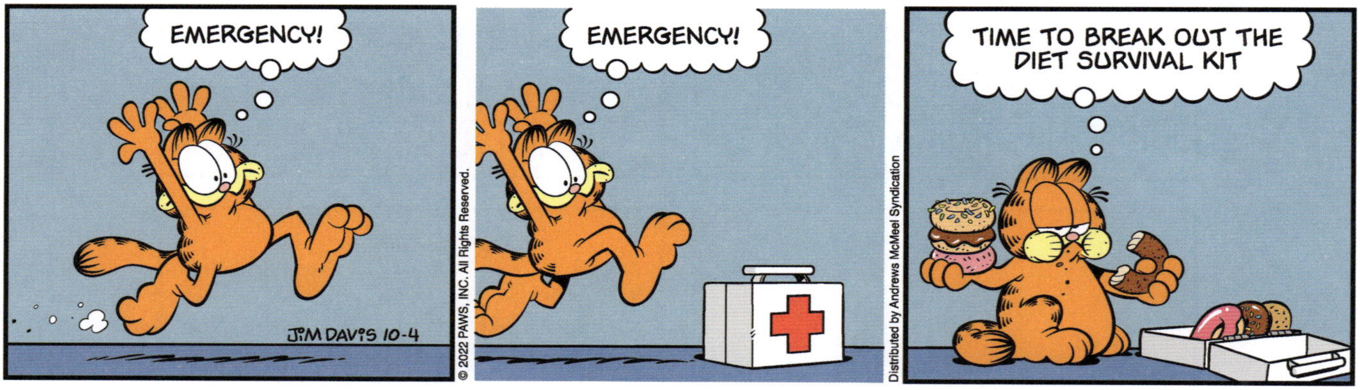
EMERGENCY!
EMERGENCY!
TIME TO BREAK OUT THE DIET SURVIVAL KIT
JIM DAVIS 10-4
© 2022 PAWS, INC. All Rights Reserved.
Distributed by Andrews McMeel Syndication

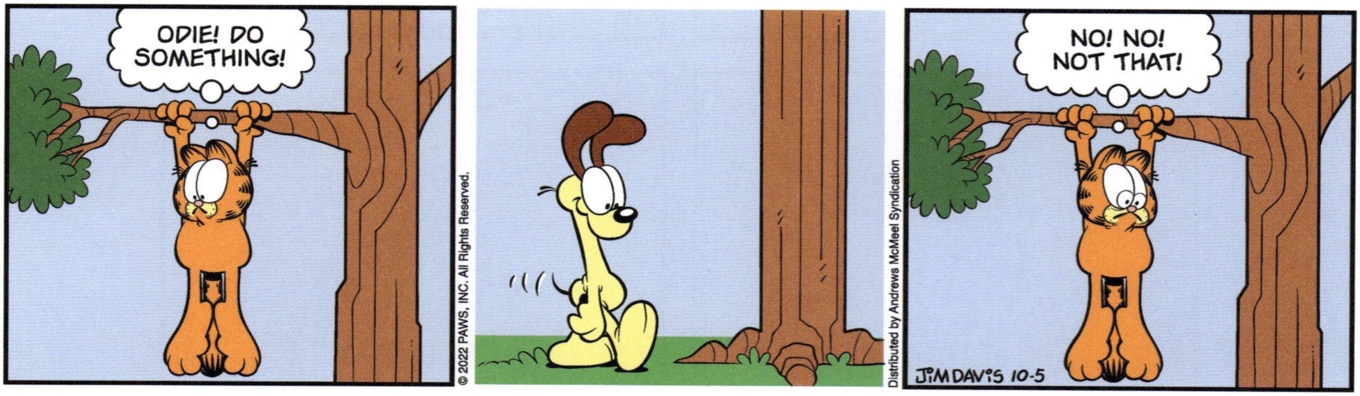
ODIE! DO SOMETHING!
NO! NO! NOT THAT!
© 2022 PAWS, INC. All Rights Reserved.
Distributed by Andrews McMeel Syndication
JIM DAVIS 10-5

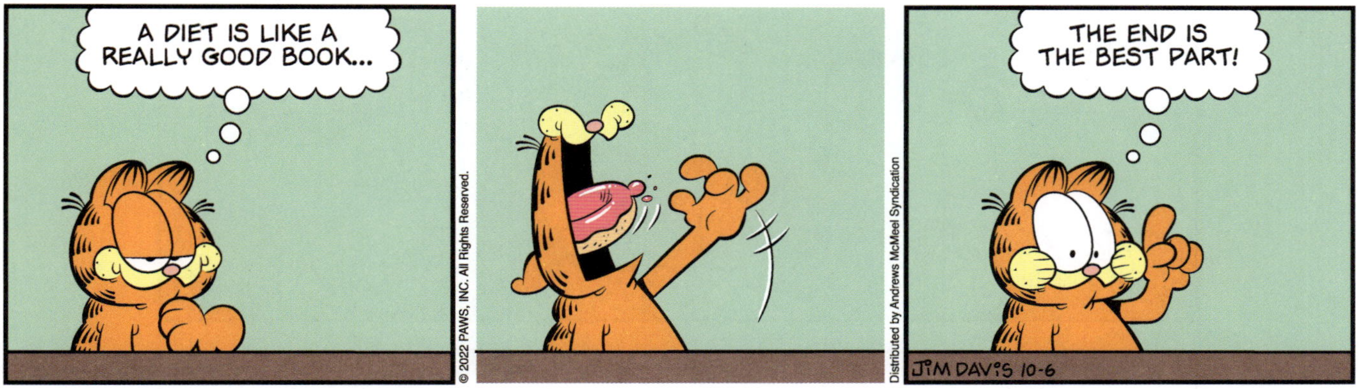
A DIET IS LIKE A REALLY GOOD BOOK...
THE END IS THE BEST PART!
© 2022 PAWS, INC. All Rights Reserved.
Distributed by Andrews McMeel Syndication
JIM DAVIS 10-6

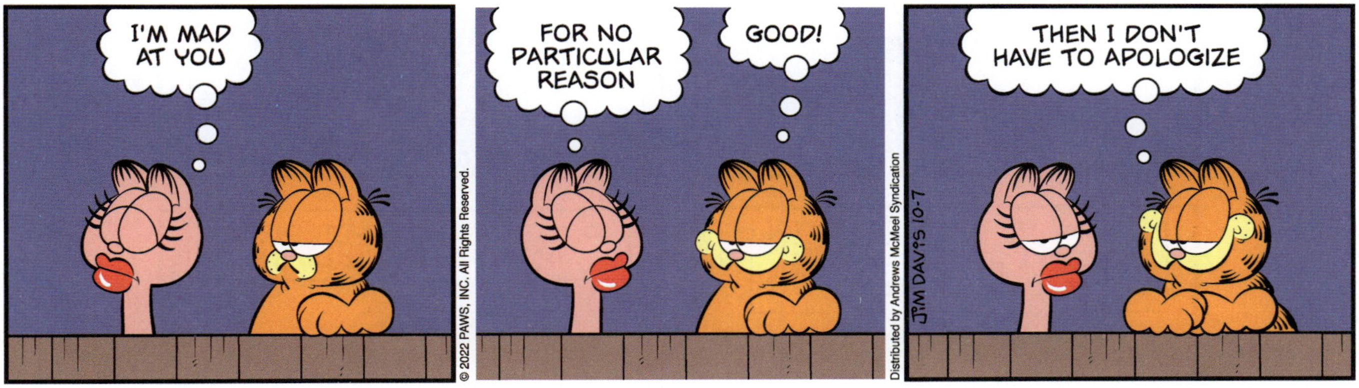
I'M MAD AT YOU
FOR NO PARTICULAR REASON
GOOD!
THEN I DON'T HAVE TO APOLOGIZE
© 2022 PAWS, INC. All Rights Reserved.
Distributed by Andrews McMeel Syndication
JIM DAVIS 10-7

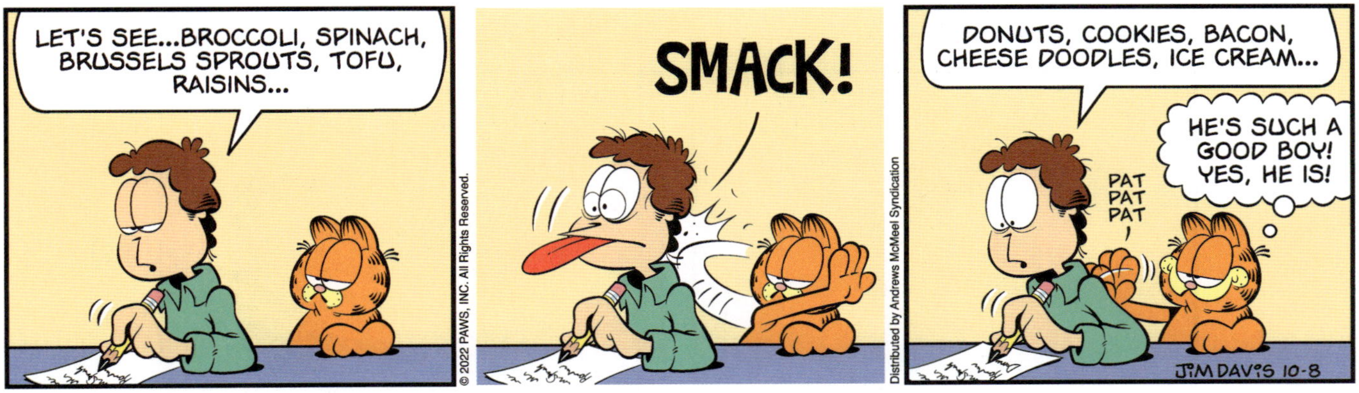
LET'S SEE...BROCCOLI, SPINACH, BRUSSELS SPROUTS, TOFU, RAISINS...
SMACK!
DONUTS, COOKIES, BACON, CHEESE DOODLES, ICE CREAM...
PAT PAT PAT
HE'S SUCH A GOOD BOY! YES, HE IS!
© 2022 PAWS, INC. All Rights Reserved.
Distributed by Andrews McMeel Syndication
JIM DAVIS 10-8

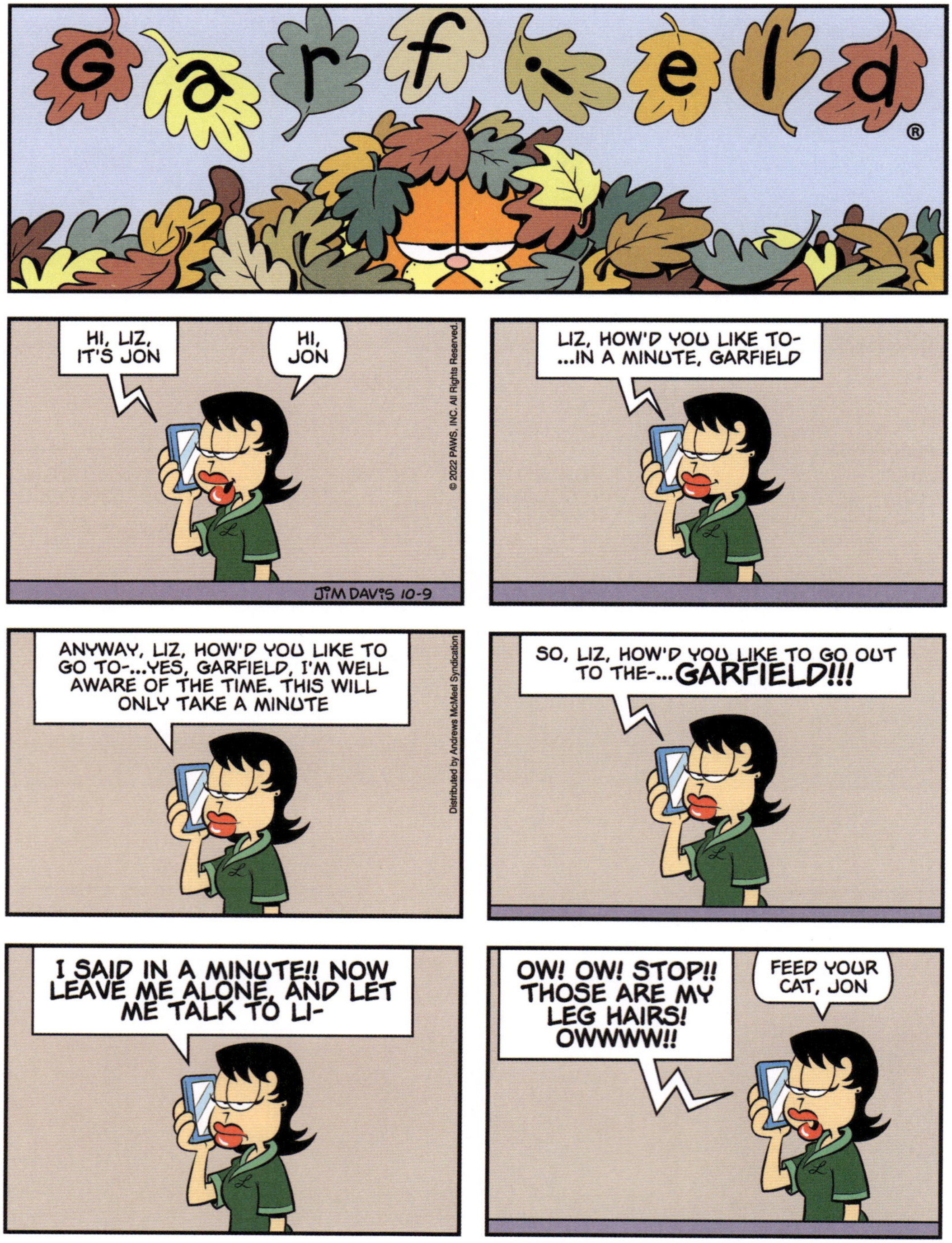
Garfield®
HI, LIZ, IT'S JON
HI, JON
© 2022 PAWS, INC. All Rights Reserved.
JIM DAVIS 10-9
LIZ, HOW'D YOU LIKE TO- ...IN A MINUTE, GARFIELD
ANYWAY, LIZ, HOW'D YOU LIKE TO GO TO-...YES, GARFIELD, I'M WELL AWARE OF THE TIME. THIS WILL ONLY TAKE A MINUTE
Distributed by Andrews McMeel Syndication
SO, LIZ, HOW'D YOU LIKE TO GO OUT TO THE-...GARFIELD!!!
I SAID IN A MINUTE!! NOW LEAVE ME ALONE, AND LET ME TALK TO LI-
OW! OW! STOP!! THOSE ARE MY LEG HAIRS! OWWWW!!
FEED YOUR CAT, JON

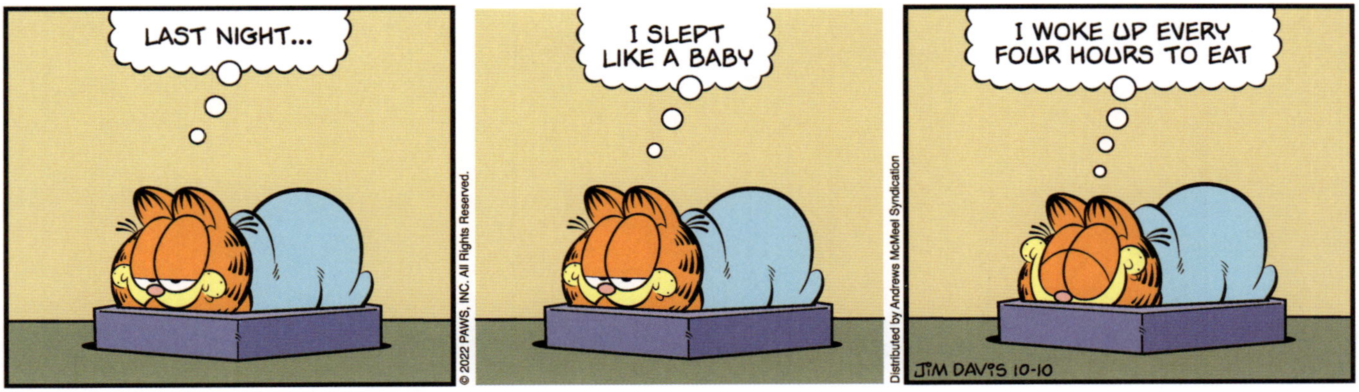
LAST NIGHT...
I SLEPT LIKE A BABY
I WOKE UP EVERY FOUR HOURS TO EAT
© 2022 PAWS, INC. All Rights Reserved.
Distributed by Andrews McMeel Syndication
JIM DAVIS 10-10

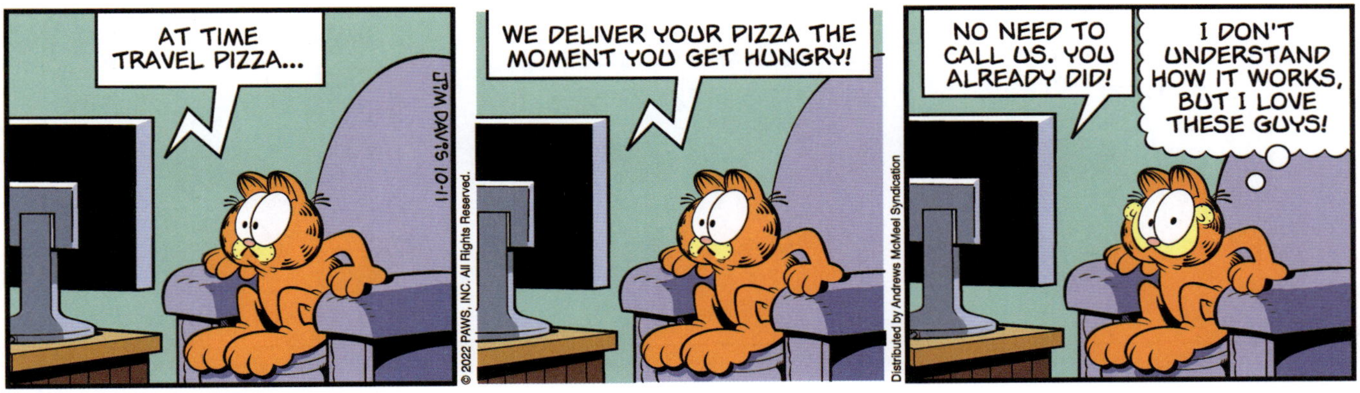
AT TIME TRAVEL PIZZA...
JIM DAVIS 10-11
WE DELIVER YOUR PIZZA THE MOMENT YOU GET HUNGRY!
NO NEED TO CALL US. YOU ALREADY DID!
I DON'T UNDERSTAND HOW IT WORKS, BUT I LOVE THESE GUYS!
© 2022 PAWS, INC. All Rights Reserved.
Distributed by Andrews McMeel Syndication

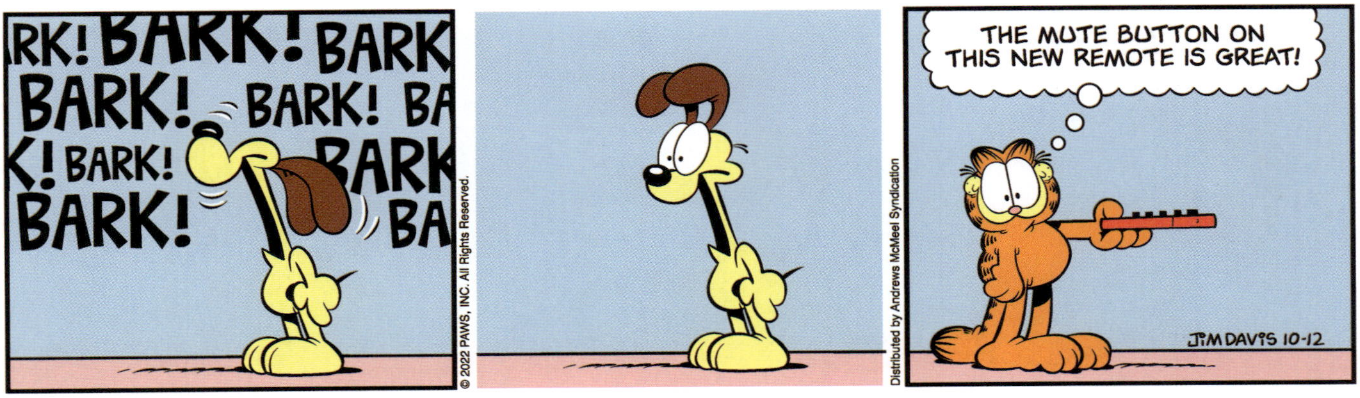
BARK! BARK! BARK! BARK!
THE MUTE BUTTON ON THIS NEW REMOTE IS GREAT!
© 2022 PAWS, INC. All Rights Reserved.
Distributed by Andrews McMeel Syndication
JIM DAVIS 10-12

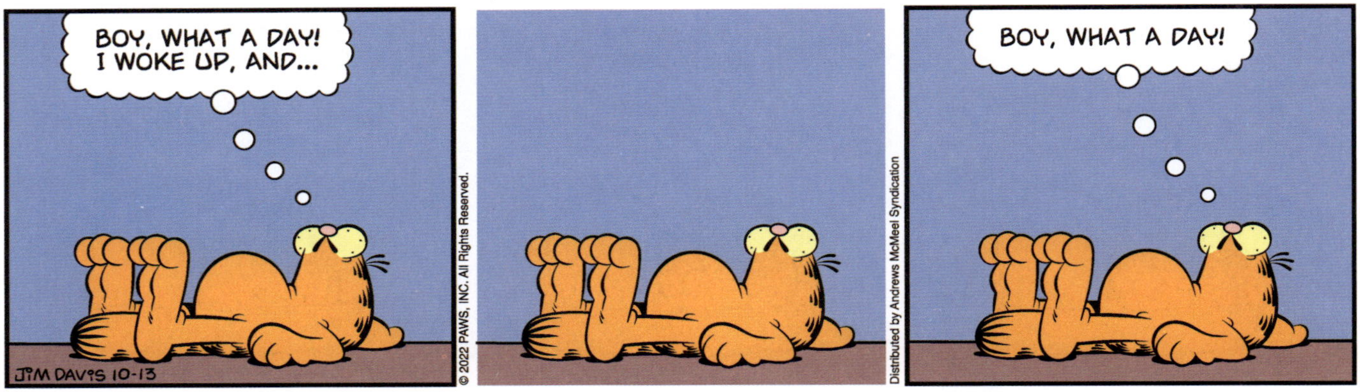
BOY, WHAT A DAY! I WOKE UP, AND...
BOY, WHAT A DAY!
JIM DAVIS 10-13
© 2022 PAWS, INC. All Rights Reserved.
Distributed by Andrews McMeel Syndication

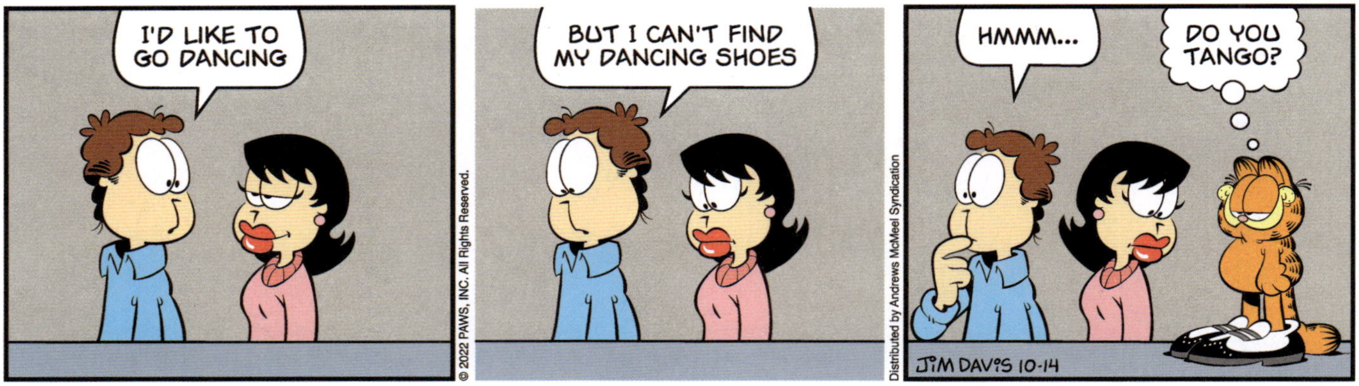
I'D LIKE TO GO DANCING
BUT I CAN'T FIND MY DANCING SHOES
HMMM...
DO YOU TANGO?
JIM DAVIS 10-14
© 2022 PAWS, INC. All Rights Reserved.
Distributed by Andrews McMeel Syndication

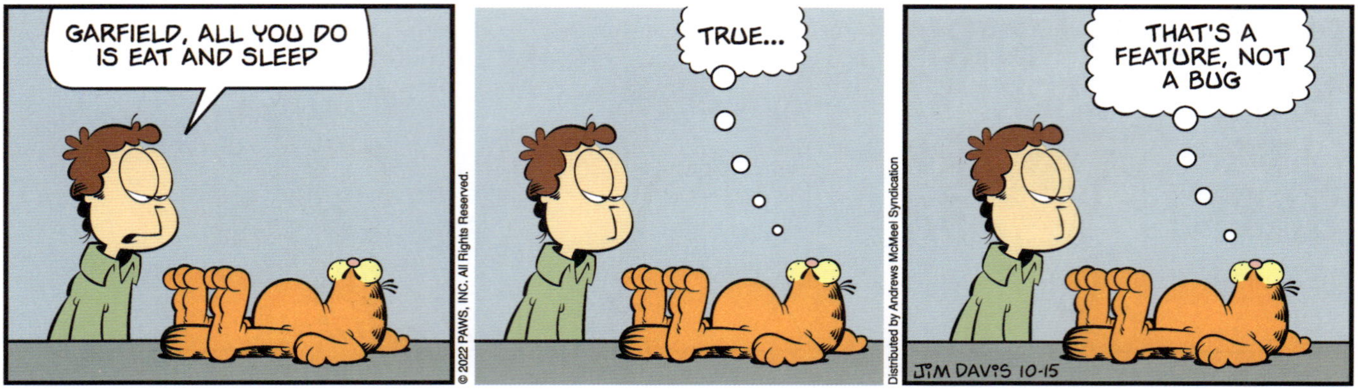
GARFIELD, ALL YOU DO IS EAT AND SLEEP
TRUE...
THAT'S A FEATURE, NOT A BUG
JIM DAVIS 10-15
© 2022 PAWS, INC. All Rights Reserved.
Distributed by Andrews McMeel Syndication

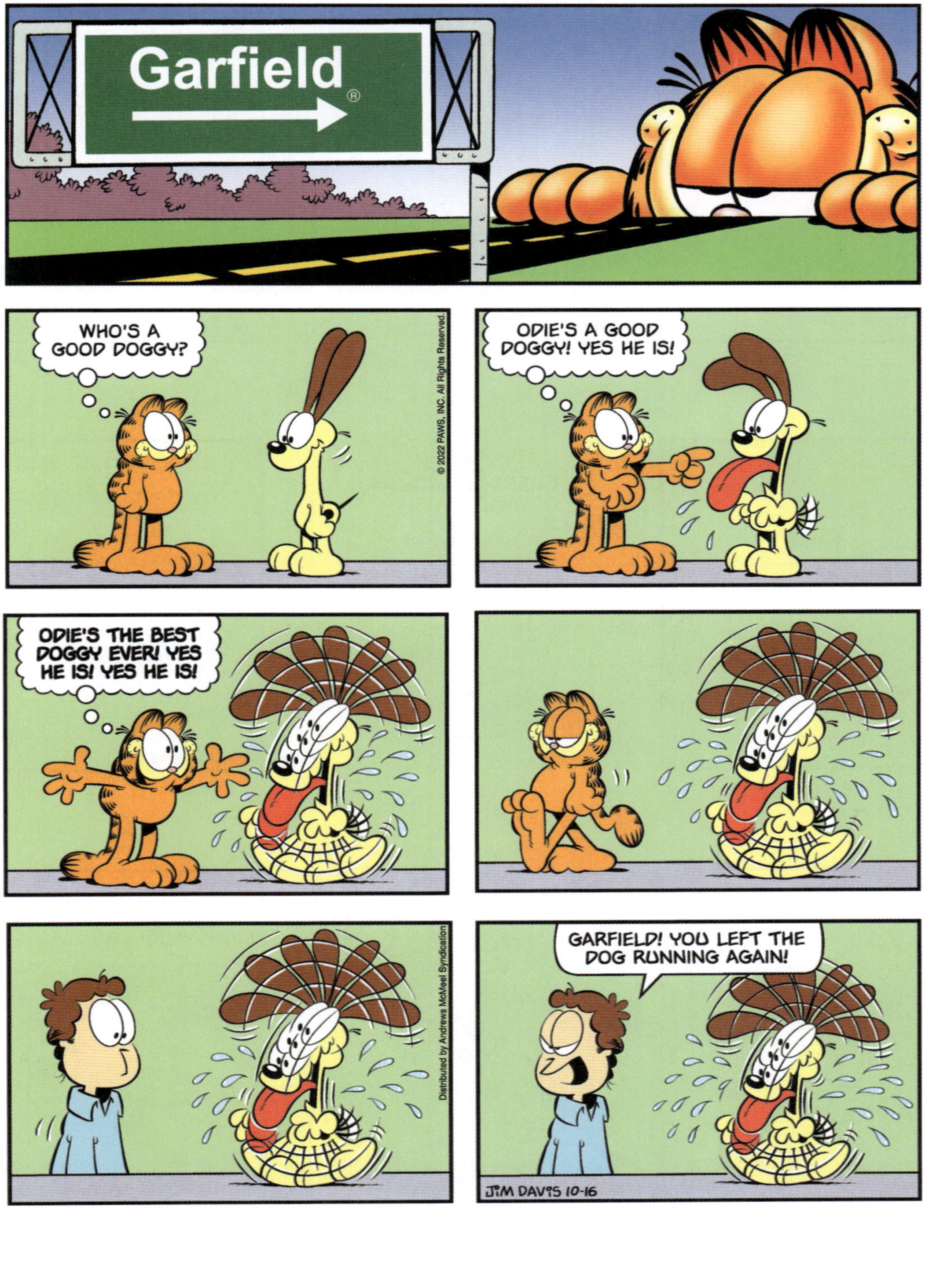
Garfield®
WHO'S A GOOD DOGGY?
© 2022 PAWS, INC. All Rights Reserved.
ODIE'S A GOOD DOGGY! YES HE IS!
ODIE'S THE BEST DOGGY EVER! YES HE IS! YES HE IS!
Distributed by Andrews McMeel Syndication
GARFIELD! YOU LEFT THE DOG RUNNING AGAIN!
JIM DAVIS 10-16

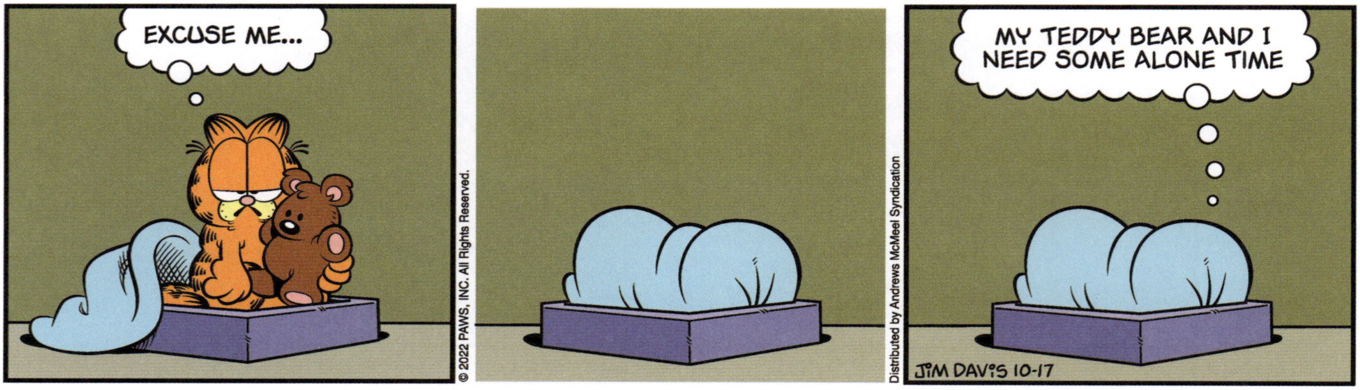
EXCUSE ME...
MY TEDDY BEAR AND I NEED SOME ALONE TIME
© 2022 PAWS, INC. All Rights Reserved.
Distributed by Andrews McMeel Syndication
JIM DAVIS 10-17

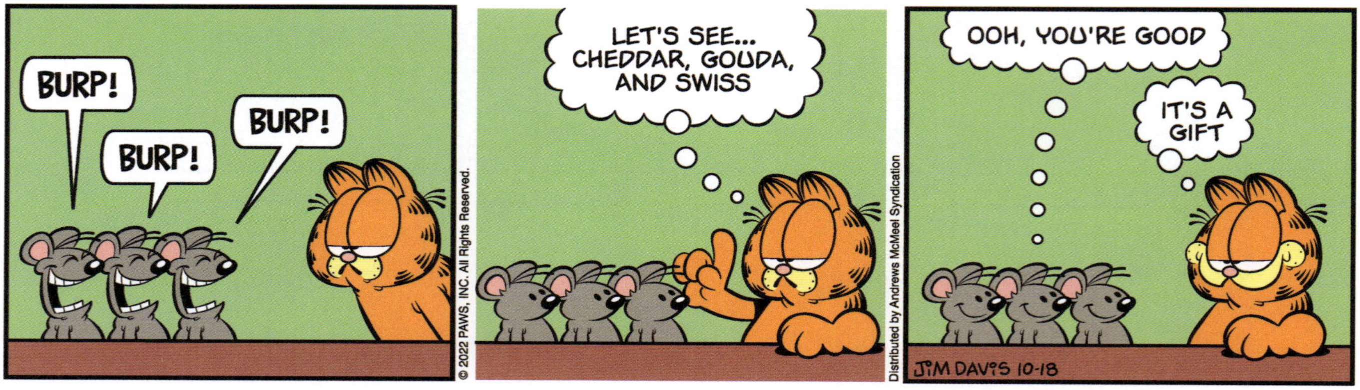
BURP!
BURP!
BURP!
LET'S SEE... CHEDDAR, GOUDA, AND SWISS
OOH, YOU'RE GOOD
IT'S A GIFT
© 2022 PAWS, INC. All Rights Reserved.
Distributed by Andrews McMeel Syndication
JIM DAVIS 10-18

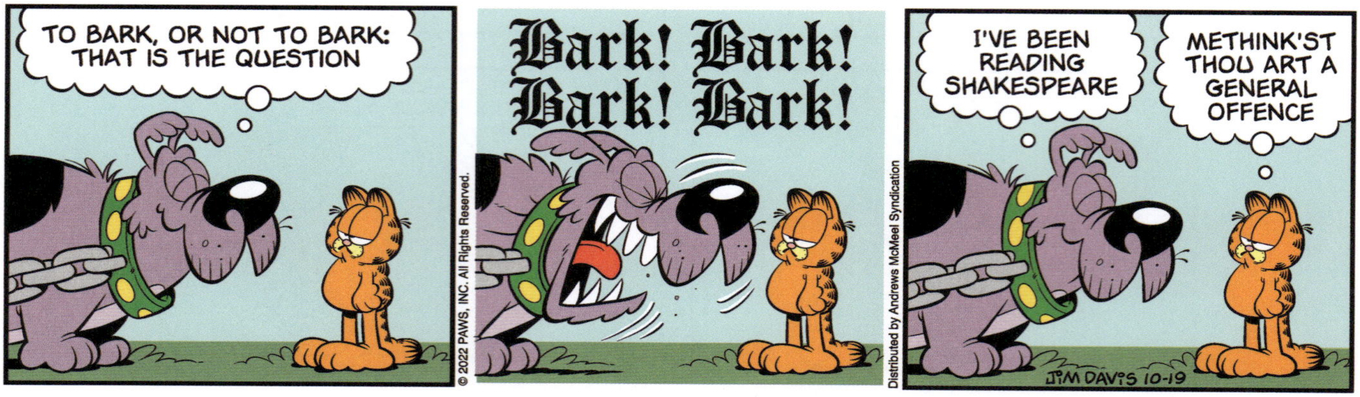
TO BARK, OR NOT TO BARK: THAT IS THE QUESTION
Bark! Bark! Bark! Bark!
I'VE BEEN READING SHAKESPEARE
METHINK'ST THOU ART A GENERAL OFFENCE
© 2022 PAWS, INC. All Rights Reserved.
Distributed by Andrews McMeel Syndication
JIM DAVIS 10-19

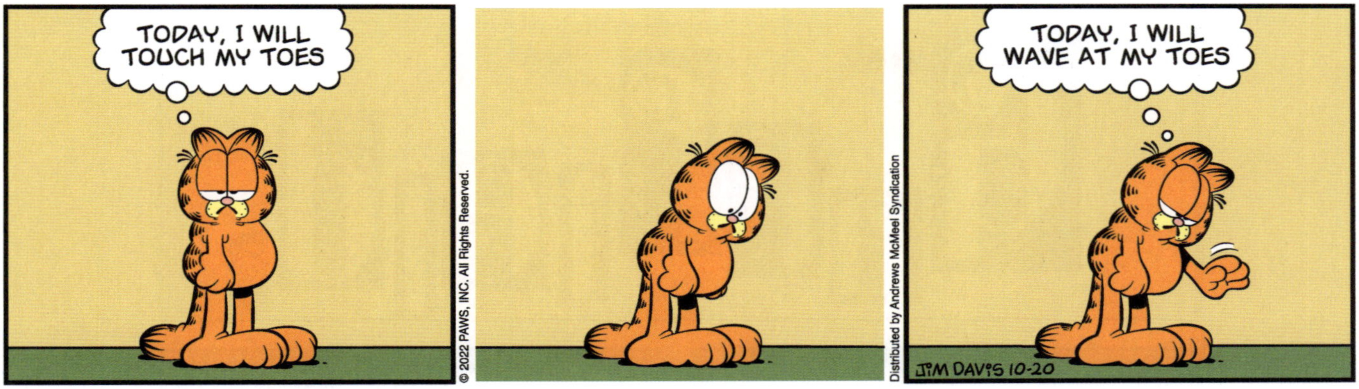
TODAY, I WILL TOUCH MY TOES
© 2022 PAWS, INC. All Rights Reserved.
Distributed by Andrews McMeel Syndication
TODAY, I WILL WAVE AT MY TOES
JIM DAVIS 10-20

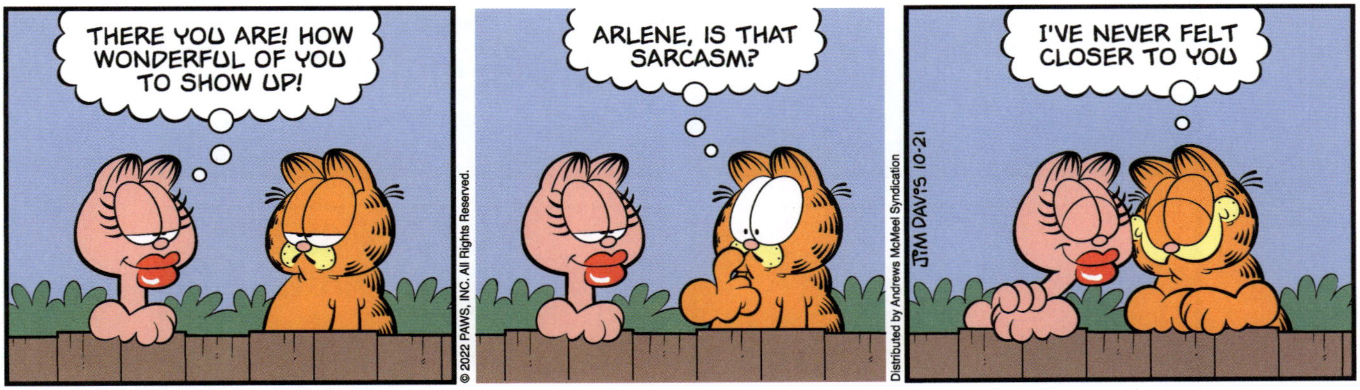
THERE YOU ARE! HOW WONDERFUL OF YOU TO SHOW UP!
© 2022 PAWS, INC. All Rights Reserved.
ARLENE, IS THAT SARCASM?
Distributed by Andrews McMeel Syndication
JIM DAVIS 10-21
I'VE NEVER FELT CLOSER TO YOU

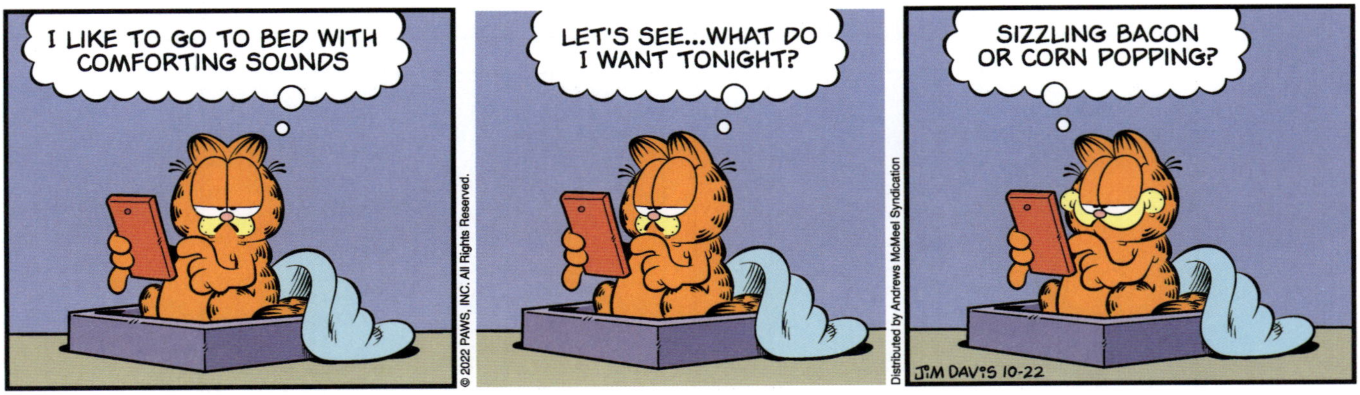
I LIKE TO GO TO BED WITH COMFORTING SOUNDS
© 2022 PAWS, INC. All Rights Reserved.
LET'S SEE...WHAT DO I WANT TONIGHT?
Distributed by Andrews McMeel Syndication
SIZZLING BACON OR CORN POPPING?
JIM DAVIS 10-22

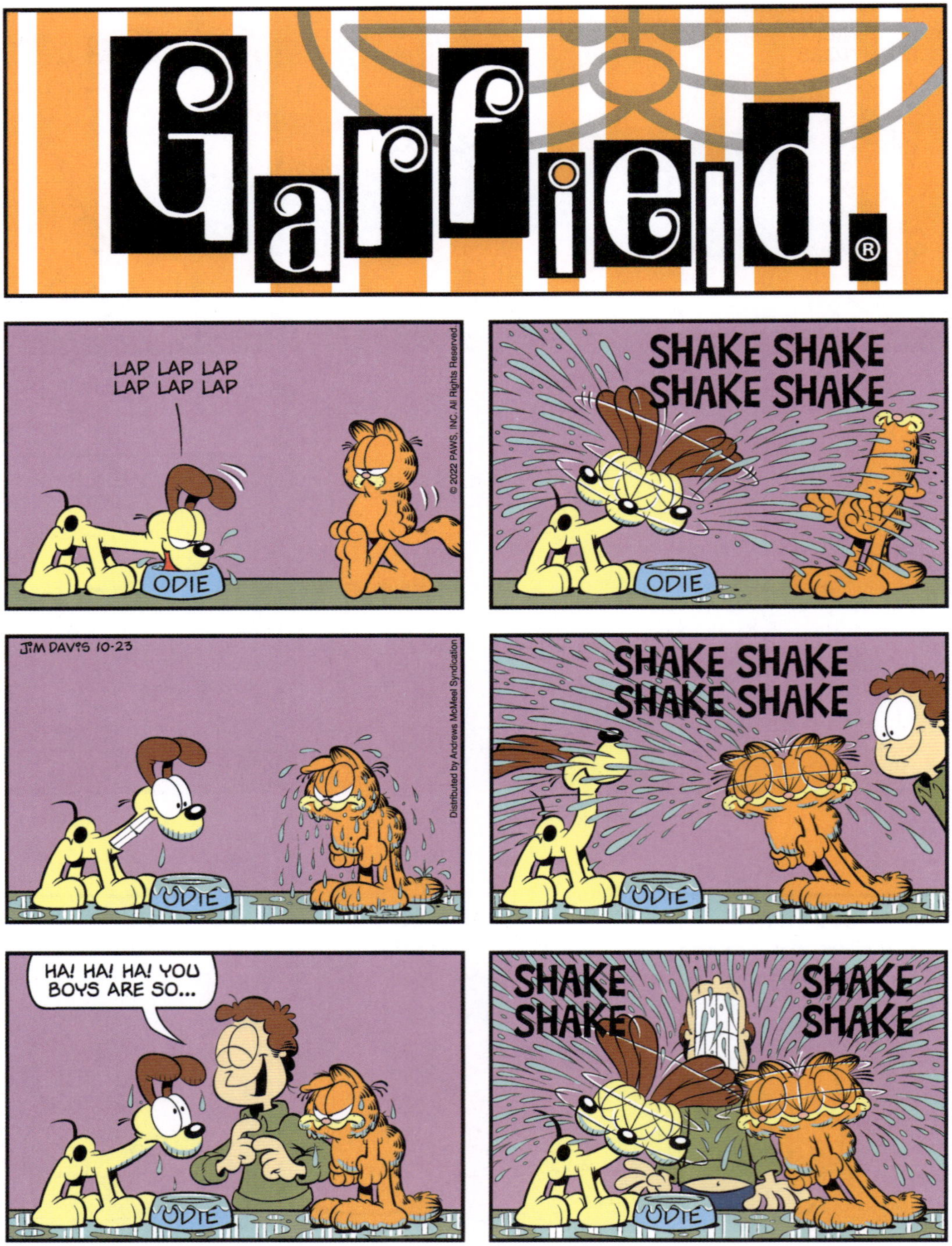
Garfield®
LAP LAP LAP
LAP LAP LAP
© 2022 PAWS, INC. All Rights Reserved.
ODIE
SHAKE SHAKE
SHAKE SHAKE
ODIE
JIM DAVIS 10-23
Distributed by Andrews McMeel Syndication
ODIE
SHAKE SHAKE
SHAKE SHAKE
ODIE
HA! HA! HA! YOU
BOYS ARE SO...
ODIE
SHAKE
SHAKE
SHAKE
SHAKE
ODIE

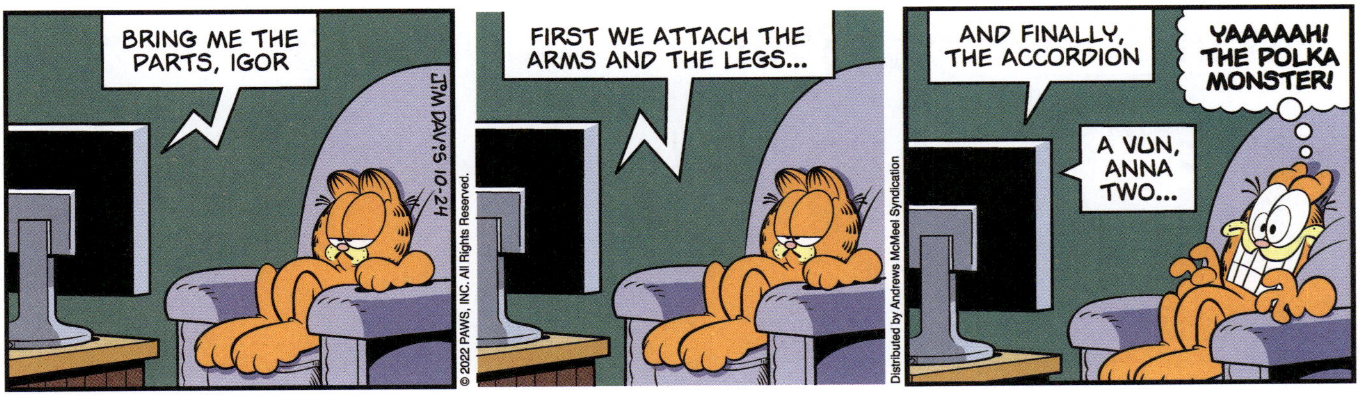
BRING ME THE PARTS, IGOR
JIM DAVIS 10-24
© 2022 PAWS, INC. All Rights Reserved.
FIRST WE ATTACH THE ARMS AND THE LEGS...
Distributed by Andrews McMeel Syndication
AND FINALLY, THE ACCORDION
A VUN, ANNA TWO...
YAAAAAH! THE POLKA MONSTER!

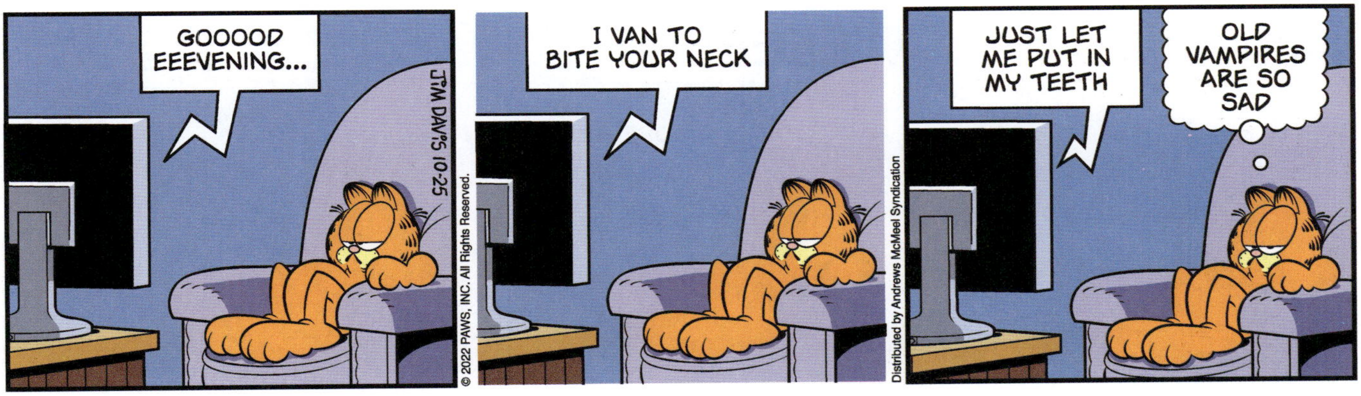
GOOOOD EEEVENING...
JIM DAVIS 10-25
© 2022 PAWS, INC. All Rights Reserved.
I VAN TO BITE YOUR NECK
Distributed by Andrews McMeel Syndication
JUST LET ME PUT IN MY TEETH
OLD VAMPIRES ARE SO SAD

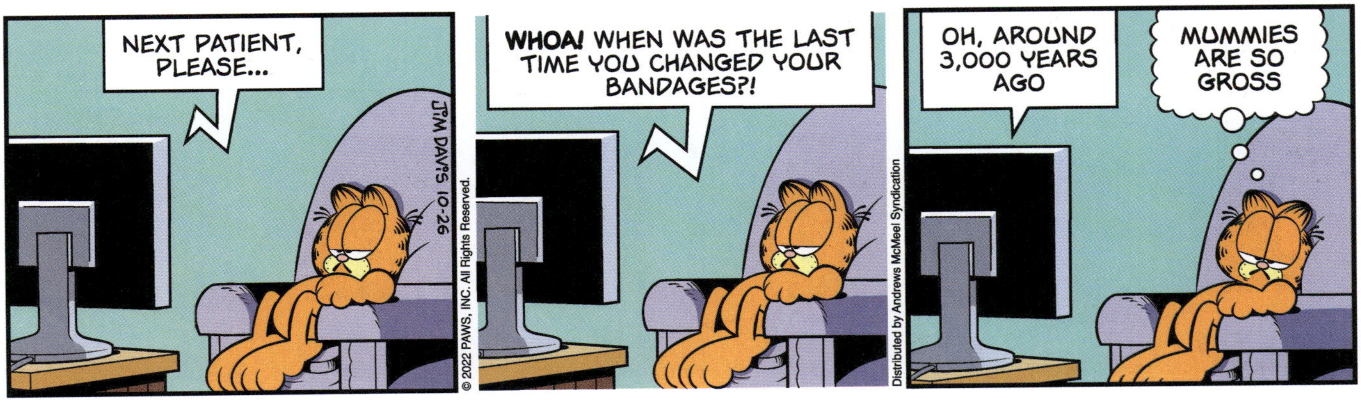
NEXT PATIENT, PLEASE...
JIM DAVIS 10-26
© 2022 PAWS, INC. All Rights Reserved.
WHOA! WHEN WAS THE LAST TIME YOU CHANGED YOUR BANDAGES?!
Distributed by Andrews McMeel Syndication
OH, AROUND 3,000 YEARS AGO
MUMMIES ARE SO GROSS

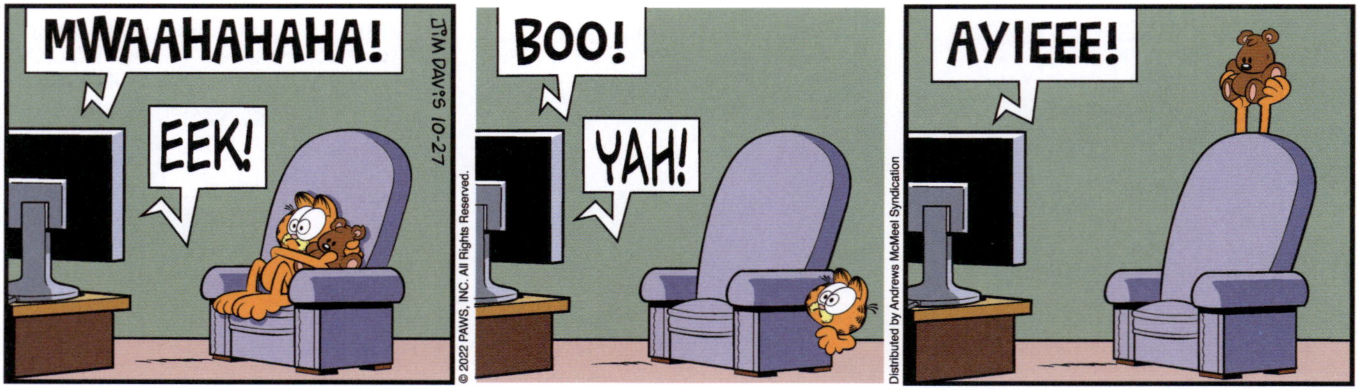
MWAAHAHAHA!
EEK!
JIM DAVIS 10-27
© 2022 PAWS, INC. All Rights Reserved.
BOO!
YAH!
Distributed by Andrews McMeel Syndication
AYIEEE!

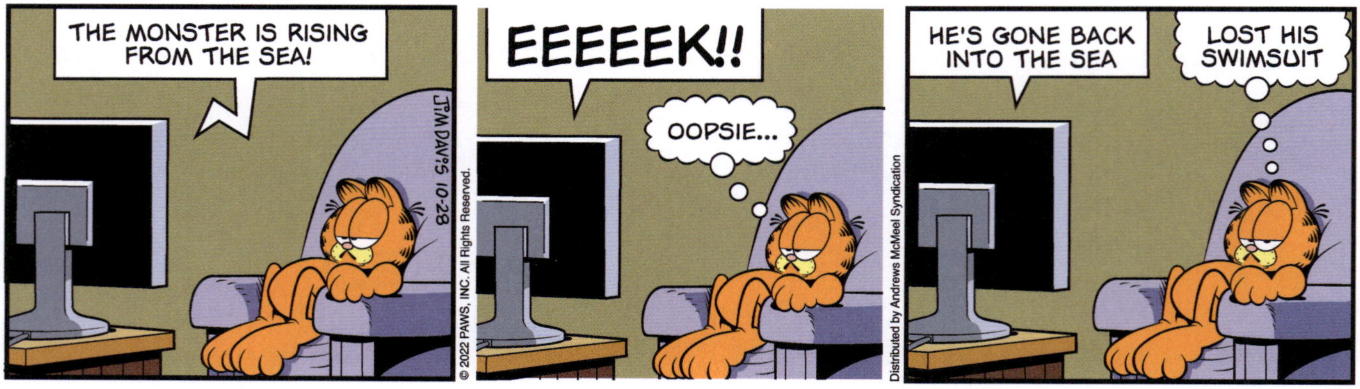
THE MONSTER IS RISING FROM THE SEA!
JIM DAVIS 10-28
© 2022 PAWS, INC. All Rights Reserved.
EEEEEK!!
OOPSIE...
Distributed by Andrews McMeel Syndication
HE'S GONE BACK INTO THE SEA
LOST HIS SWIMSUIT

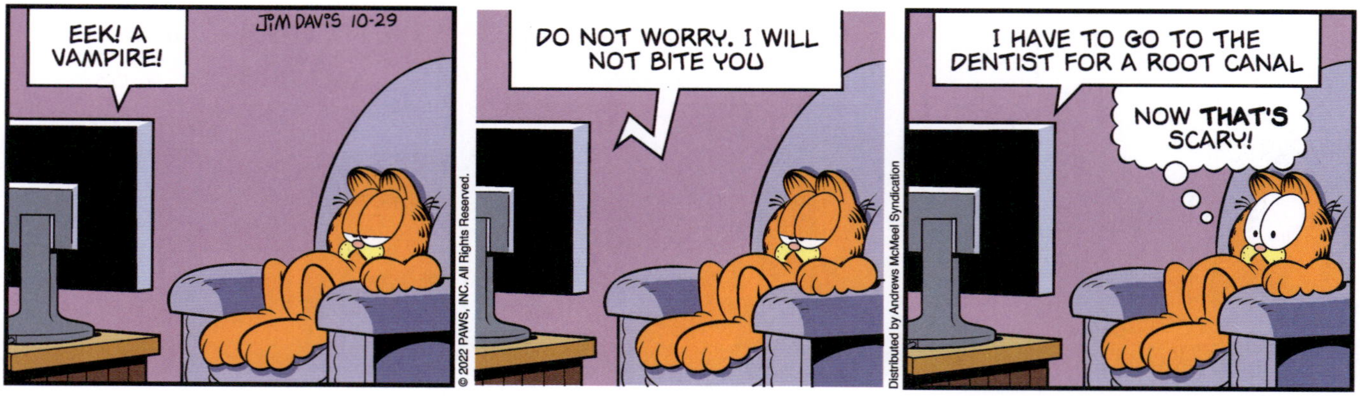
EEK! A VAMPIRE!
JIM DAVIS 10-29
© 2022 PAWS, INC. All Rights Reserved.
DO NOT WORRY. I WILL NOT BITE YOU
Distributed by Andrews McMeel Syndication
I HAVE TO GO TO THE DENTIST FOR A ROOT CANAL
NOW THAT'S SCARY!

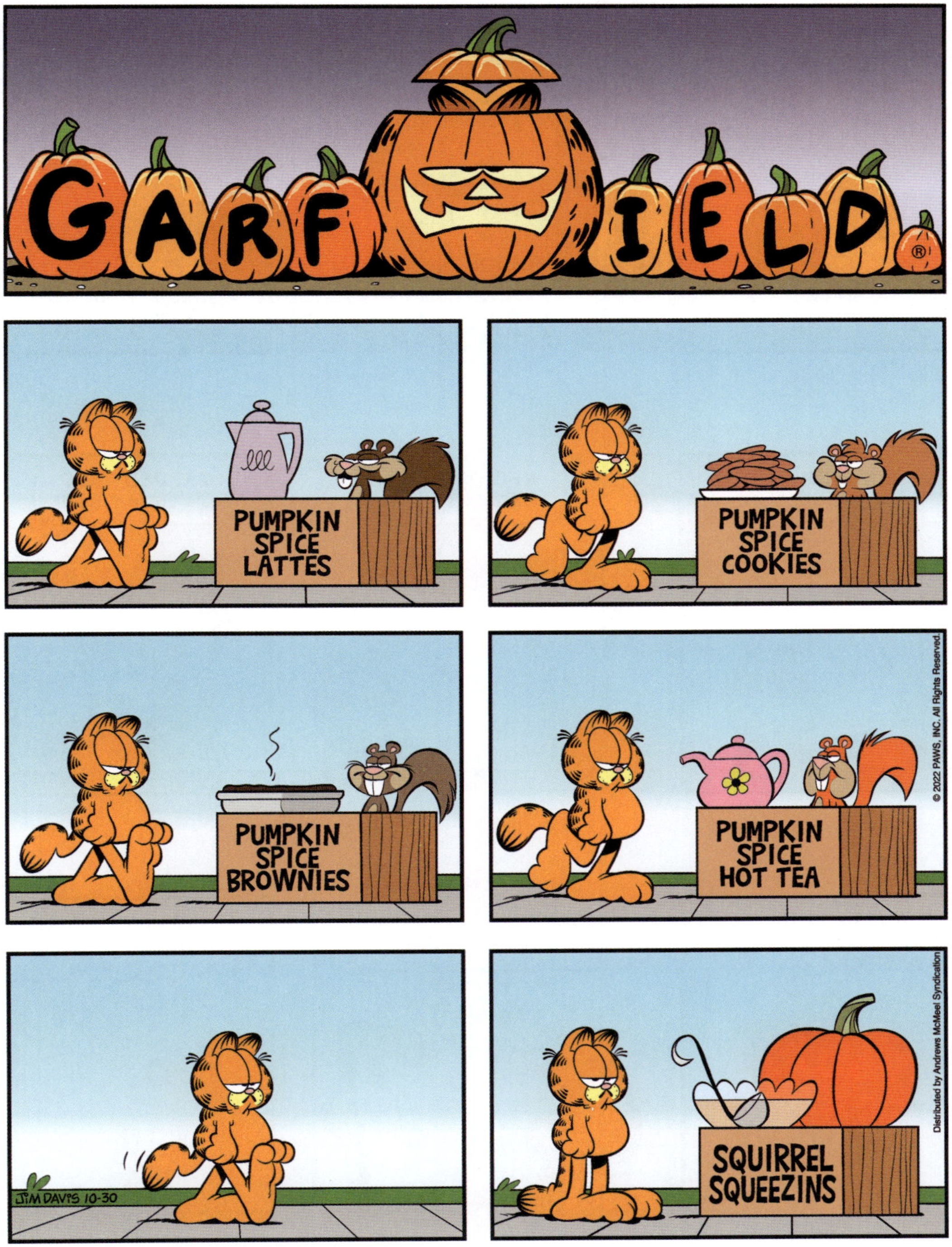
GARFIELD®
PUMPKIN SPICE LATTES
PUMPKIN SPICE COOKIES
PUMPKIN SPICE BROWNIES
PUMPKIN SPICE HOT TEA
JIM DAVIS 10-30
SQUIRREL SQUEEZINS
© 2022 PAWS, INC. All Rights Reserved.
Distributed by Andrews McMeel Syndication

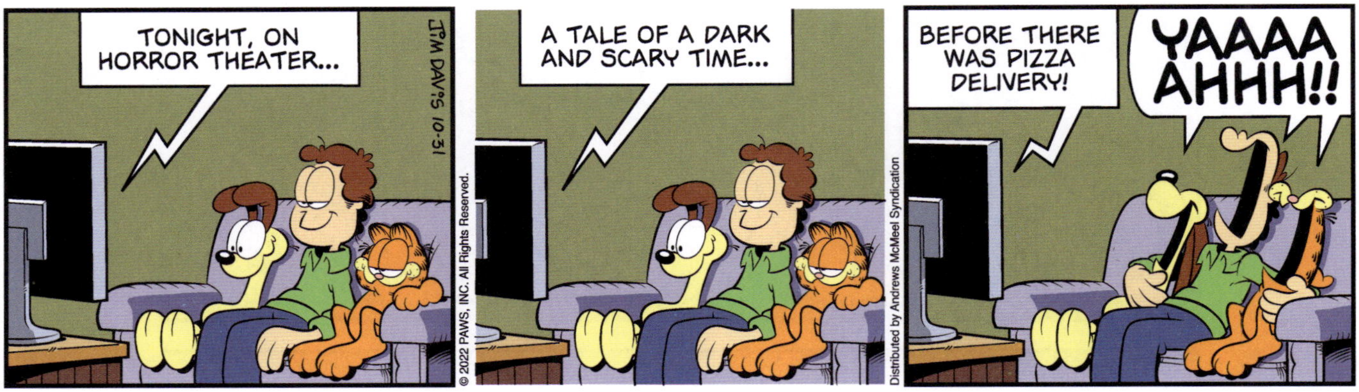
TONIGHT, ON HORROR THEATER...
JIM DAVIS 10-31
A TALE OF A DARK AND SCARY TIME...
BEFORE THERE WAS PIZZA DELIVERY!
YAAAA AHHH!!
© 2022 PAWS, INC. All Rights Reserved.
Distributed by Andrews McMeel Syndication

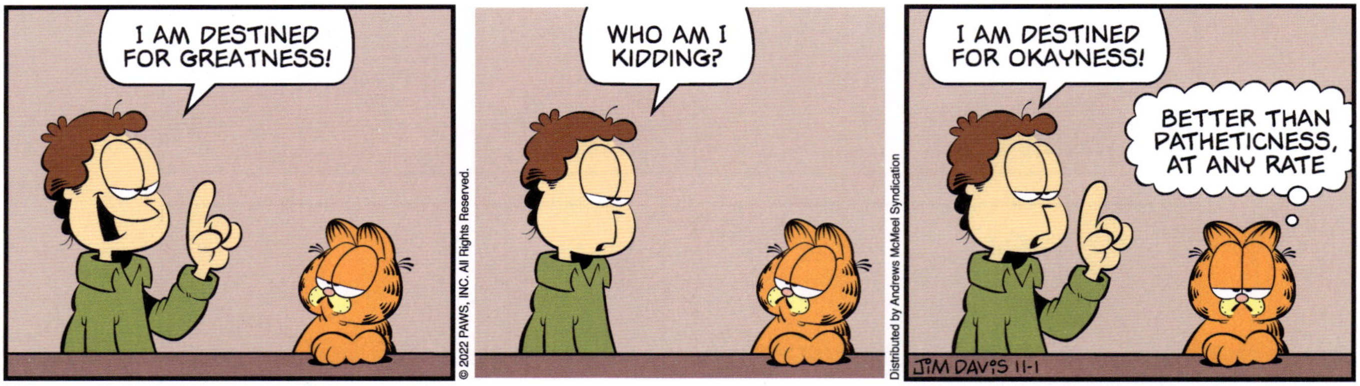
I AM DESTINED FOR GREATNESS!
WHO AM I KIDDING?
I AM DESTINED FOR OKAYNESS!
BETTER THAN PATHETICNESS, AT ANY RATE
JIM DAVIS 11-1
© 2022 PAWS, INC. All Rights Reserved.
Distributed by Andrews McMeel Syndication

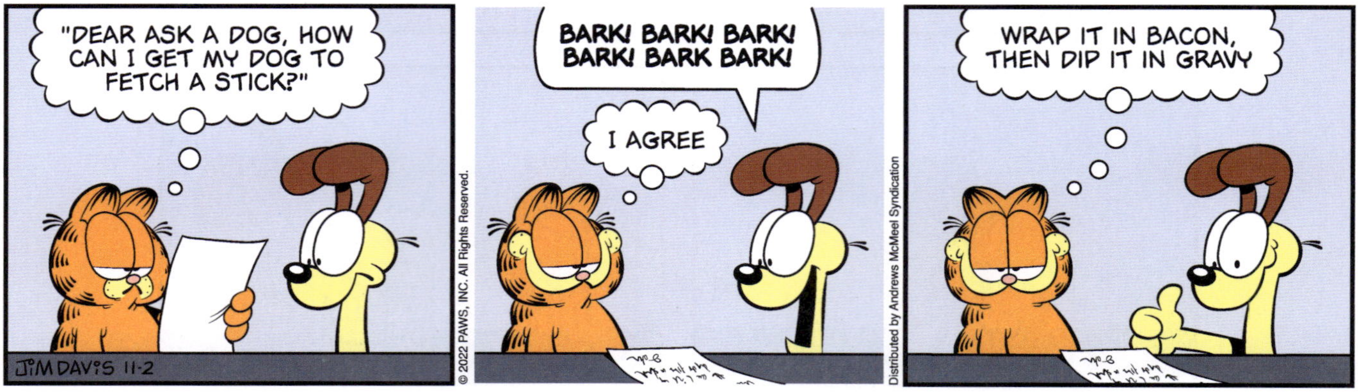
"DEAR ASK A DOG, HOW CAN I GET MY DOG TO FETCH A STICK?"
JIM DAVIS 11-2
BARK! BARK! BARK! BARK! BARK BARK!
I AGREE
WRAP IT IN BACON, THEN DIP IT IN GRAVY
© 2022 PAWS, INC. All Rights Reserved.
Distributed by Andrews McMeel Syndication

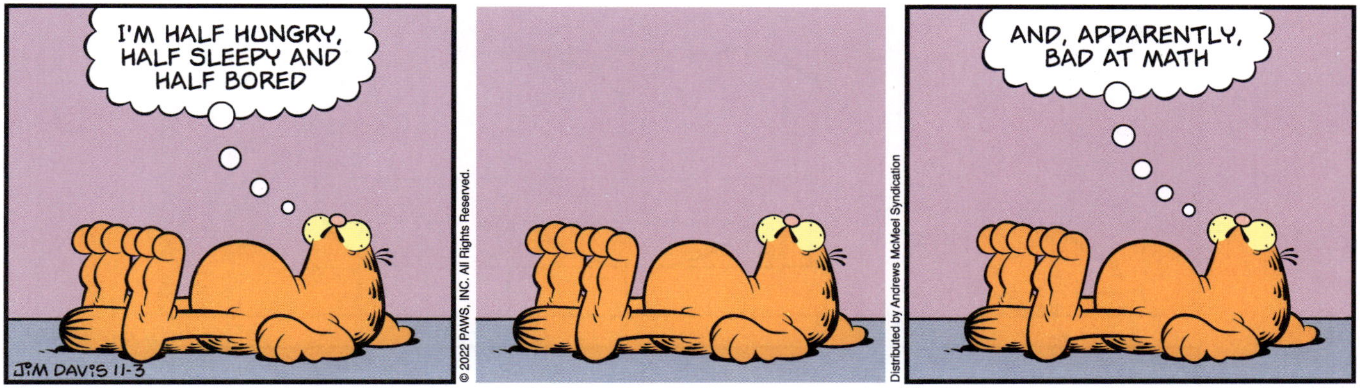
I'M HALF HUNGRY, HALF SLEEPY AND HALF BORED
AND, APPARENTLY, BAD AT MATH
JIM DAVIS 11-3
© 2022 PAWS, INC. All Rights Reserved.
Distributed by Andrews McMeel Syndication

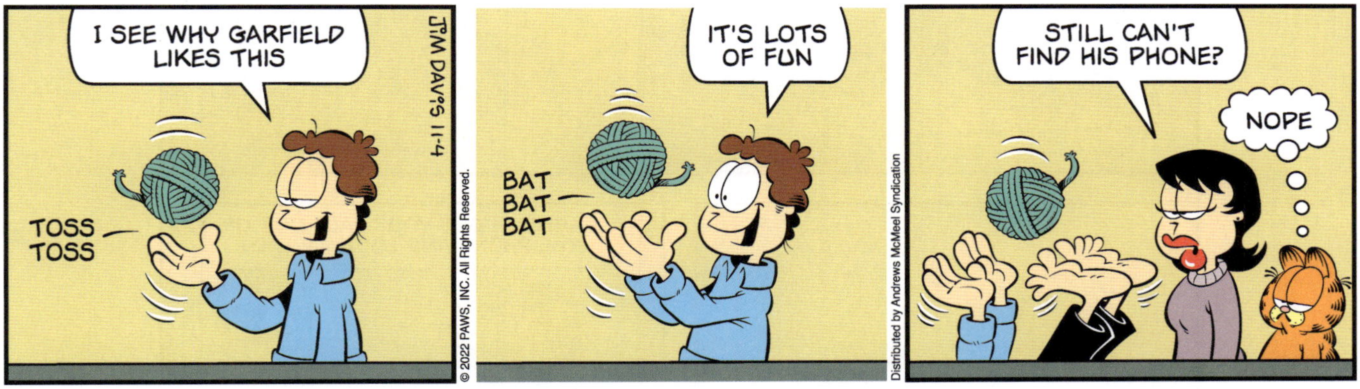
I SEE WHY GARFIELD LIKES THIS
TOSS TOSS
JIM DAVIS 11-4
IT'S LOTS OF FUN
BAT BAT BAT
STILL CAN'T FIND HIS PHONE?
NOPE
© 2022 PAWS, INC. All Rights Reserved.
Distributed by Andrews McMeel Syndication

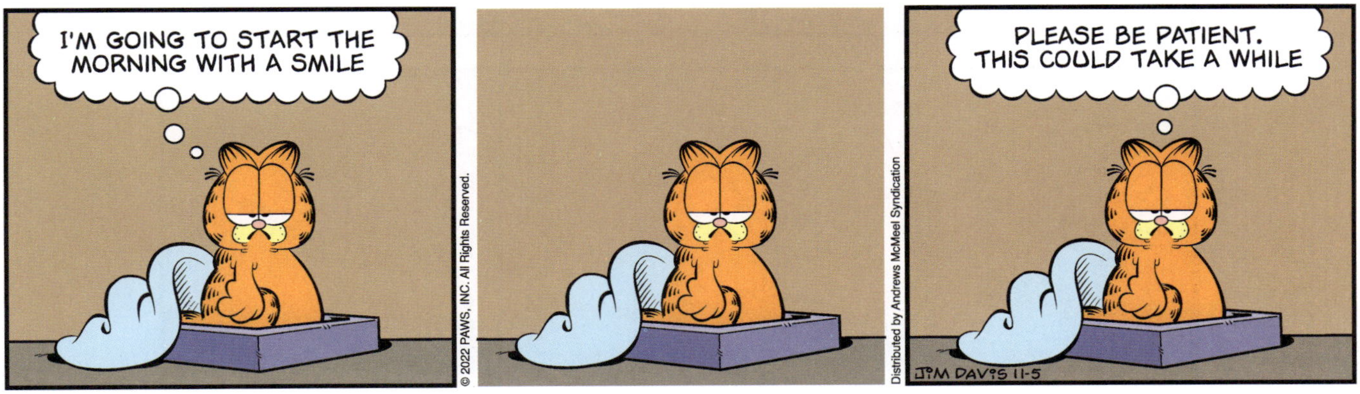
I'M GOING TO START THE MORNING WITH A SMILE
PLEASE BE PATIENT. THIS COULD TAKE A WHILE
JIM DAVIS 11-5
© 2022 PAWS, INC. All Rights Reserved.
Distributed by Andrews McMeel Syndication

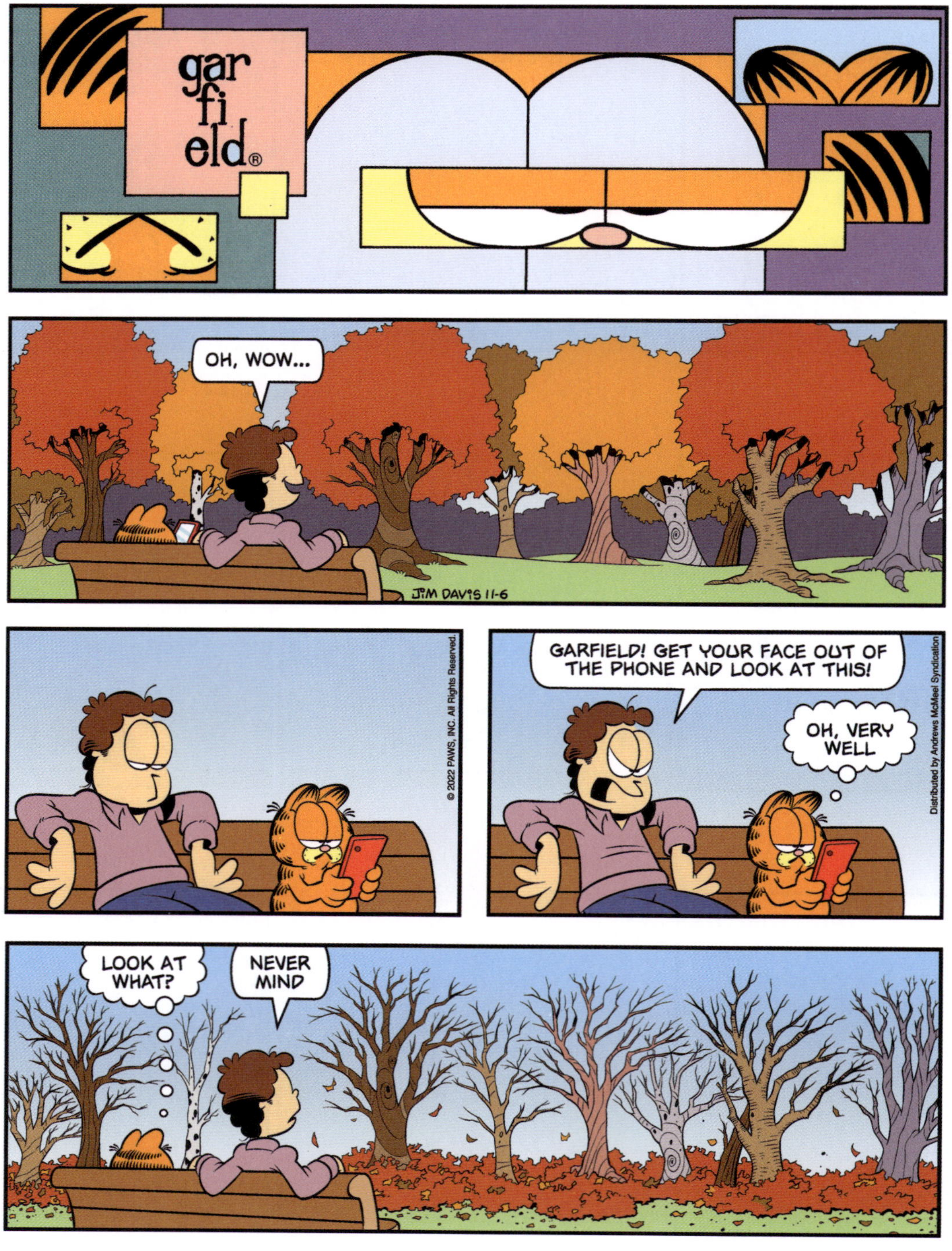
garfield®
OH, WOW...
JIM DAVIS 11-6
© 2022 PAWS, INC. All Rights Reserved.
GARFIELD! GET YOUR FACE OUT OF THE PHONE AND LOOK AT THIS!
OH, VERY WELL
Distributed by Andrews McMeel Syndication
LOOK AT WHAT?
NEVER MIND

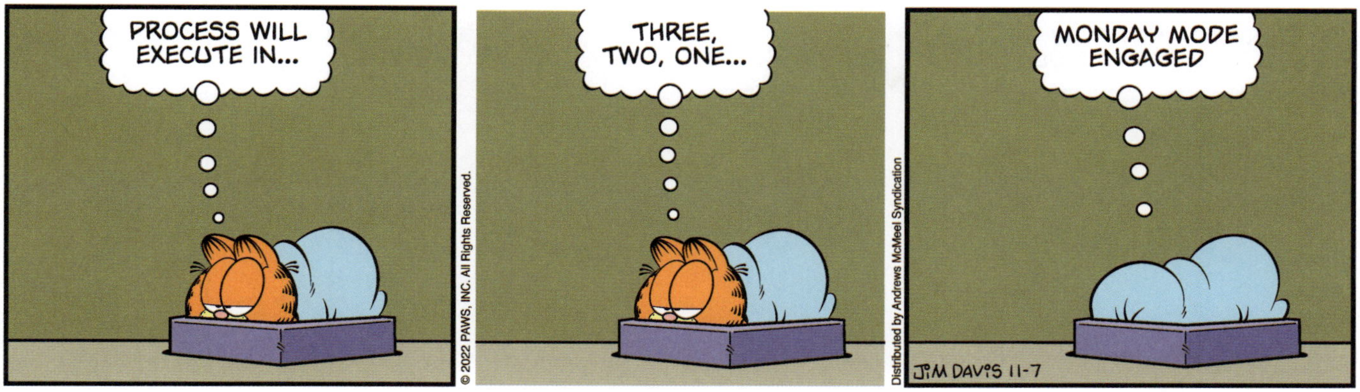
PROCESS WILL EXECUTE IN...
THREE, TWO, ONE...
MONDAY MODE ENGAGED
© 2022 PAWS, INC. All Rights Reserved.
Distributed by Andrews McMeel Syndication
JIM DAVIS 11-7

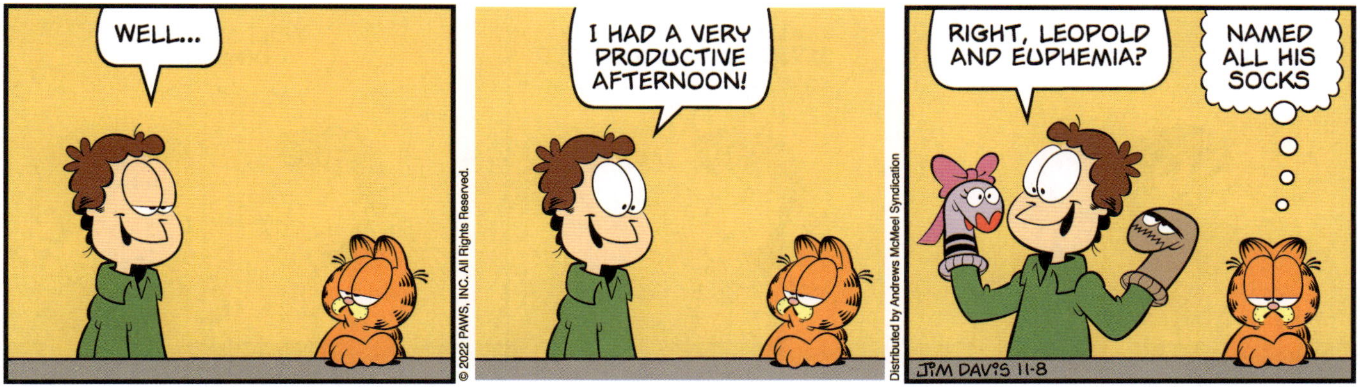
WELL...
I HAD A VERY PRODUCTIVE AFTERNOON!
RIGHT, LEOPOLD AND EUPHEMIA?
NAMED ALL HIS SOCKS
© 2022 PAWS, INC. All Rights Reserved.
Distributed by Andrews McMeel Syndication
JIM DAVIS 11-8

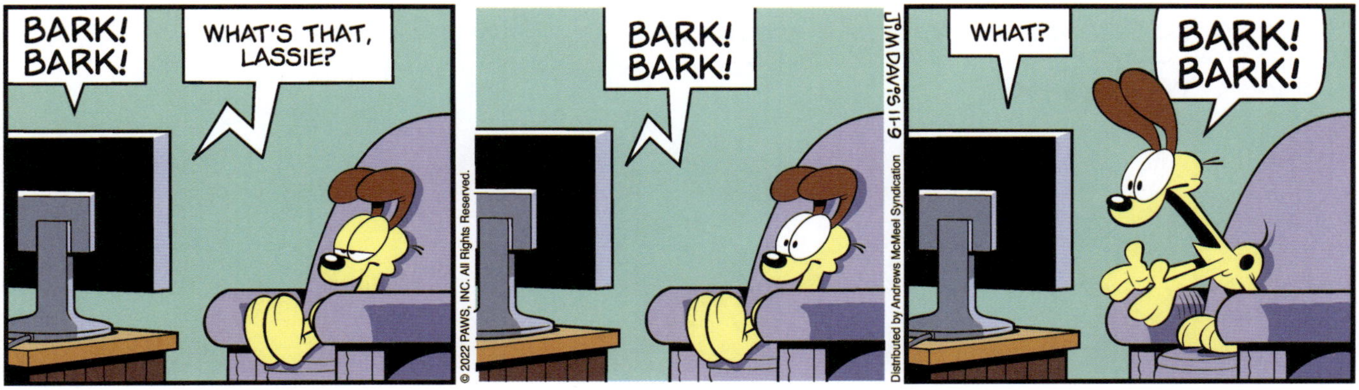
BARK! BARK!
WHAT'S THAT, LASSIE?
BARK! BARK!
WHAT?
BARK! BARK!
© 2022 PAWS, INC. All Rights Reserved.
Distributed by Andrews McMeel Syndication
JIM DAVIS 11-9

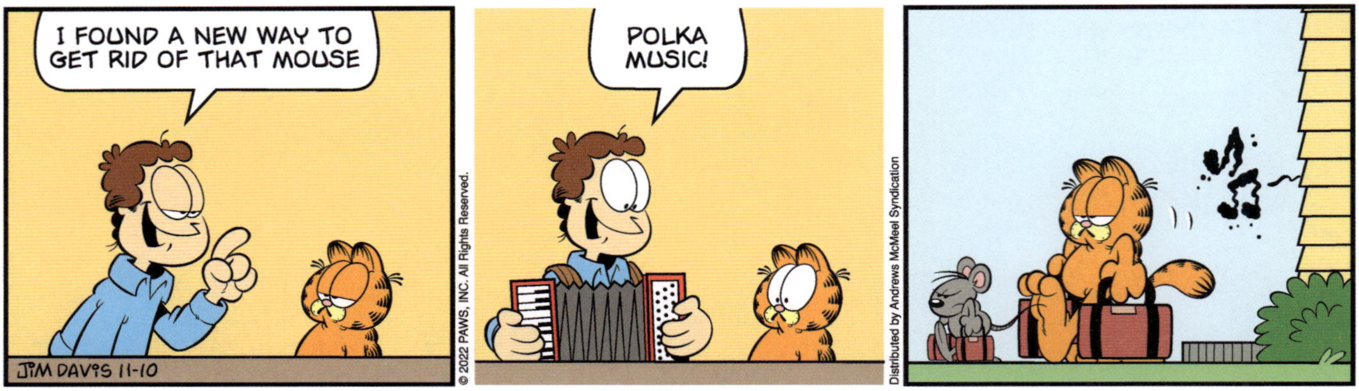
I FOUND A NEW WAY TO GET RID OF THAT MOUSE
JIM DAVIS 11-10
POLKA MUSIC!
© 2022 PAWS, INC. All Rights Reserved.
Distributed by Andrews McMeel Syndication

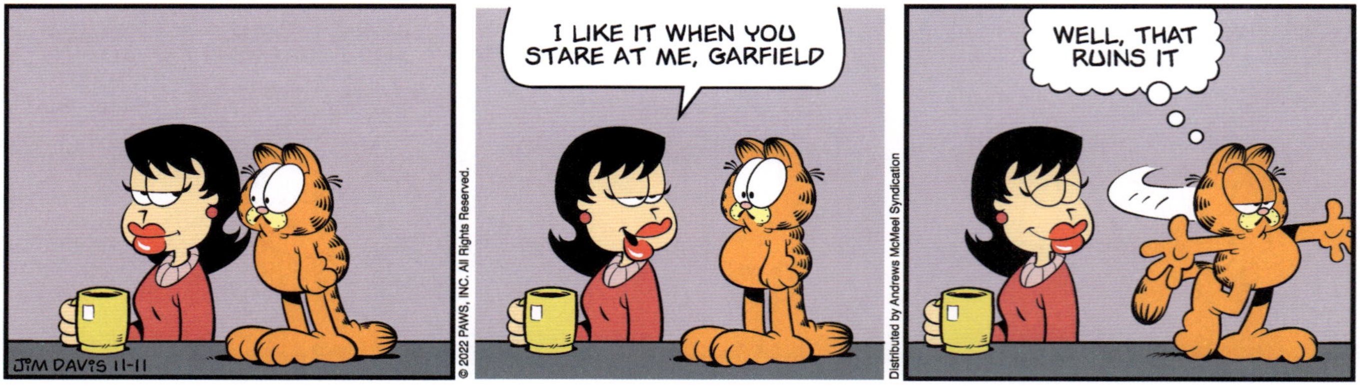
JIM DAVIS 11-11
I LIKE IT WHEN YOU STARE AT ME, GARFIELD
© 2022 PAWS, INC. All Rights Reserved.
WELL, THAT RUINS IT
Distributed by Andrews McMeel Syndication

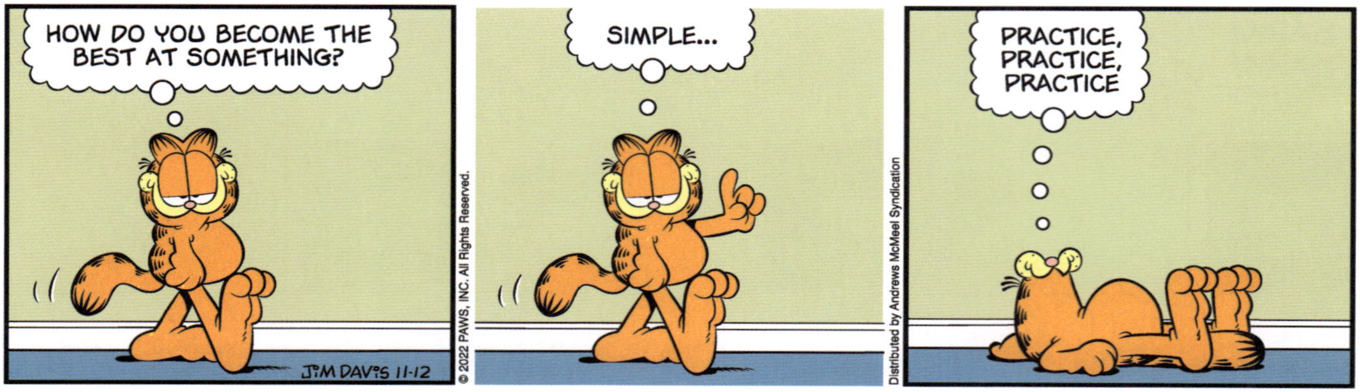
HOW DO YOU BECOME THE BEST AT SOMETHING?
JIM DAVIS 11-12
SIMPLE...
© 2022 PAWS, INC. All Rights Reserved.
PRACTICE, PRACTICE, PRACTICE
Distributed by Andrews McMeel Syndication

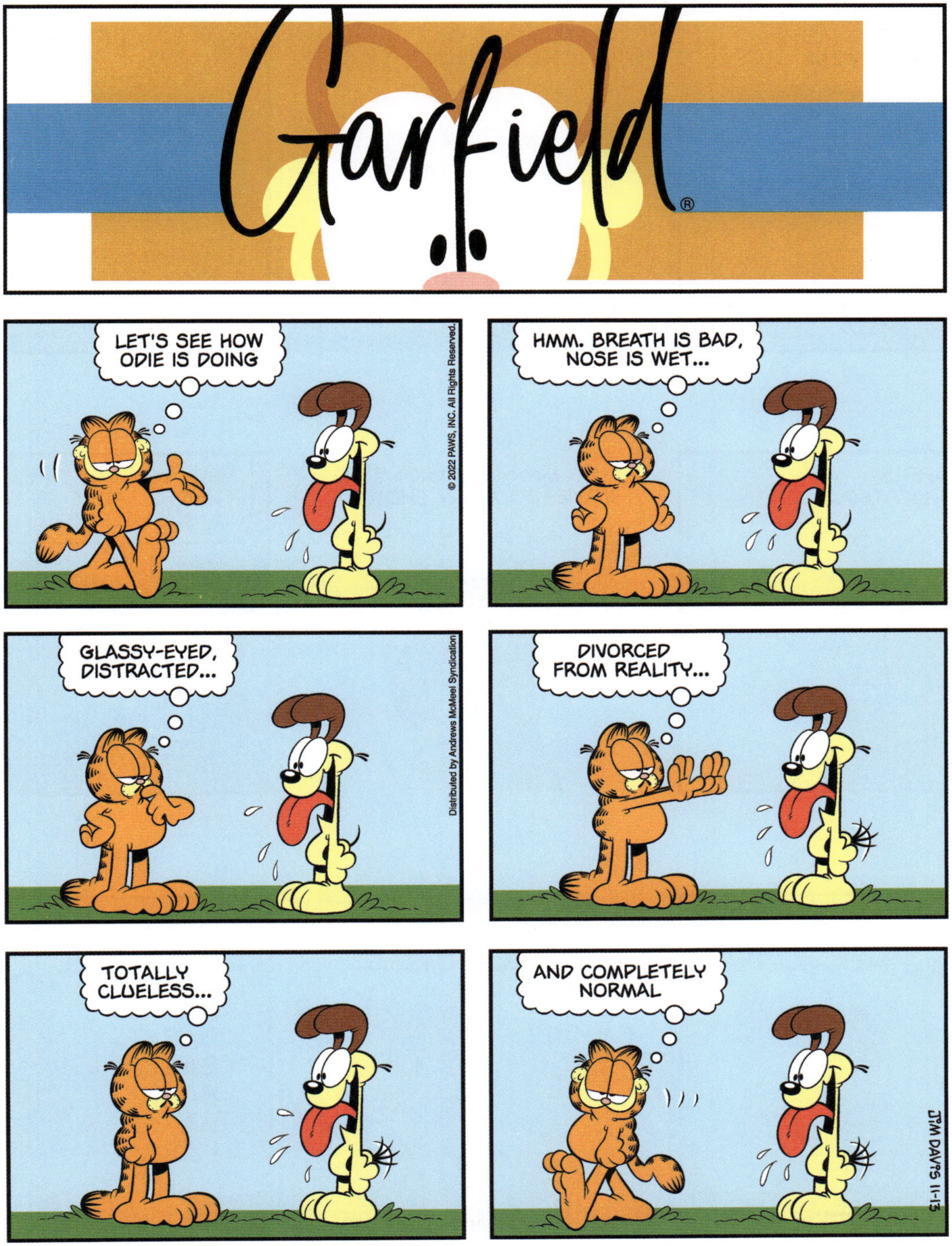
Garfield®
LET'S SEE HOW ODIE IS DOING
© 2022 PAWS, INC. All Rights Reserved.
HMM. BREATH IS BAD, NOSE IS WET...
GLASSY-EYED, DISTRACTED...
Distributed by Andrews McMeel Syndication
DIVORCED FROM REALITY...
TOTALLY CLUELESS...
AND COMPLETELY NORMAL
JPM DAVPS 11-13

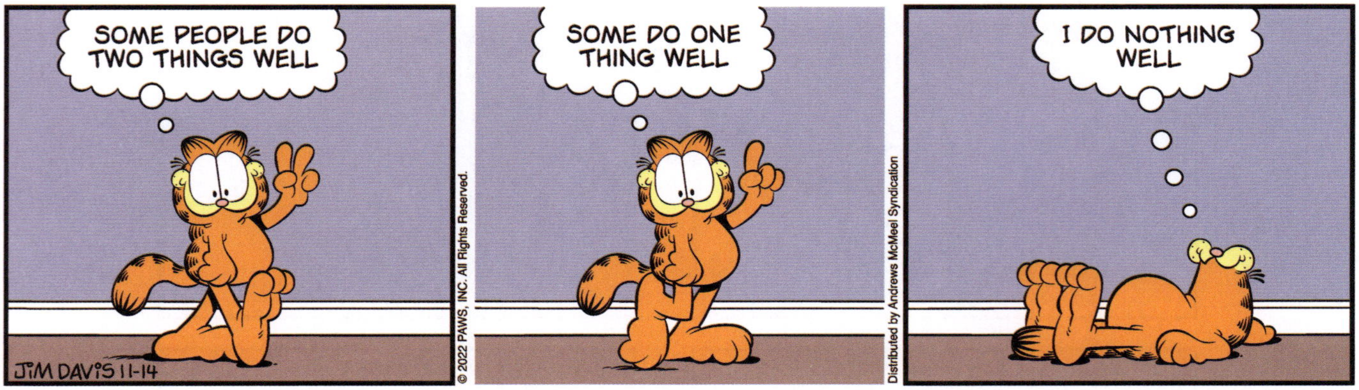
SOME PEOPLE DO TWO THINGS WELL
JIM DAVIS 11-14
© 2022 PAWS, INC. All Rights Reserved.
SOME DO ONE THING WELL
Distributed by Andrews McMeel Syndication
I DO NOTHING WELL

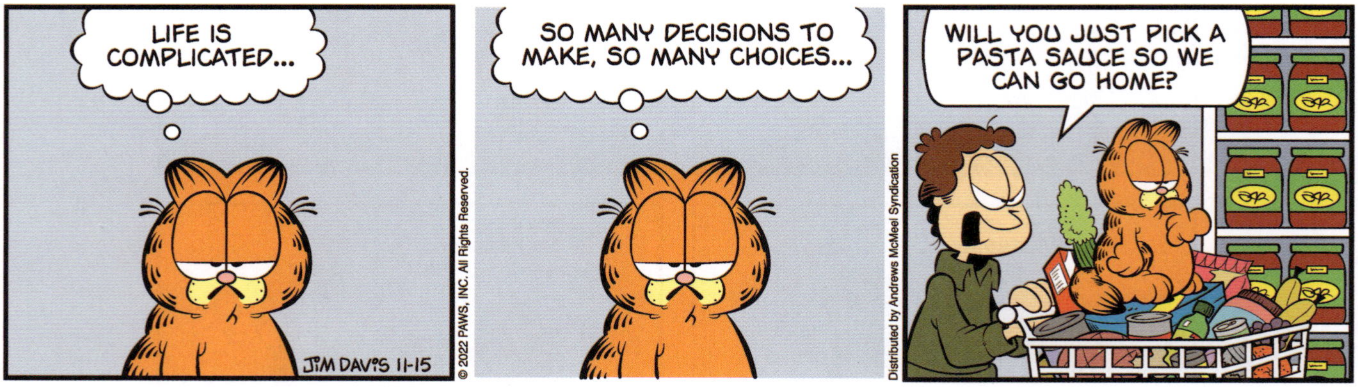
LIFE IS COMPLICATED...
JIM DAVIS 11-15
© 2022 PAWS, INC. All Rights Reserved.
SO MANY DECISIONS TO MAKE, SO MANY CHOICES...
Distributed by Andrews McMeel Syndication
WILL YOU JUST PICK A PASTA SAUCE SO WE CAN GO HOME?

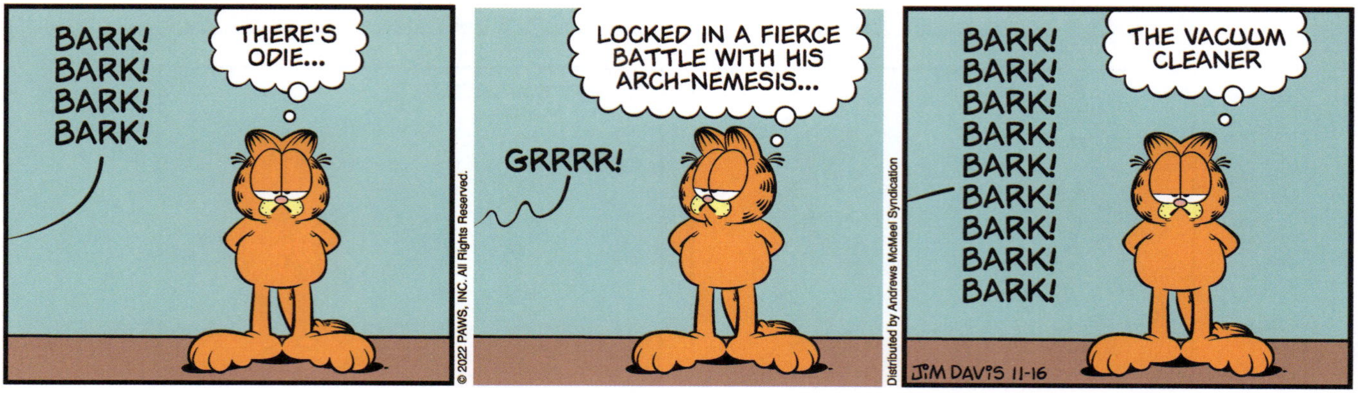
BARK! BARK! BARK! BARK!
THERE'S ODIE...
© 2022 PAWS, INC. All Rights Reserved.
GRRRR!
LOCKED IN A FIERCE BATTLE WITH HIS ARCH-NEMESIS...
Distributed by Andrews McMeel Syndication
BARK! BARK! BARK! BARK! BARK! BARK! BARK! BARK! BARK!
THE VACUUM CLEANER
JIM DAVIS 11-16

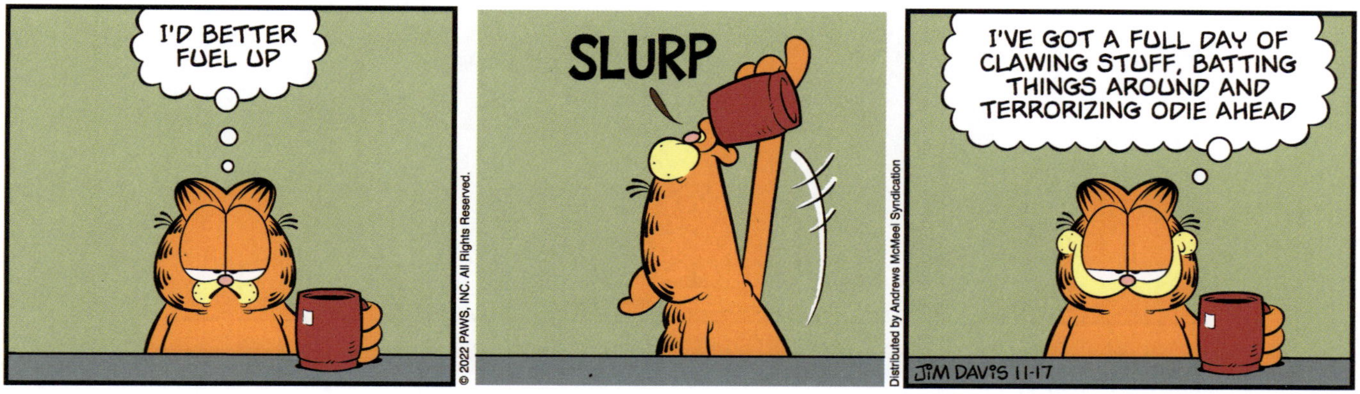
I'D BETTER FUEL UP
SLURP
I'VE GOT A FULL DAY OF CLAWING STUFF, BATTING THINGS AROUND AND TERRORIZING ODIE AHEAD
© 2022 PAWS, INC. All Rights Reserved.
Distributed by Andrews McMeel Syndication
JIM DAVIS 11-17

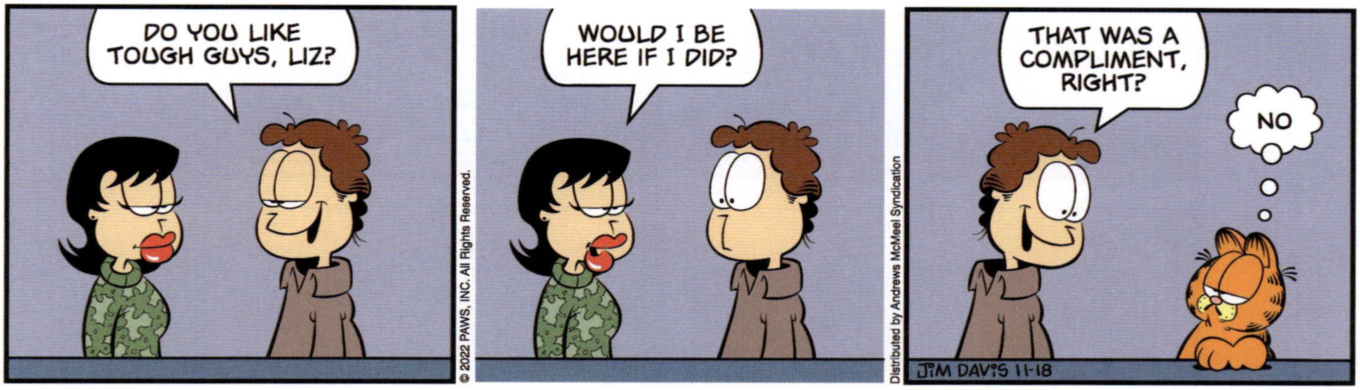
DO YOU LIKE TOUGH GUYS, LIZ?
WOULD I BE HERE IF I DID?
THAT WAS A COMPLIMENT, RIGHT?
NO
© 2022 PAWS, INC. All Rights Reserved.
Distributed by Andrews McMeel Syndication
JIM DAVIS 11-18

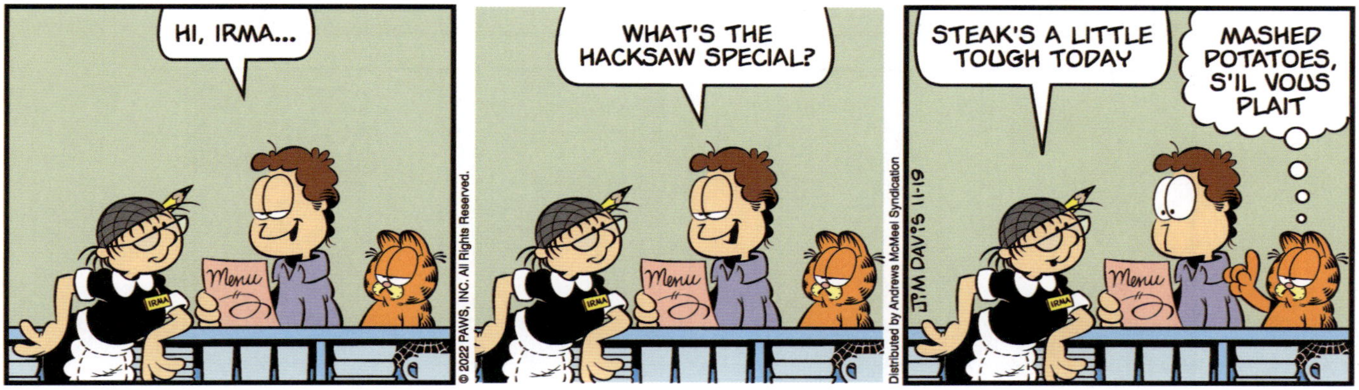
HI, IRMA...
WHAT'S THE HACKSAW SPECIAL?
STEAK'S A LITTLE TOUGH TODAY
MASHED POTATOES, S'IL VOUS PLAIT
Menu
IRMA
© 2022 PAWS, INC. All Rights Reserved.
Distributed by Andrews McMeel Syndication
JIM DAVIS 11-19

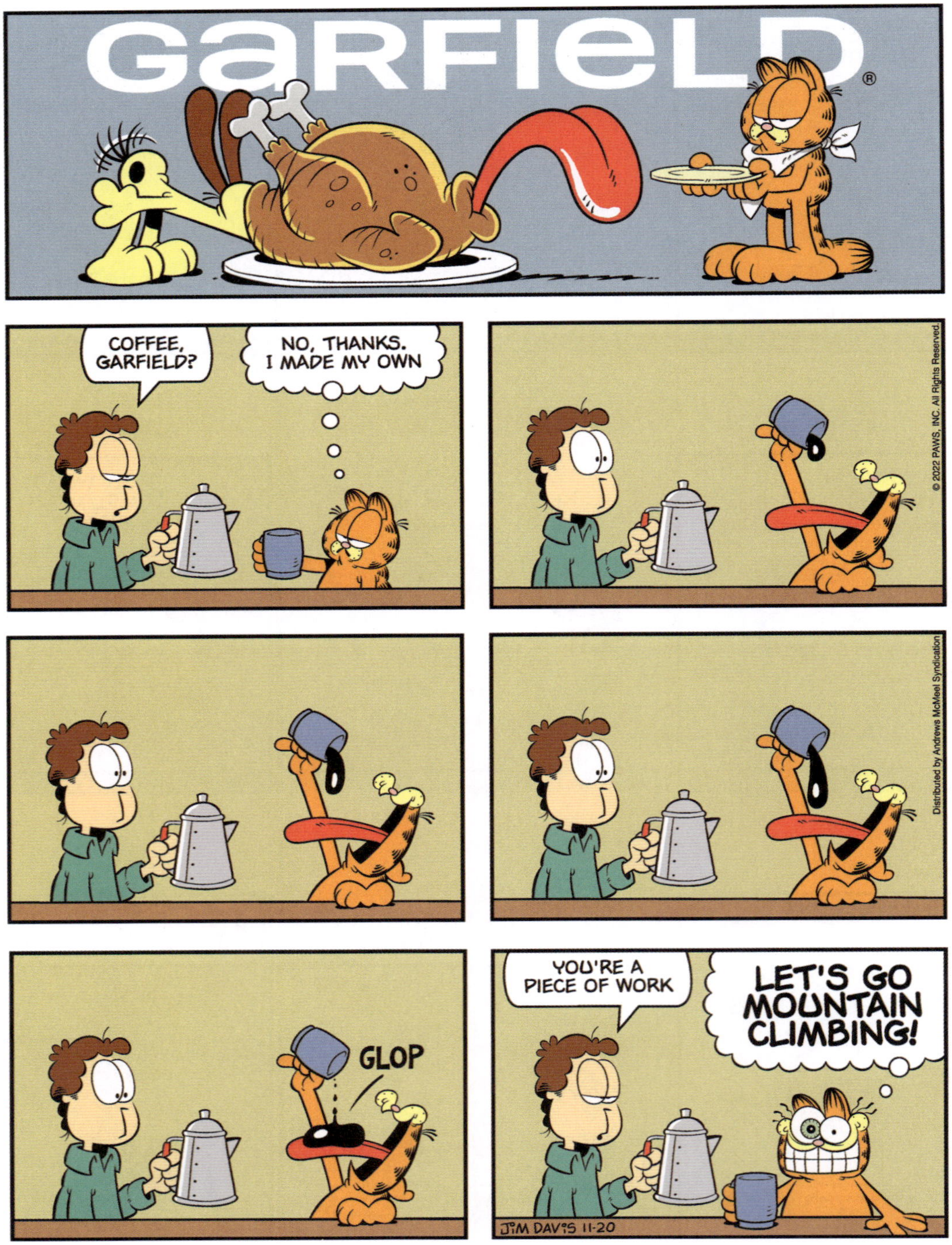
GARFIELD®
COFFEE, GARFIELD?
NO, THANKS. I MADE MY OWN
© 2022 PAWS, INC. All Rights Reserved.
Distributed by Andrews McMeel Syndication
GLOP
YOU'RE A PIECE OF WORK
LET'S GO MOUNTAIN CLIMBING!
JIM DAVIS 11-20

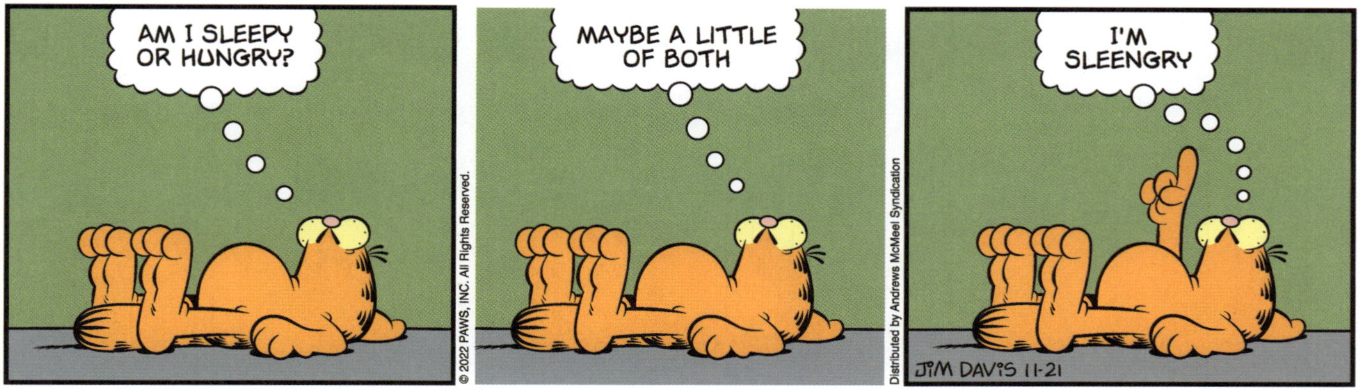
AM I SLEEPY OR HUNGRY?
MAYBE A LITTLE OF BOTH
I'M SLEENGRY
© 2022 PAWS, INC. All Rights Reserved.
Distributed by Andrews McMeel Syndication
JIM DAVIS 11-21

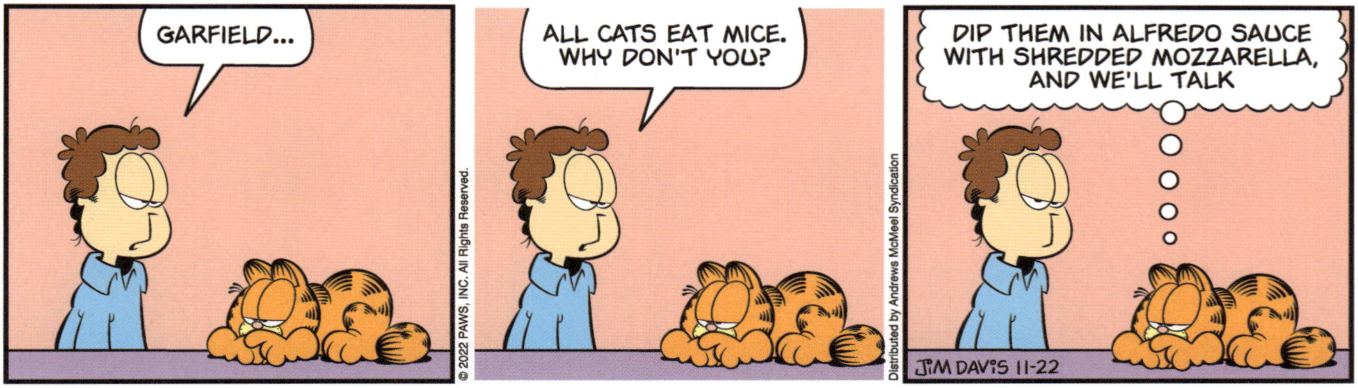
GARFIELD...
ALL CATS EAT MICE. WHY DON'T YOU?
DIP THEM IN ALFREDO SAUCE WITH SHREDDED MOZZARELLA, AND WE'LL TALK
© 2022 PAWS, INC. All Rights Reserved.
Distributed by Andrews McMeel Syndication
JIM DAVIS 11-22

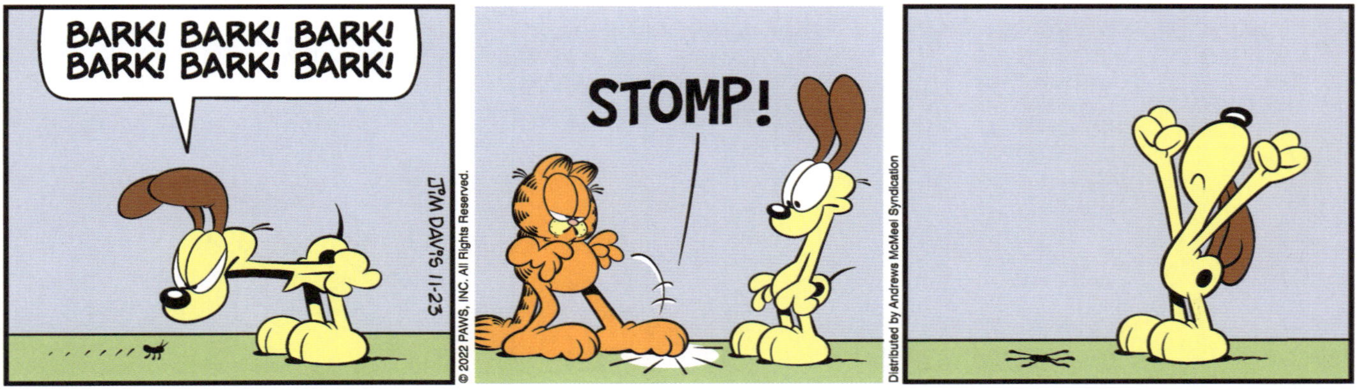
BARK! BARK! BARK! BARK! BARK! BARK!
JIM DAVIS 11-23
© 2022 PAWS, INC. All Rights Reserved.
STOMP!
Distributed by Andrews McMeel Syndication

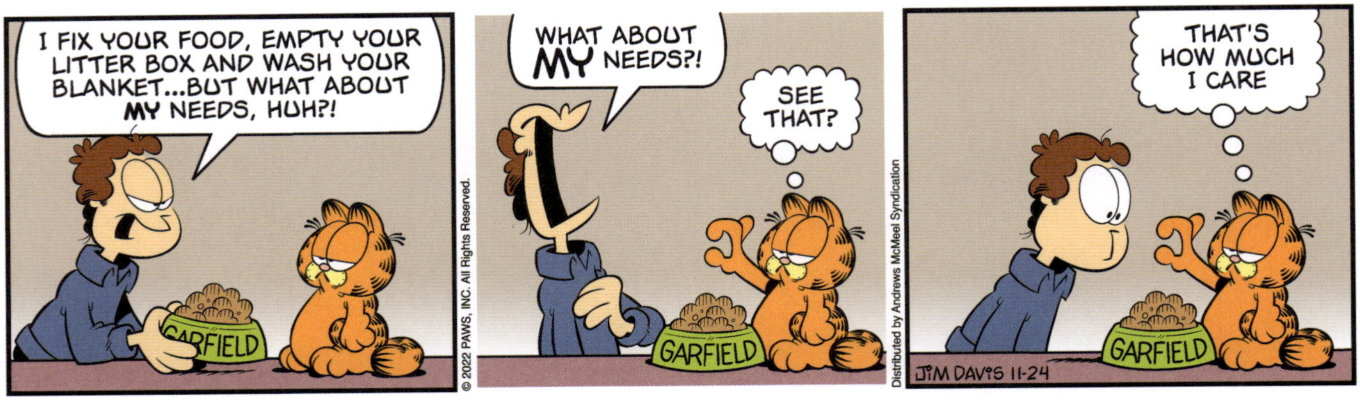
I FIX YOUR FOOD, EMPTY YOUR LITTER BOX AND WASH YOUR BLANKET...BUT WHAT ABOUT MY NEEDS, HUH?!
GARFIELD
© 2022 PAWS, INC. All Rights Reserved.
WHAT ABOUT MY NEEDS?!
SEE THAT?
GARFIELD
Distributed by Andrews McMeel Syndication
THAT'S HOW MUCH I CARE
GARFIELD
JIM DAVIS 11-24

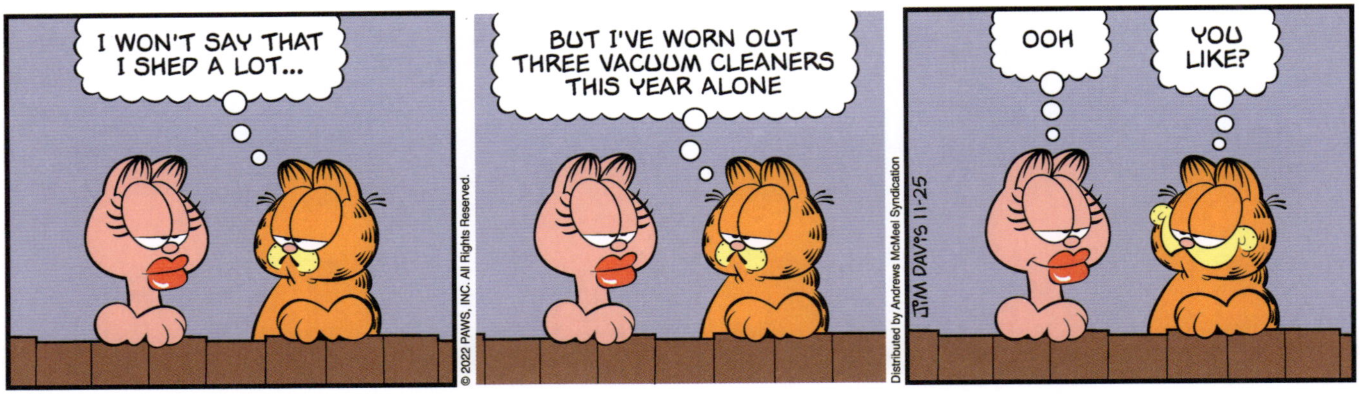
I WON'T SAY THAT I SHED A LOT...
© 2022 PAWS, INC. All Rights Reserved.
BUT I'VE WORN OUT THREE VACUUM CLEANERS THIS YEAR ALONE
Distributed by Andrews McMeel Syndication
JIM DAVIS 11-25
OOH
YOU LIKE?

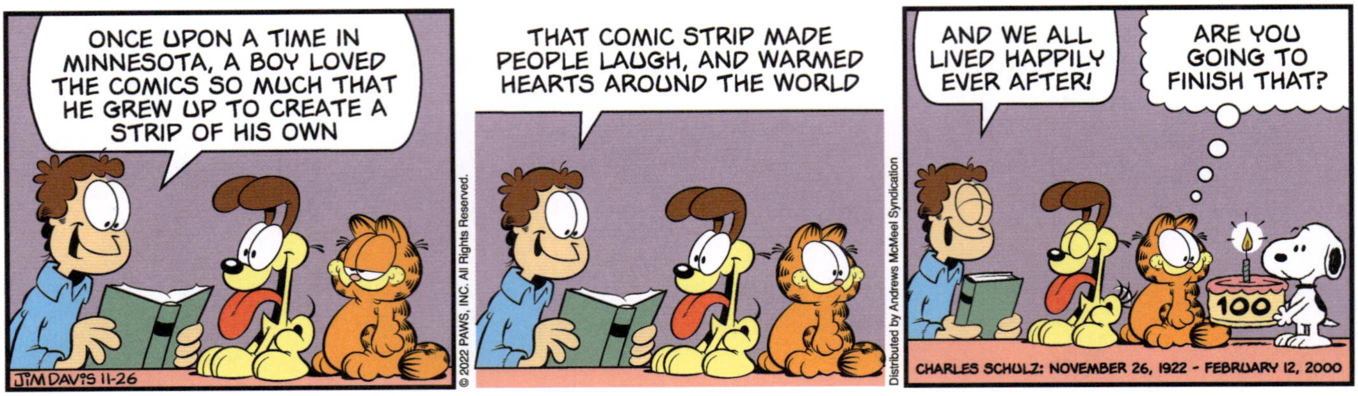
ONCE UPON A TIME IN MINNESOTA, A BOY LOVED THE COMICS SO MUCH THAT HE GREW UP TO CREATE A STRIP OF HIS OWN
JIM DAVIS 11-26
© 2022 PAWS, INC. All Rights Reserved.
THAT COMIC STRIP MADE PEOPLE LAUGH, AND WARMED HEARTS AROUND THE WORLD
Distributed by Andrews McMeel Syndication
AND WE ALL LIVED HAPPILY EVER AFTER!
ARE YOU GOING TO FINISH THAT?
100
CHARLES SCHULZ: NOVEMBER 26, 1922 - FEBRUARY 12, 2000

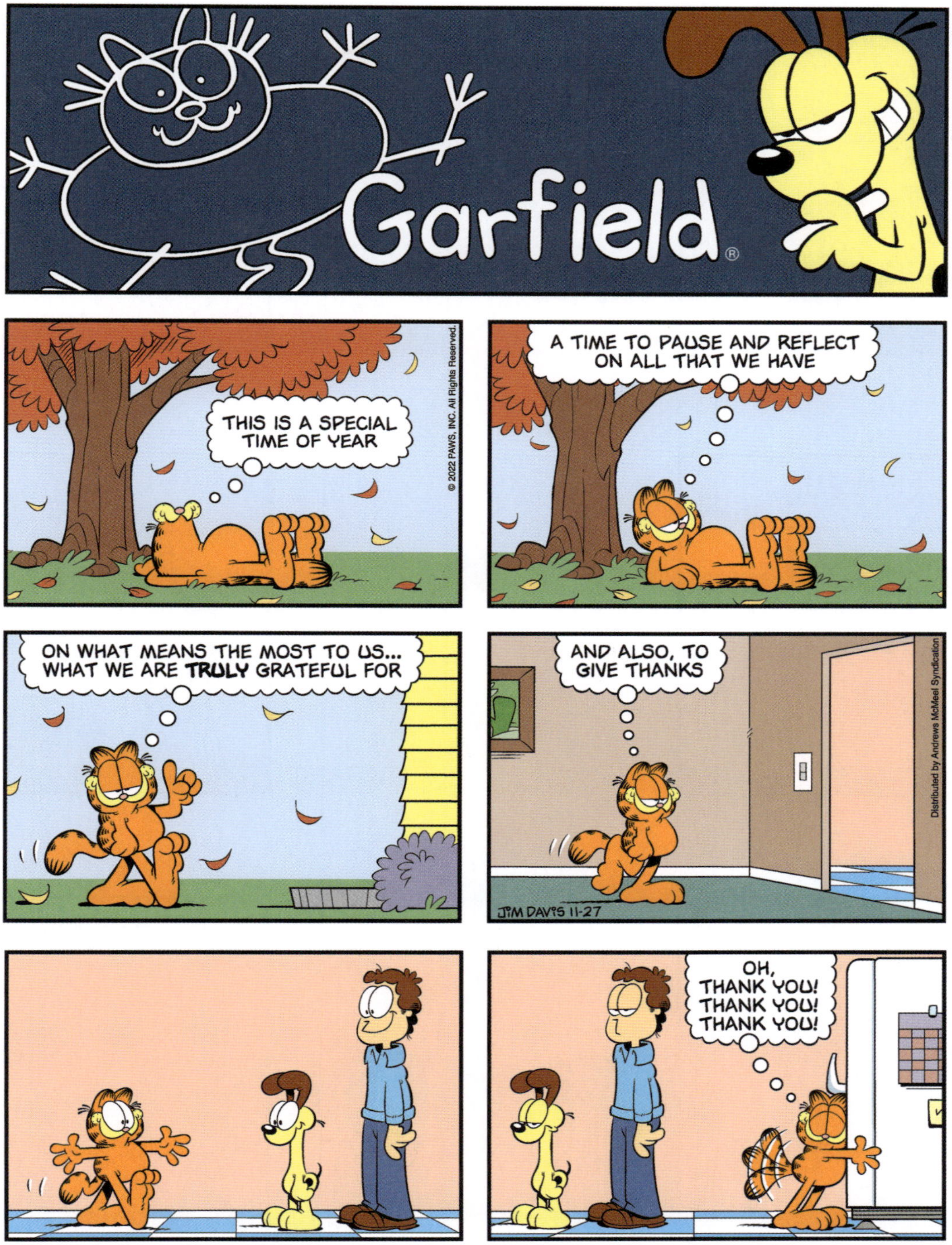
Garfield®
THIS IS A SPECIAL TIME OF YEAR
© 2022 PAWS, INC. All Rights Reserved.
A TIME TO PAUSE AND REFLECT ON ALL THAT WE HAVE
ON WHAT MEANS THE MOST TO US... WHAT WE ARE TRULY GRATEFUL FOR
AND ALSO, TO GIVE THANKS
JIM DAVIS 11-27
Distributed by Andrews McMeel Syndication
OH, THANK YOU! THANK YOU! THANK YOU!

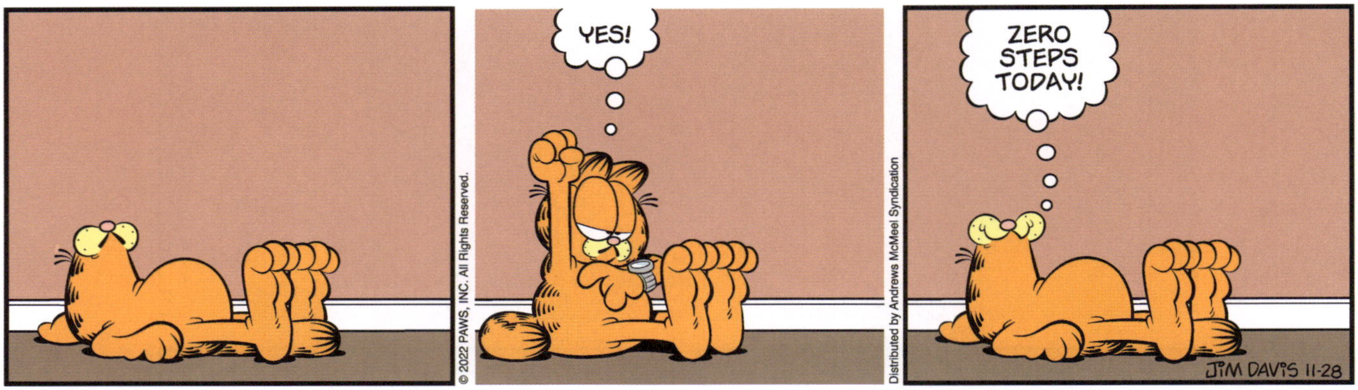
YES!
ZERO STEPS TODAY!
© 2022 PAWS, INC. All Rights Reserved.
Distributed by Andrews McMeel Syndication
JIM DAVIS 11-28

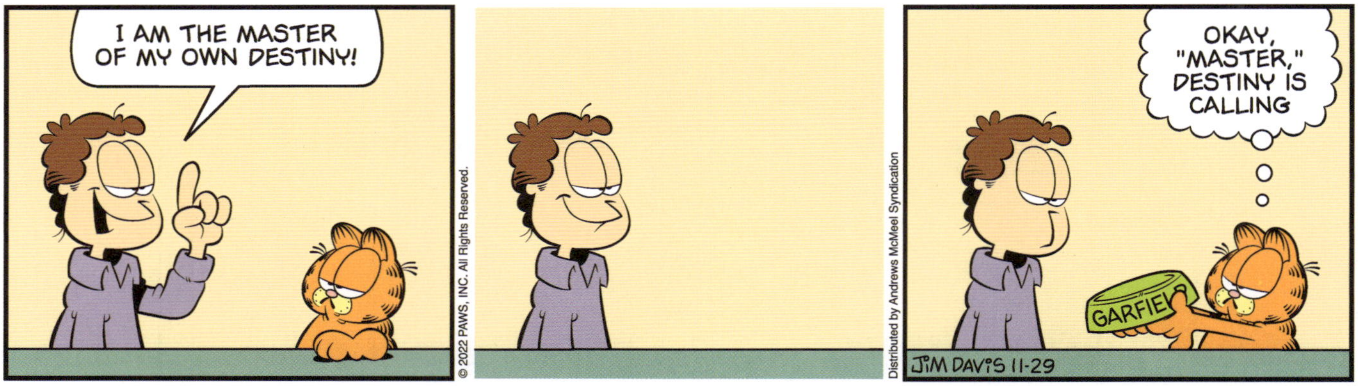
I AM THE MASTER OF MY OWN DESTINY!
OKAY, "MASTER," DESTINY IS CALLING
© 2022 PAWS, INC. All Rights Reserved.
Distributed by Andrews McMeel Syndication
JIM DAVIS 11-29

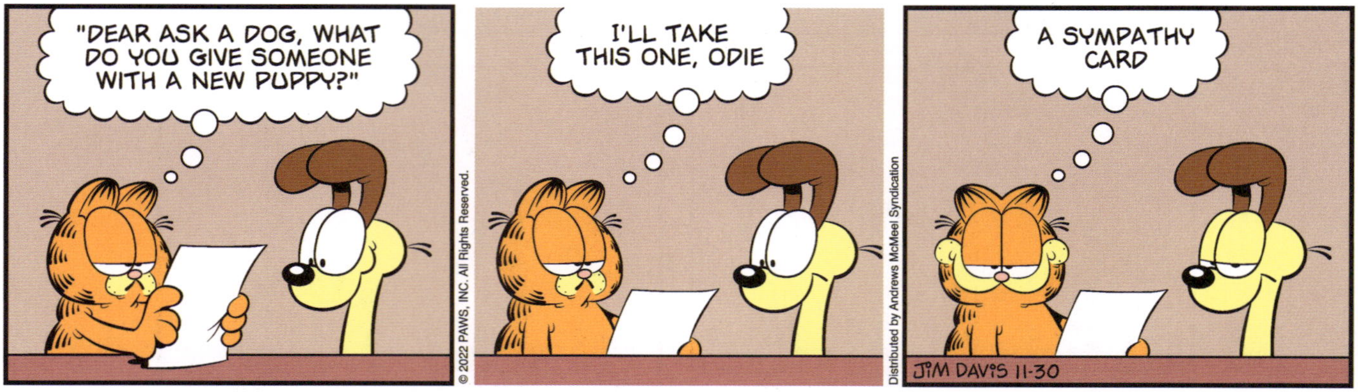
"DEAR ASK A DOG, WHAT DO YOU GIVE SOMEONE WITH A NEW PUPPY?"
I'LL TAKE THIS ONE, ODIE
A SYMPATHY CARD
© 2022 PAWS, INC. All Rights Reserved.
Distributed by Andrews McMeel Syndication
JIM DAVIS 11-30

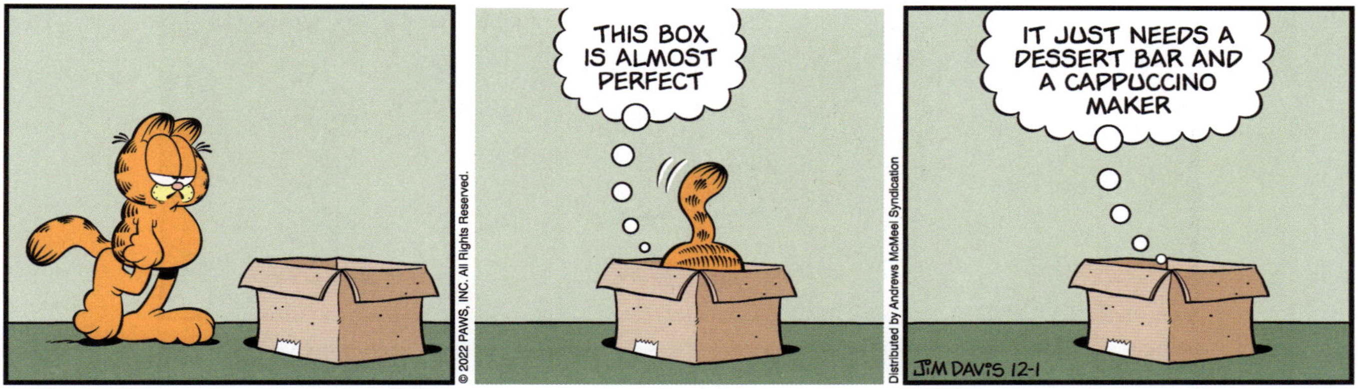
THIS BOX IS ALMOST PERFECT
IT JUST NEEDS A DESSERT BAR AND A CAPPUCCINO MAKER
© 2022 PAWS, INC. All Rights Reserved.
Distributed by Andrews McMeel Syndication
JIM DAVIS 12-1

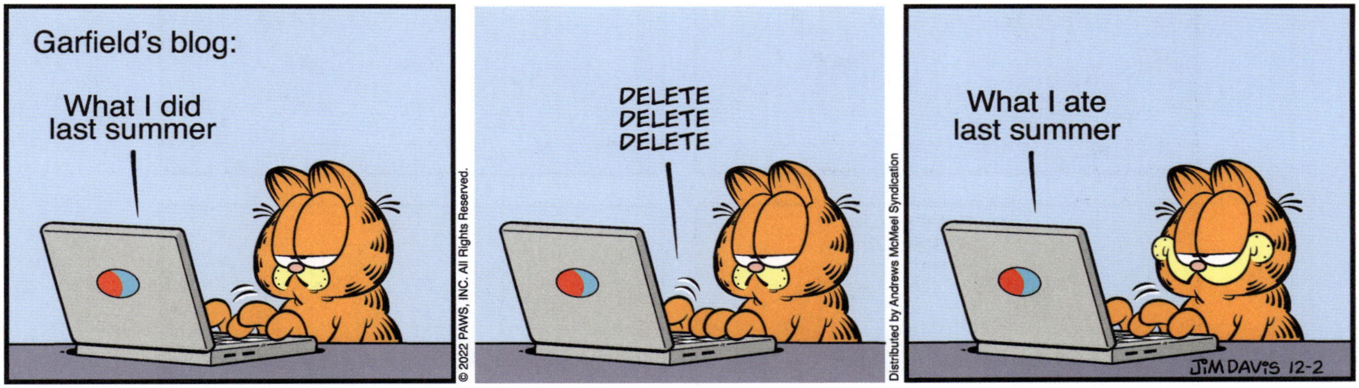
Garfield's blog:
What I did last summer
DELETE DELETE DELETE
What I ate last summer
© 2022 PAWS, INC. All Rights Reserved.
Distributed by Andrews McMeel Syndication
JIM DAVIS 12-2

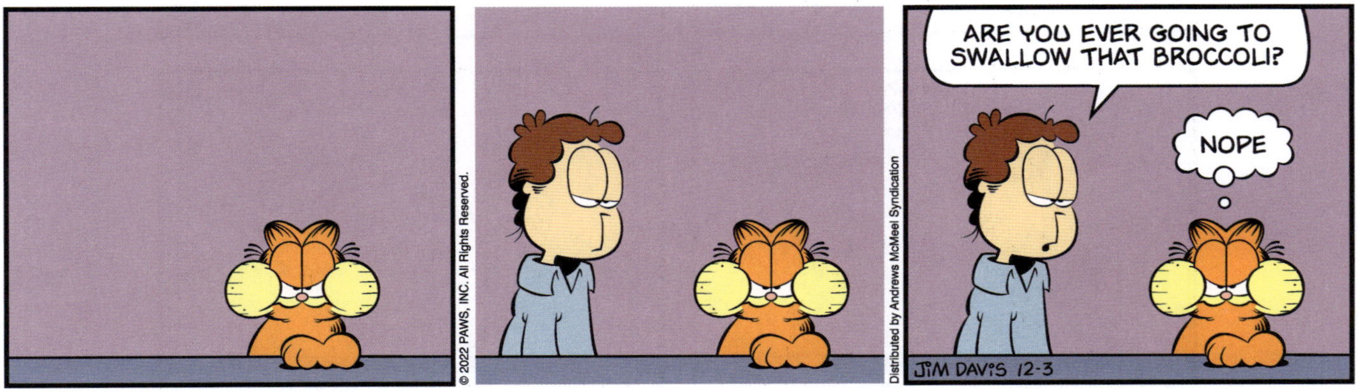
ARE YOU EVER GOING TO SWALLOW THAT BROCCOLI?
NOPE
© 2022 PAWS, INC. All Rights Reserved.
Distributed by Andrews McMeel Syndication
JIM DAVIS 12-3

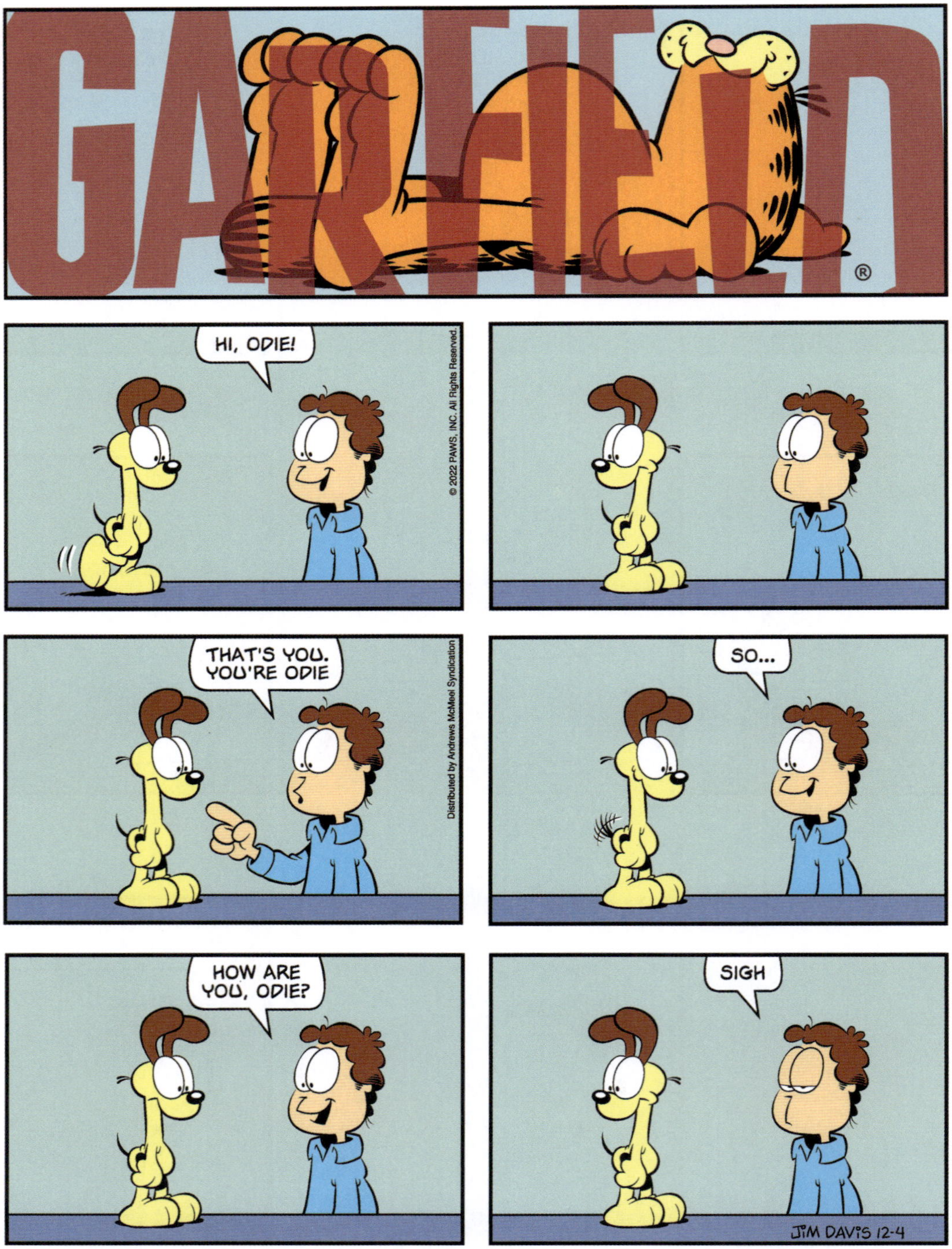
GARFIELD®
HI, ODIE!
© 2022 PAWS, INC. All Rights Reserved.
THAT'S YOU. YOU'RE ODIE
Distributed by Andrews McMeel Syndication
SO...
HOW ARE YOU, ODIE?
SIGH
JIM DAVIS 12-4

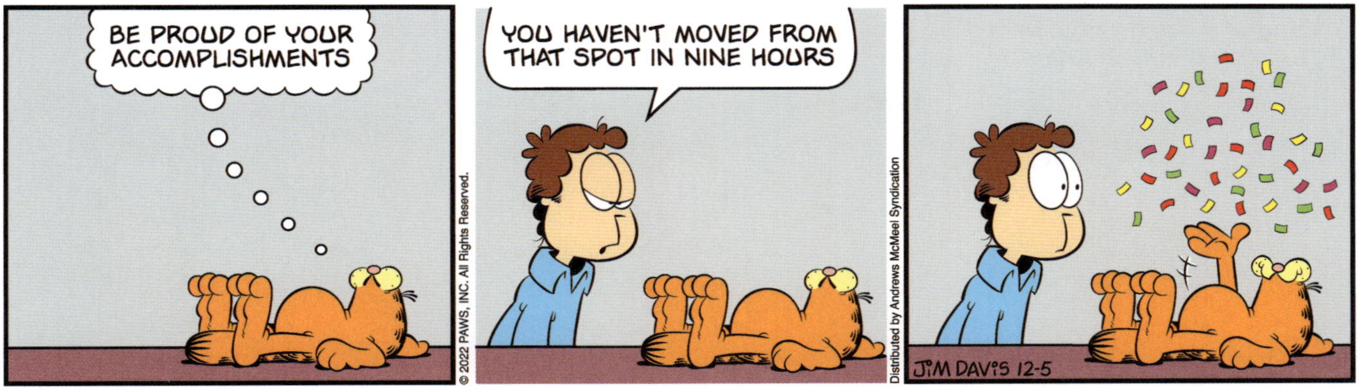
BE PROUD OF YOUR ACCOMPLISHMENTS
YOU HAVEN'T MOVED FROM THAT SPOT IN NINE HOURS
© 2022 PAWS, INC. All Rights Reserved.
Distributed by Andrews McMeel Syndication
JIM DAVIS 12-5

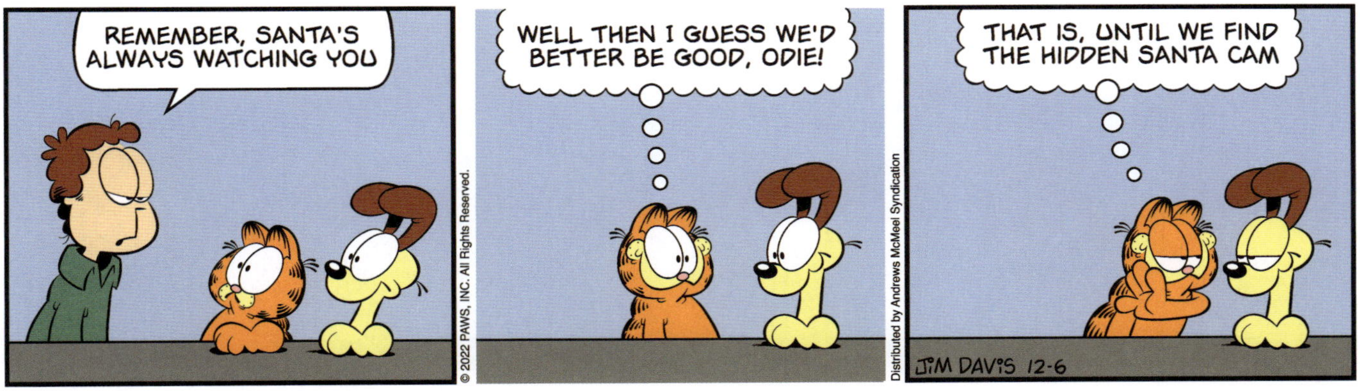
REMEMBER, SANTA'S ALWAYS WATCHING YOU
WELL THEN I GUESS WE'D BETTER BE GOOD, ODIE!
THAT IS, UNTIL WE FIND THE HIDDEN SANTA CAM
© 2022 PAWS, INC. All Rights Reserved.
Distributed by Andrews McMeel Syndication
JIM DAVIS 12-6

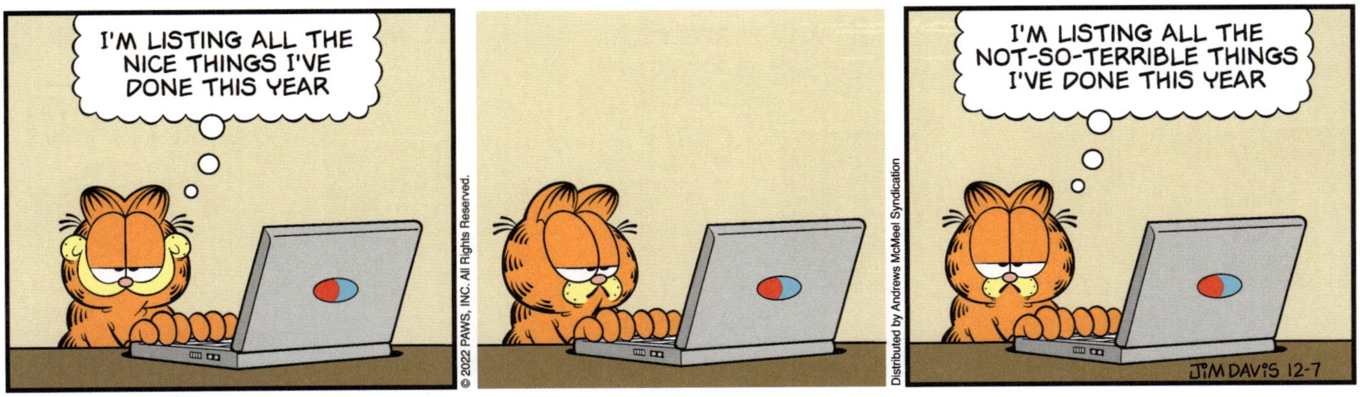
I'M LISTING ALL THE NICE THINGS I'VE DONE THIS YEAR
I'M LISTING ALL THE NOT-SO-TERRIBLE THINGS I'VE DONE THIS YEAR
© 2022 PAWS, INC. All Rights Reserved.
Distributed by Andrews McMeel Syndication
JIM DAVIS 12-7

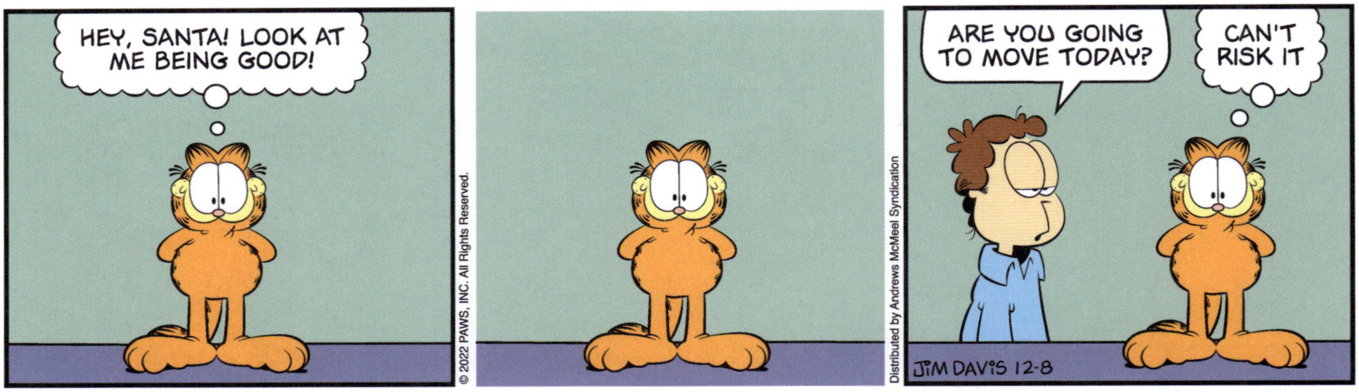
HEY, SANTA! LOOK AT ME BEING GOOD!
© 2022 PAWS, INC. All Rights Reserved.
Distributed by Andrews McMeel Syndication
ARE YOU GOING TO MOVE TODAY?
CAN'T RISK IT
JIM DAVIS 12-8

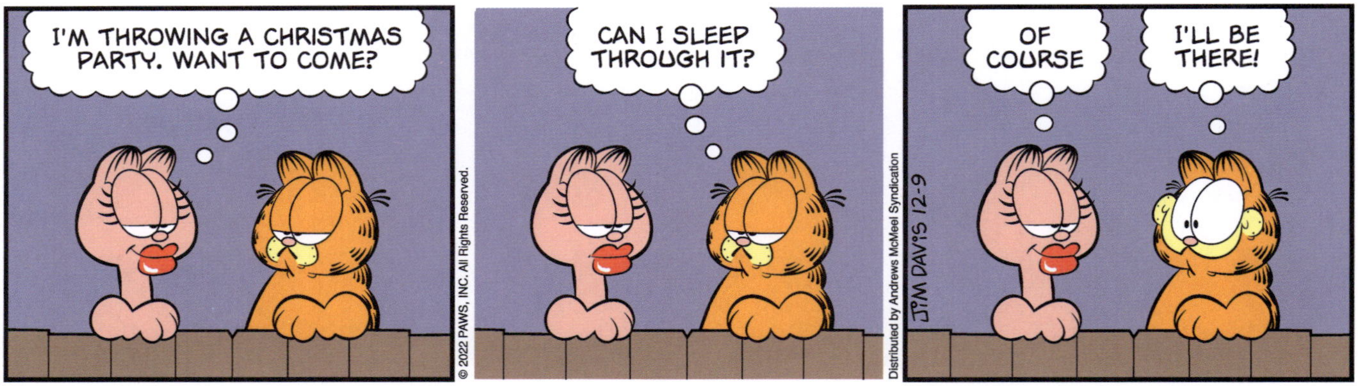
I'M THROWING A CHRISTMAS PARTY. WANT TO COME?
© 2022 PAWS, INC. All Rights Reserved.
CAN I SLEEP THROUGH IT?
Distributed by Andrews McMeel Syndication
JIM DAVIS 12-9
OF COURSE
I'LL BE THERE!

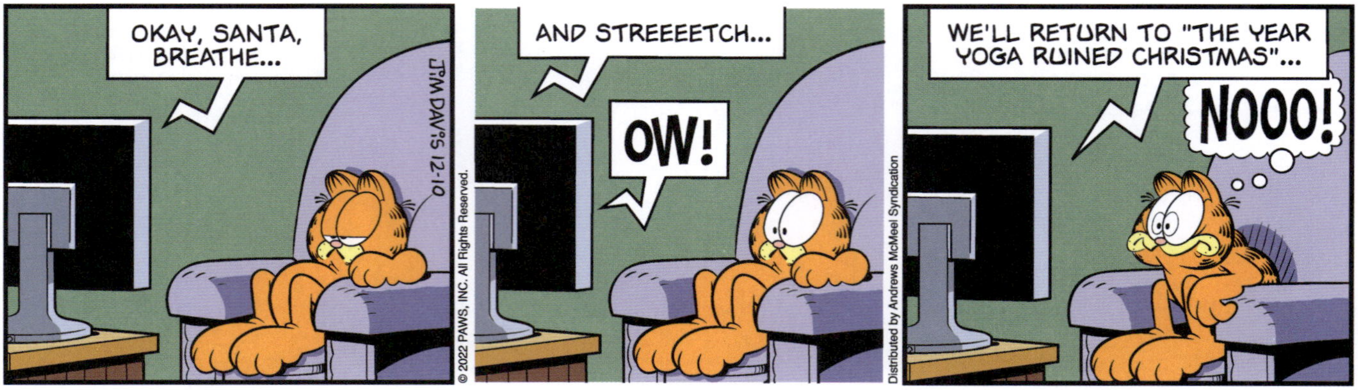
OKAY, SANTA, BREATHE...
JIM DAVIS 12-10
© 2022 PAWS, INC. All Rights Reserved.
AND STREEEETCH...
OW!
Distributed by Andrews McMeel Syndication
WE'LL RETURN TO "THE YEAR YOGA RUINED CHRISTMAS"...
NOOO!

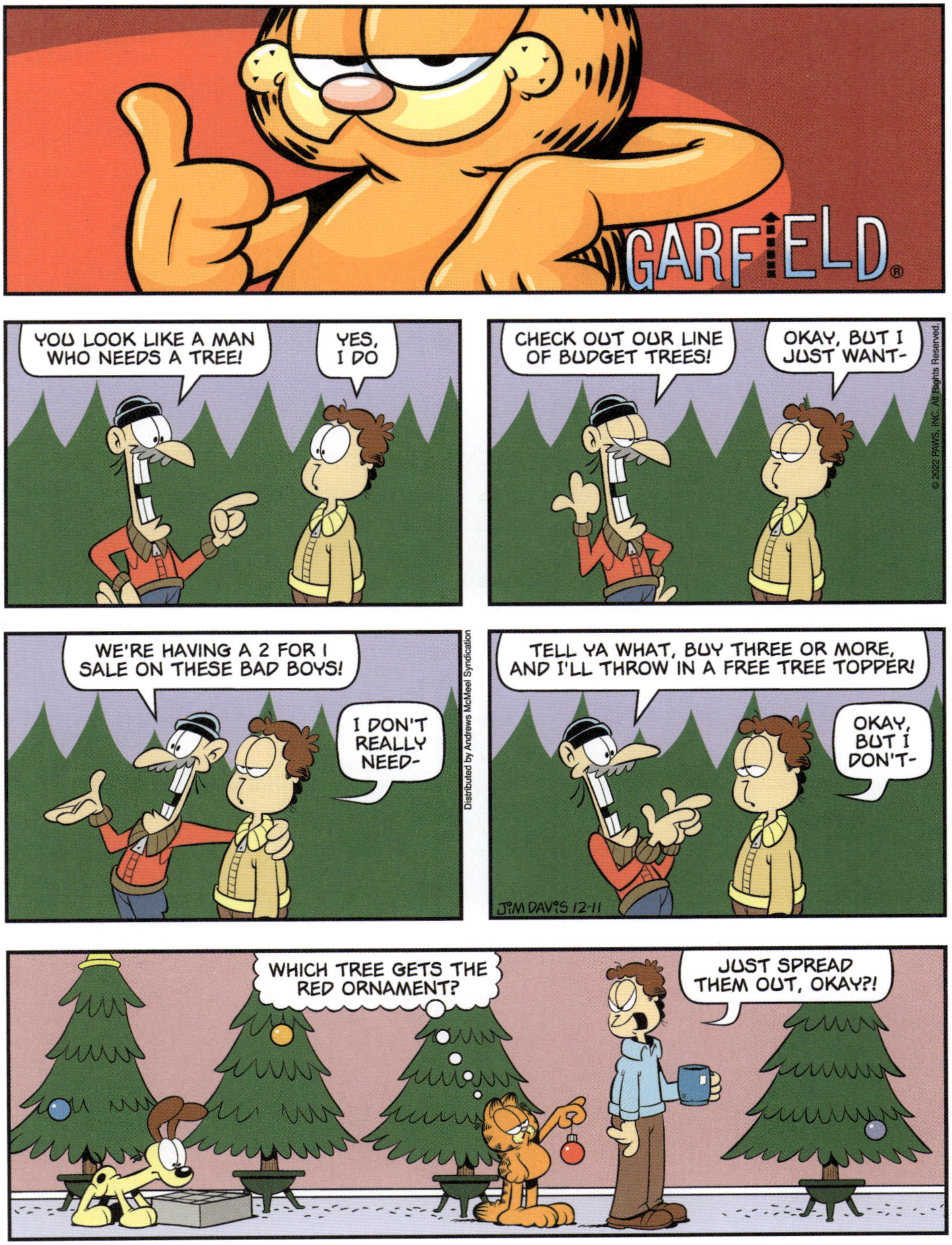
GARFIELD®
YOU LOOK LIKE A MAN WHO NEEDS A TREE!
YES, I DO
CHECK OUT OUR LINE OF BUDGET TREES!
OKAY, BUT I JUST WANT-
© 2022 PAWS, INC. All Rights Reserved.
WE'RE HAVING A 2 FOR 1 SALE ON THESE BAD BOYS!
I DON'T REALLY NEED-
Distributed by Andrews McMeel Syndication
TELL YA WHAT, BUY THREE OR MORE, AND I'LL THROW IN A FREE TREE TOPPER!
OKAY, BUT I DON'T-
JIM DAVIS 12-11
WHICH TREE GETS THE RED ORNAMENT?
JUST SPREAD THEM OUT, OKAY?!

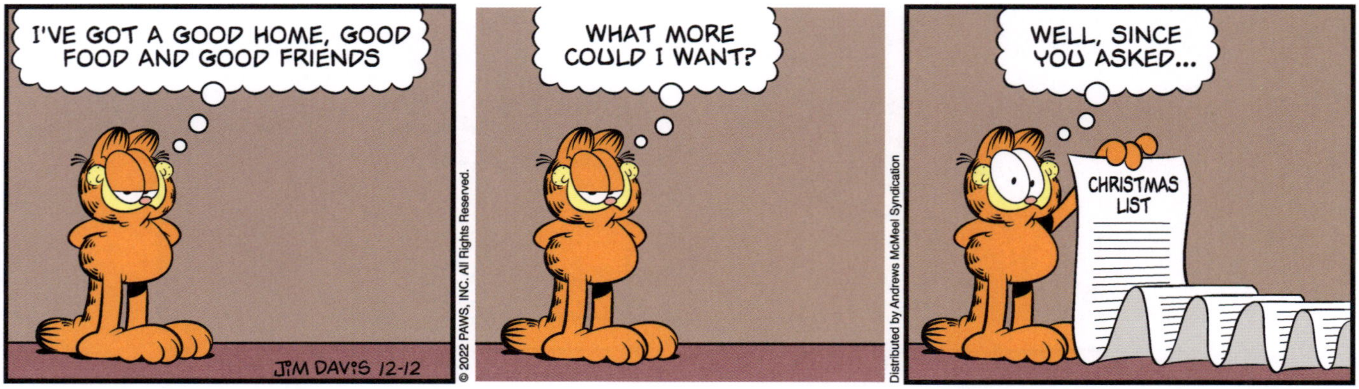
I'VE GOT A GOOD HOME, GOOD FOOD AND GOOD FRIENDS
JIM DAVIS 12-12
© 2022 PAWS, INC. All Rights Reserved.
WHAT MORE COULD I WANT?
Distributed by Andrews McMeel Syndication
WELL, SINCE YOU ASKED...
CHRISTMAS LIST

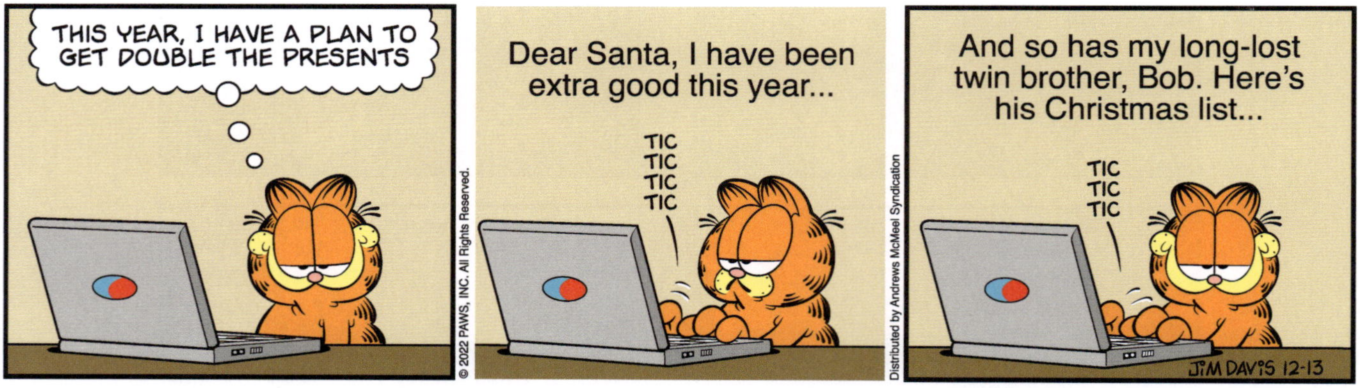
THIS YEAR, I HAVE A PLAN TO GET DOUBLE THE PRESENTS
© 2022 PAWS, INC. All Rights Reserved.
Dear Santa, I have been extra good this year...
TIC TIC TIC TIC
Distributed by Andrews McMeel Syndication
And so has my long-lost twin brother, Bob. Here's his Christmas list...
TIC TIC TIC
JIM DAVIS 12-13

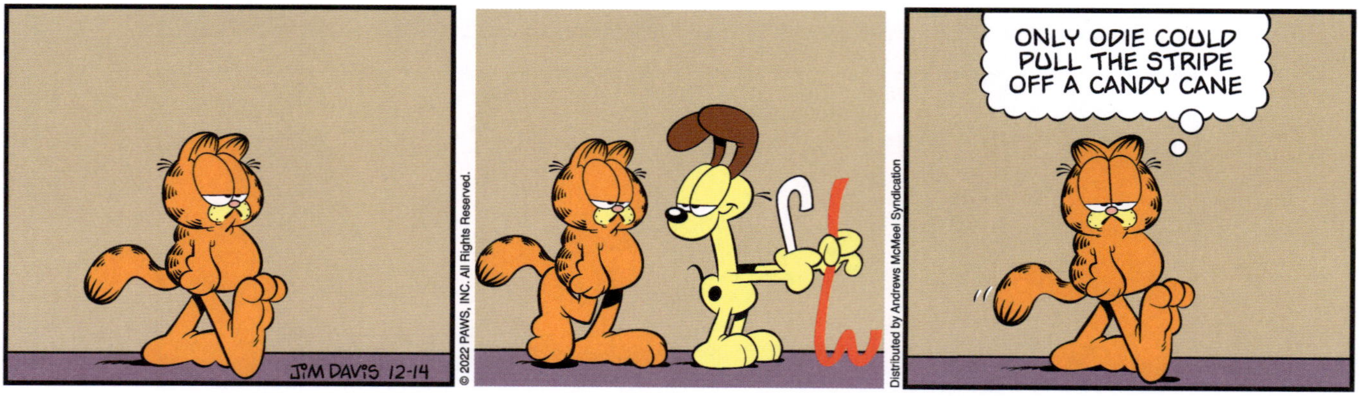
JIM DAVIS 12-14
© 2022 PAWS, INC. All Rights Reserved.
Distributed by Andrews McMeel Syndication
ONLY ODIE COULD PULL THE STRIPE OFF A CANDY CANE

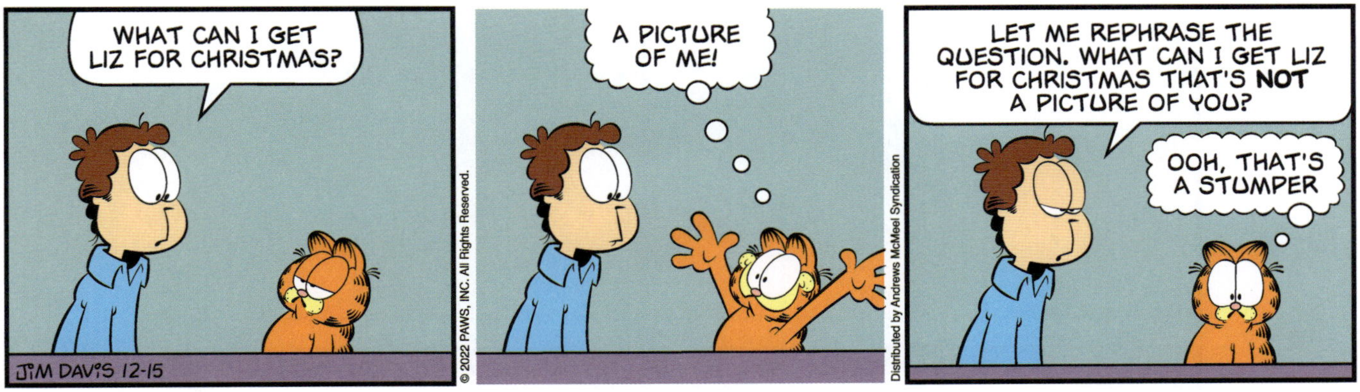
WHAT CAN I GET LIZ FOR CHRISTMAS?
JIM DAVIS 12-15
© 2022 PAWS, INC. All Rights Reserved.
A PICTURE OF ME!
Distributed by Andrews McMeel Syndication
LET ME REPHRASE THE QUESTION. WHAT CAN I GET LIZ FOR CHRISTMAS THAT'S **NOT** A PICTURE OF YOU?
OOH, THAT'S A STUMPER

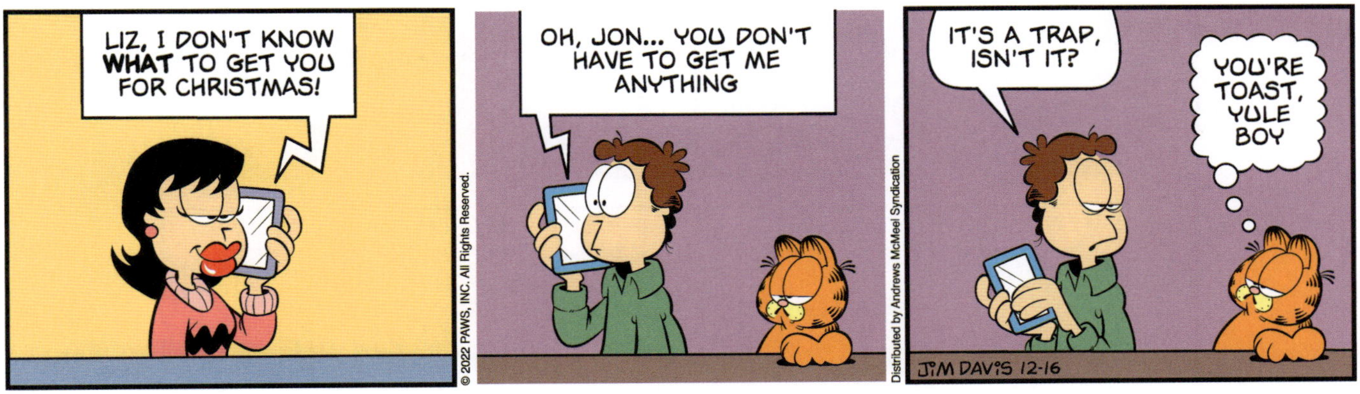
LIZ, I DON'T KNOW **WHAT** TO GET YOU FOR CHRISTMAS!
© 2022 PAWS, INC. All Rights Reserved.
OH, JON... YOU DON'T HAVE TO GET ME ANYTHING
Distributed by Andrews McMeel Syndication
IT'S A TRAP, ISN'T IT?
YOU'RE TOAST, YULE BOY
JIM DAVIS 12-16

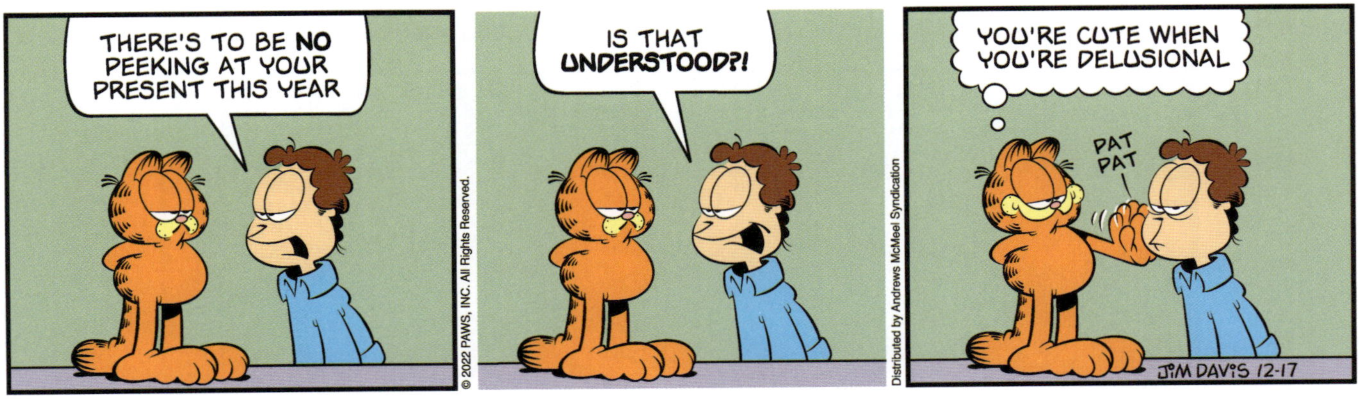
THERE'S TO BE **NO** PEEKING AT YOUR PRESENT THIS YEAR
© 2022 PAWS, INC. All Rights Reserved.
IS THAT **UNDERSTOOD?!**
Distributed by Andrews McMeel Syndication
YOU'RE CUTE WHEN YOU'RE DELUSIONAL
PAT PAT
JIM DAVIS 12-17

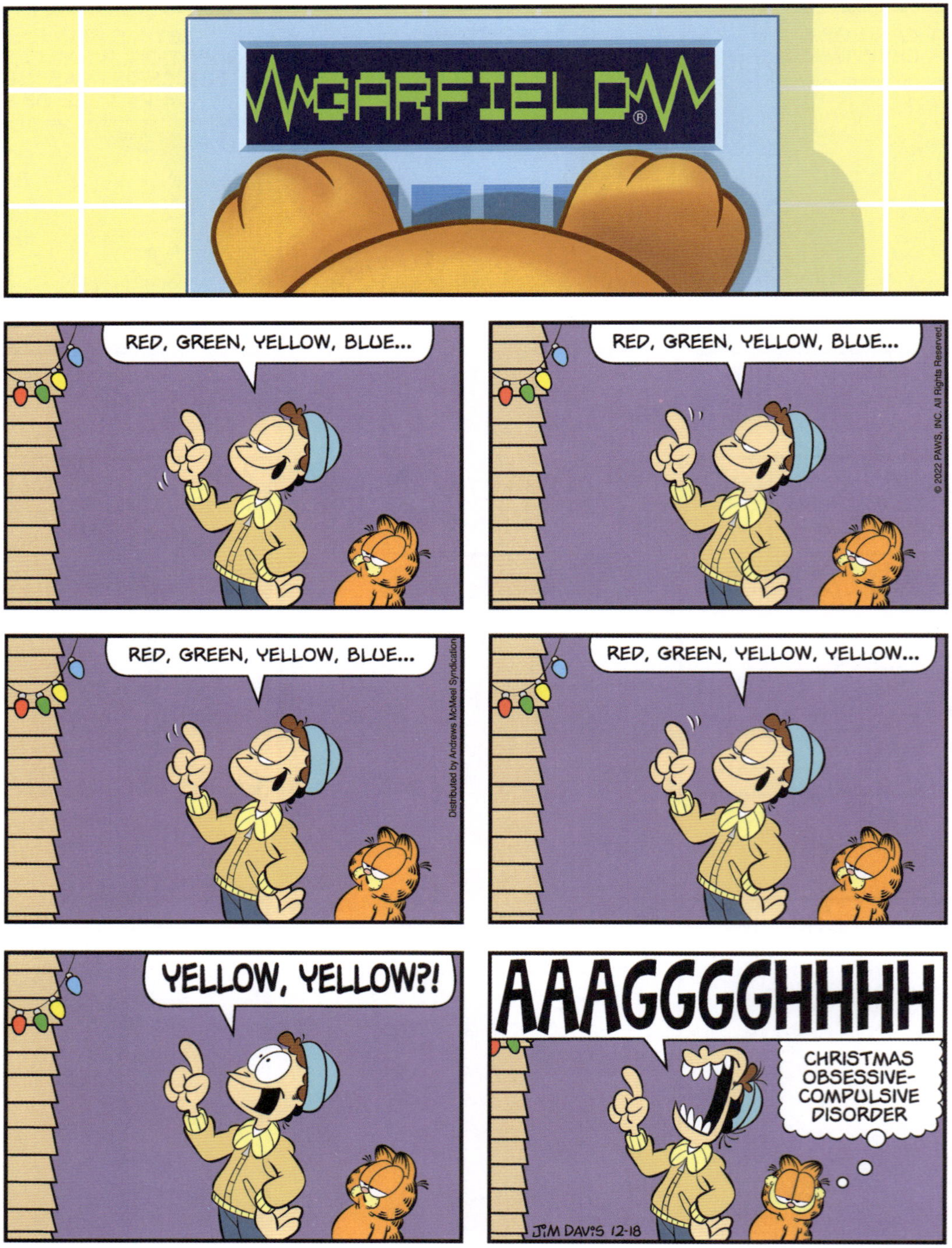
GARFIELD®
RED, GREEN, YELLOW, BLUE...
RED, GREEN, YELLOW, BLUE...
© 2022 PAWS, INC. All Rights Reserved.
RED, GREEN, YELLOW, BLUE...
Distributed by Andrews McMeel Syndication
RED, GREEN, YELLOW, YELLOW...
YELLOW, YELLOW?!
AAAGGGGHHHH
CHRISTMAS OBSESSIVE-COMPULSIVE DISORDER
JIM DAVIS 12-18

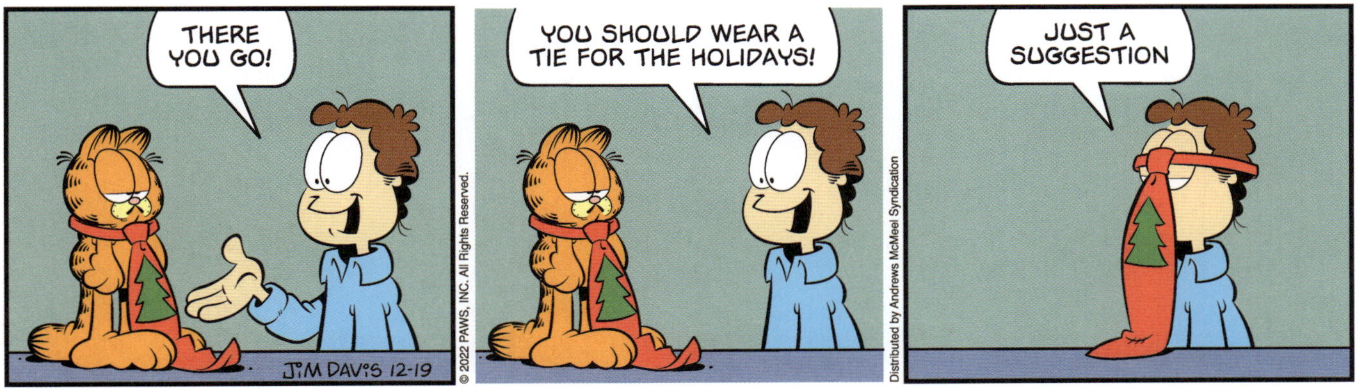
THERE YOU GO!
JIM DAVIS 12-19
© 2022 PAWS, INC. All Rights Reserved.
YOU SHOULD WEAR A TIE FOR THE HOLIDAYS!
Distributed by Andrews McMeel Syndication
JUST A SUGGESTION

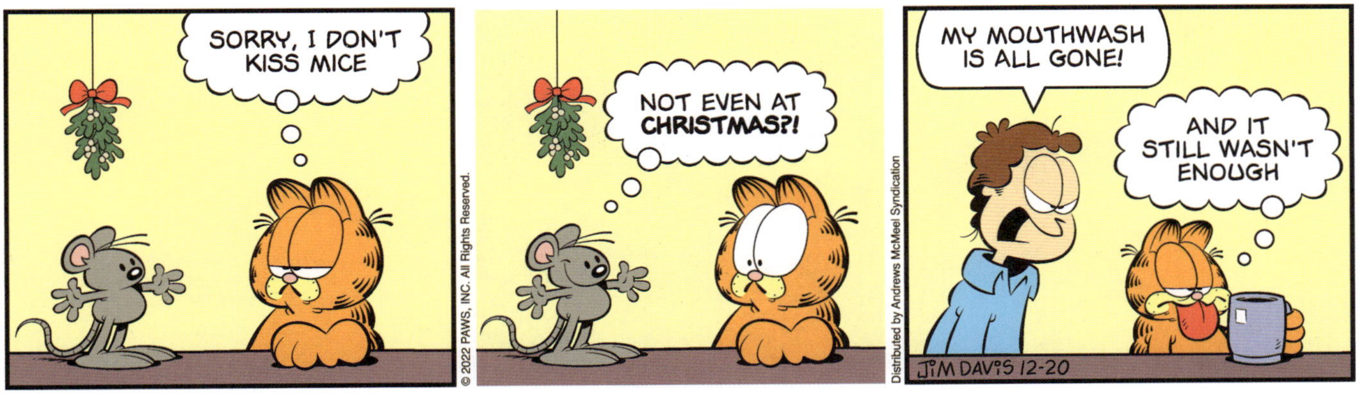
SORRY, I DON'T KISS MICE
© 2022 PAWS, INC. All Rights Reserved.
NOT EVEN AT **CHRISTMAS?!**
Distributed by Andrews McMeel Syndication
MY MOUTHWASH IS ALL GONE!
AND IT STILL WASN'T ENOUGH
JIM DAVIS 12-20

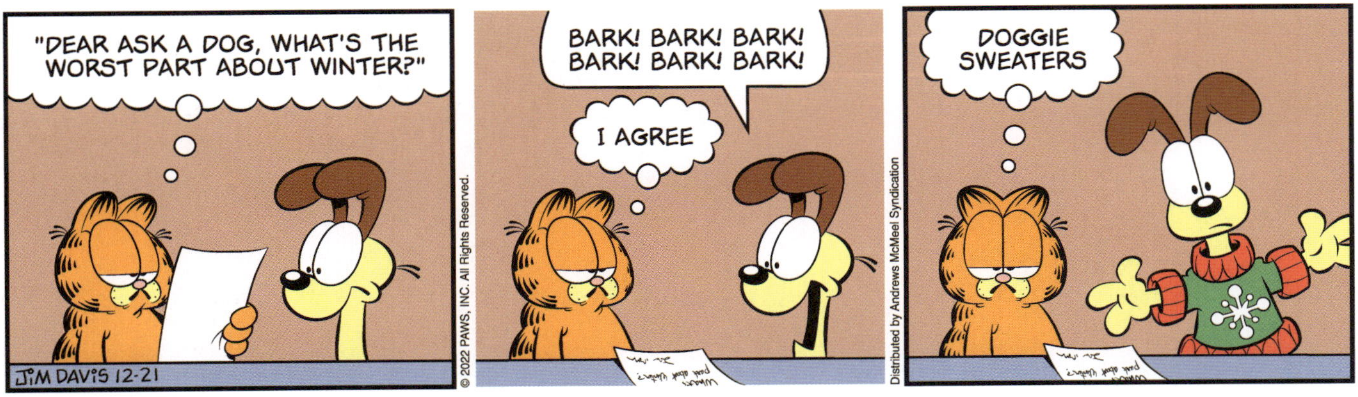
"DEAR ASK A DOG, WHAT'S THE WORST PART ABOUT WINTER?"
JIM DAVIS 12-21
© 2022 PAWS, INC. All Rights Reserved.
BARK! BARK! BARK! BARK! BARK! BARK!
I AGREE
Distributed by Andrews McMeel Syndication
DOGGIE SWEATERS

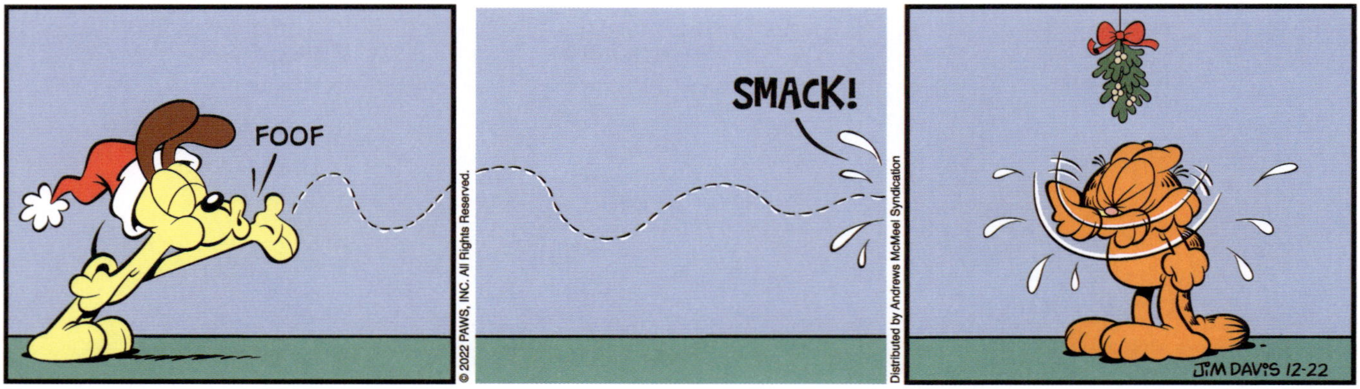
FOOF
SMACK!
© 2022 PAWS, INC. All Rights Reserved.
Distributed by Andrews McMeel Syndication
JIM DAVIS 12-22

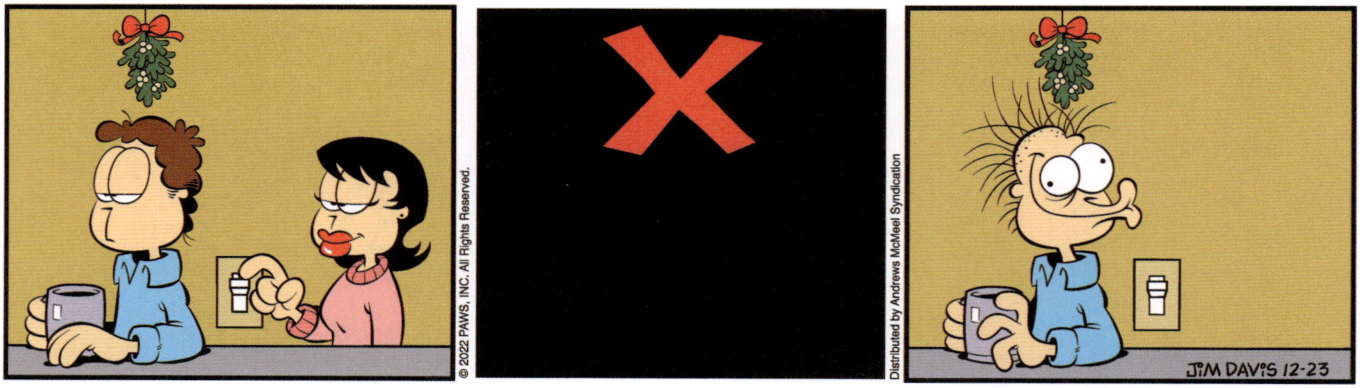
© 2022 PAWS, INC. All Rights Reserved.
Distributed by Andrews McMeel Syndication
JIM DAVIS 12-23

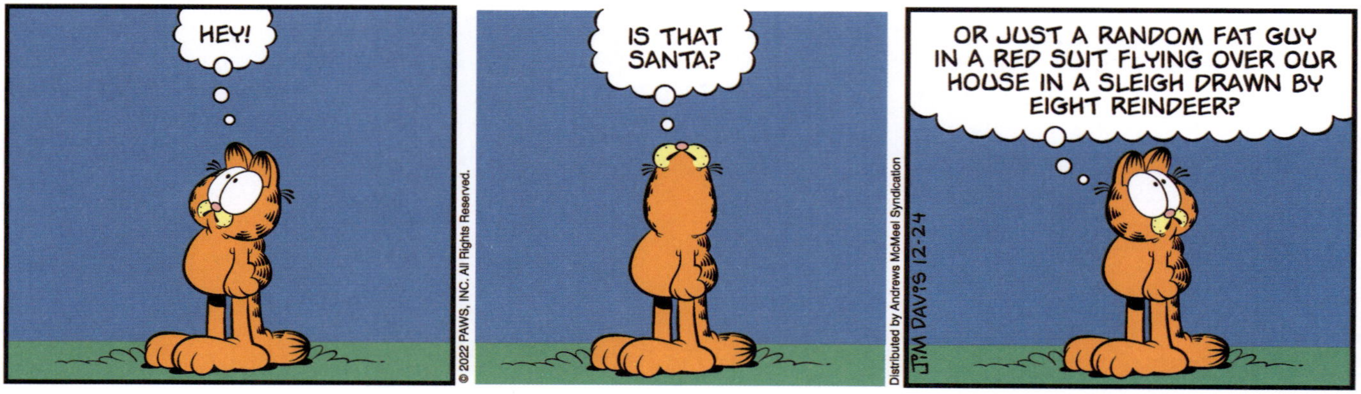
HEY!
IS THAT SANTA?
OR JUST A RANDOM FAT GUY IN A RED SUIT FLYING OVER OUR HOUSE IN A SLEIGH DRAWN BY EIGHT REINDEER?
© 2022 PAWS, INC. All Rights Reserved.
Distributed by Andrews McMeel Syndication
JIM DAVIS 12-24

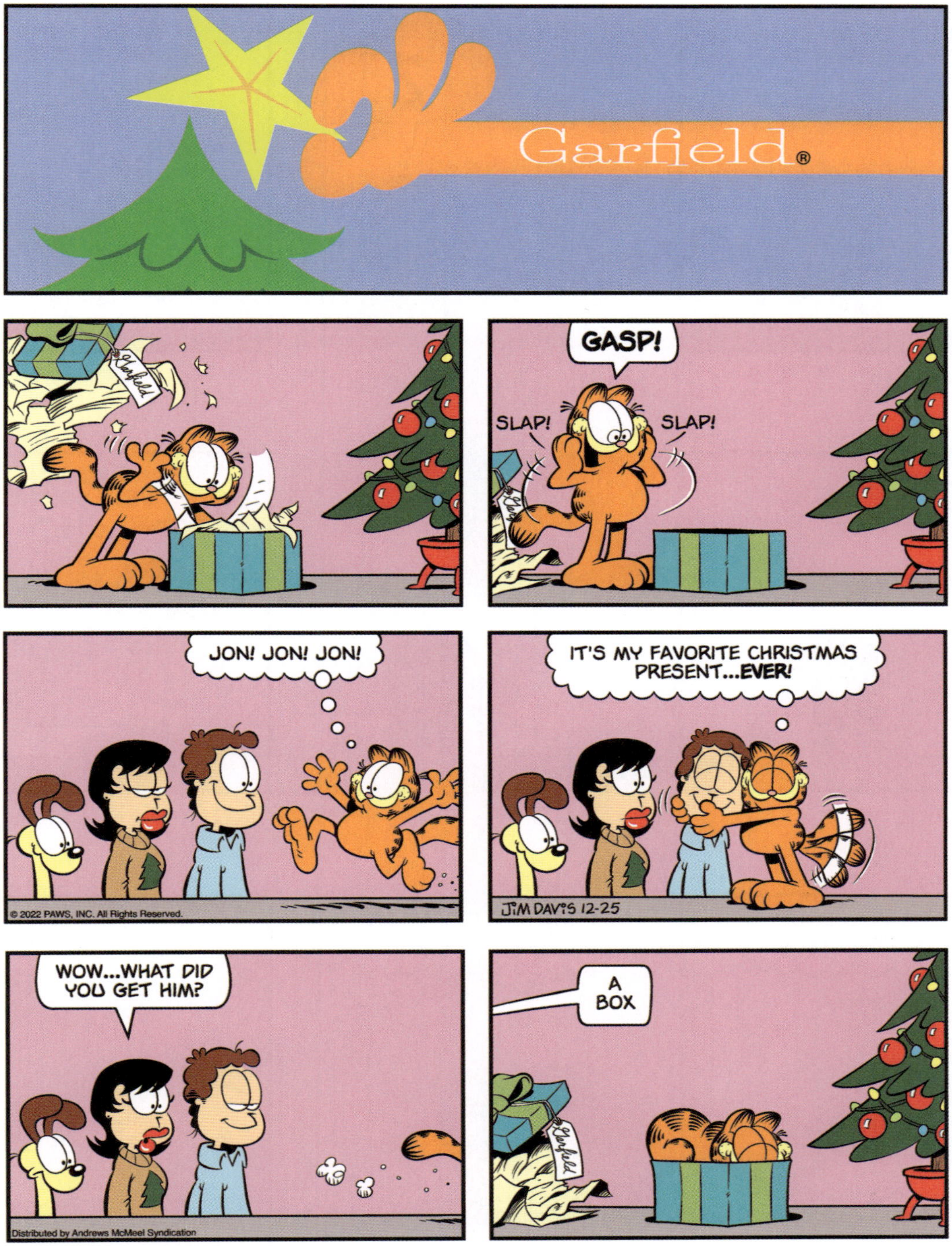
Garfield®
GASP!
SLAP!
SLAP!
JON! JON! JON!
© 2022 PAWS, INC. All Rights Reserved.
IT'S MY FAVORITE CHRISTMAS PRESENT...EVER!
JIM DAVIS 12-25
WOW...WHAT DID YOU GET HIM?
Distributed by Andrews McMeel Syndication
A BOX

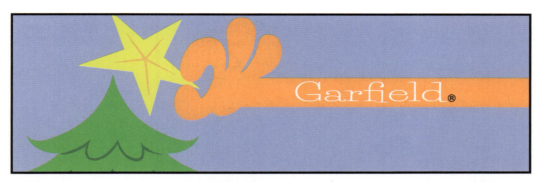

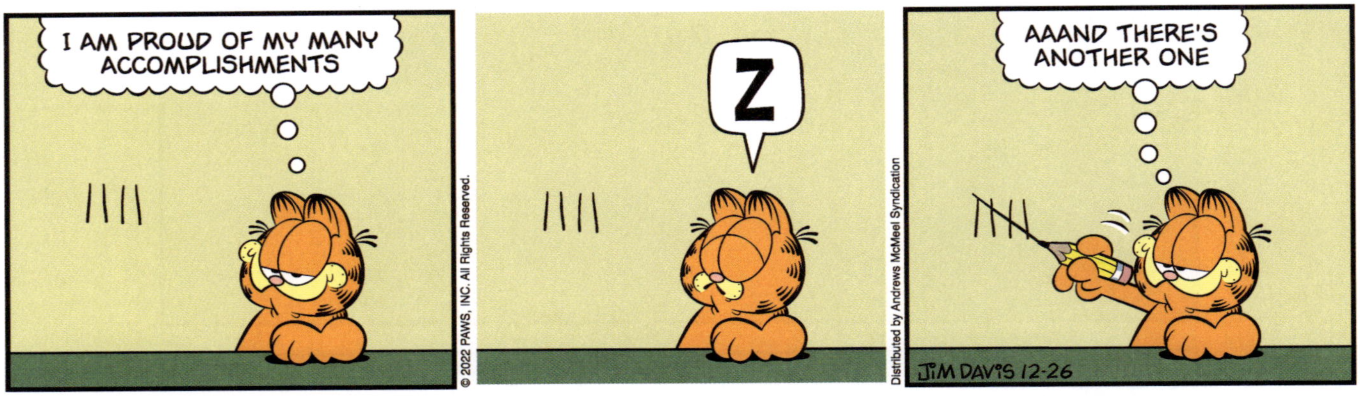
I AM PROUD OF MY MANY ACCOMPLISHMENTS
Z
AAAND THERE'S ANOTHER ONE
© 2022 PAWS, INC. All Rights Reserved.
Distributed by Andrews McMeel Syndication
JIM DAVIS 12-26

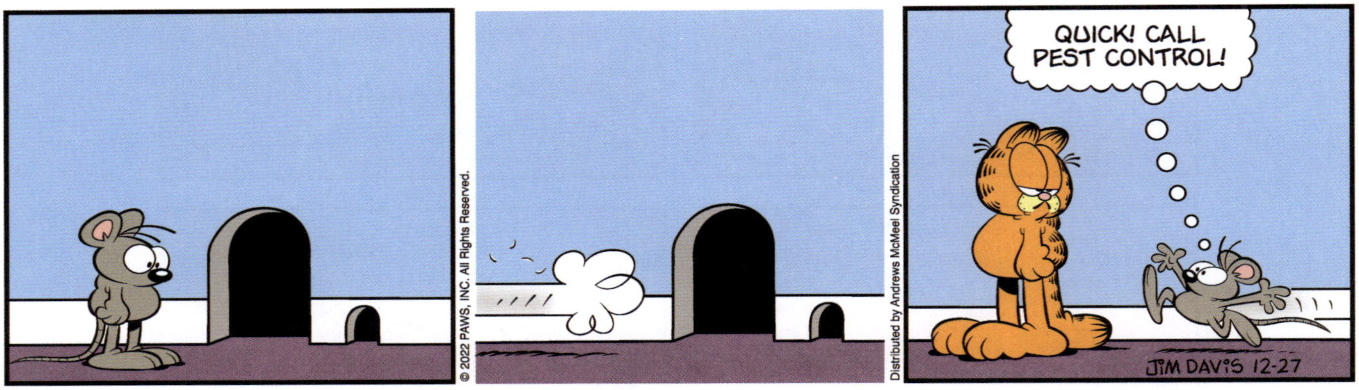
QUICK! CALL PEST CONTROL!
© 2022 PAWS, INC. All Rights Reserved.
Distributed by Andrews McMeel Syndication
JIM DAVIS 12-27

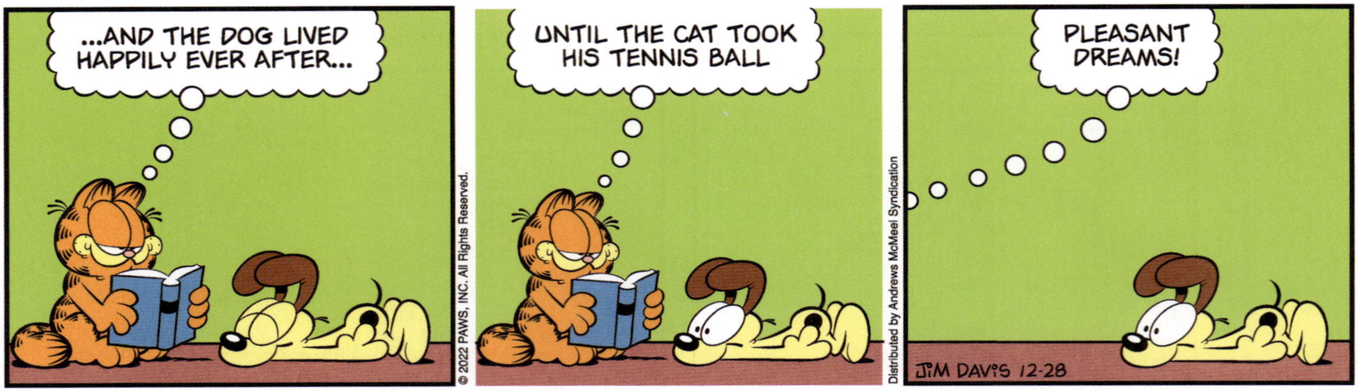
...AND THE DOG LIVED HAPPILY EVER AFTER...
UNTIL THE CAT TOOK HIS TENNIS BALL
PLEASANT DREAMS!
© 2022 PAWS, INC. All Rights Reserved.
Distributed by Andrews McMeel Syndication
JIM DAVIS 12-28

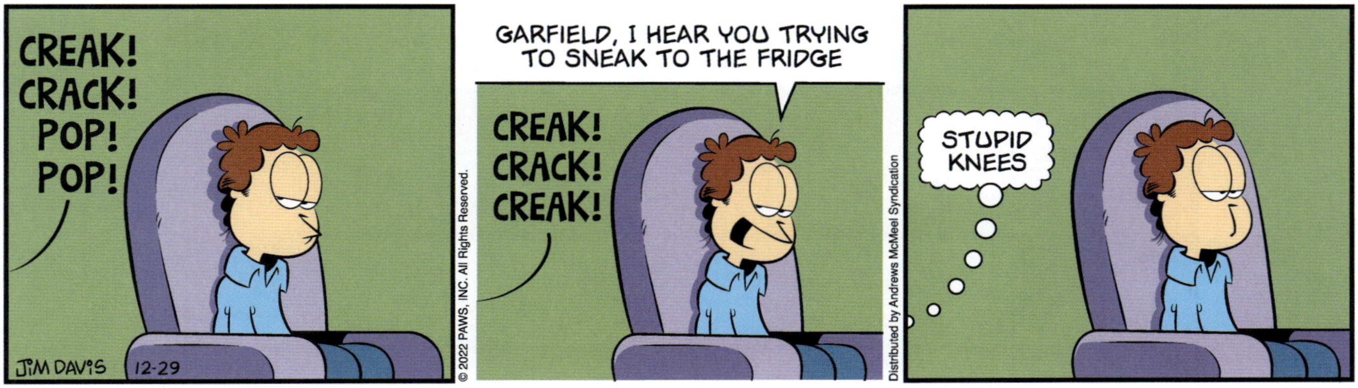
CREAK! CRACK! POP! POP!
JIM DAVIS 12-29
© 2022 PAWS, INC. All Rights Reserved.
GARFIELD, I HEAR YOU TRYING TO SNEAK TO THE FRIDGE
CREAK! CRACK! CREAK!
Distributed by Andrews McMeel Syndication
STUPID KNEES

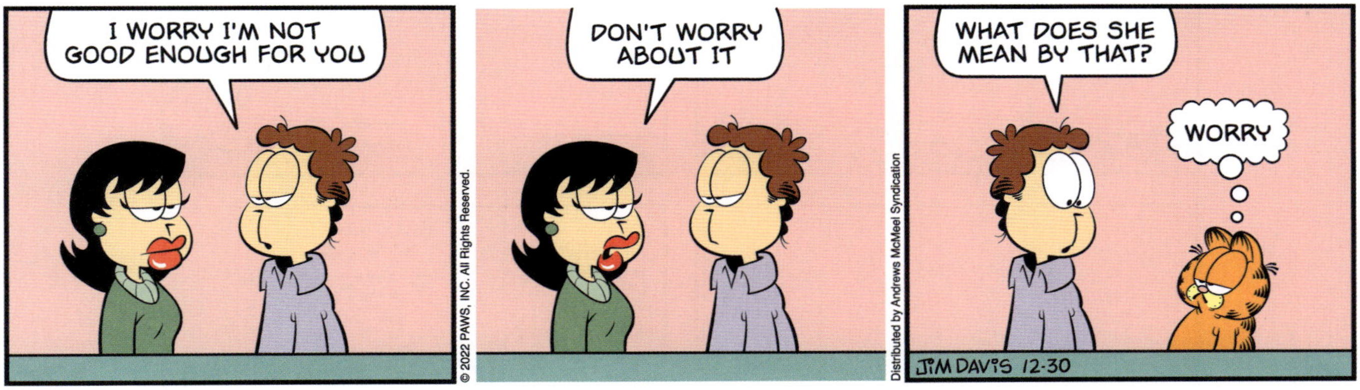
I WORRY I'M NOT GOOD ENOUGH FOR YOU
© 2022 PAWS, INC. All Rights Reserved.
DON'T WORRY ABOUT IT
Distributed by Andrews McMeel Syndication
WHAT DOES SHE MEAN BY THAT?
WORRY
JIM DAVIS 12-30

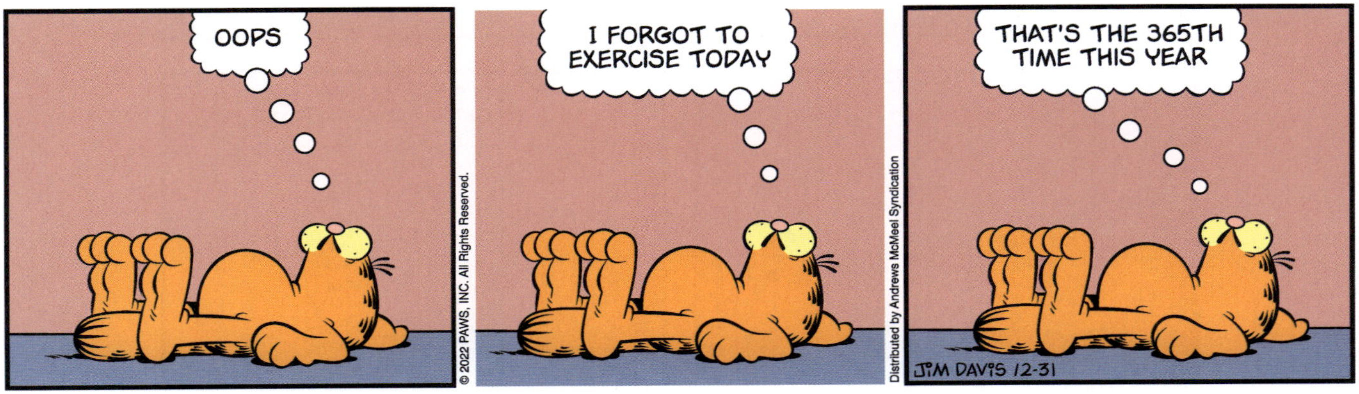
OOPS
© 2022 PAWS, INC. All Rights Reserved.
I FORGOT TO EXERCISE TODAY
Distributed by Andrews McMeel Syndication
THAT'S THE 365TH TIME THIS YEAR
JIM DAVIS 12-31

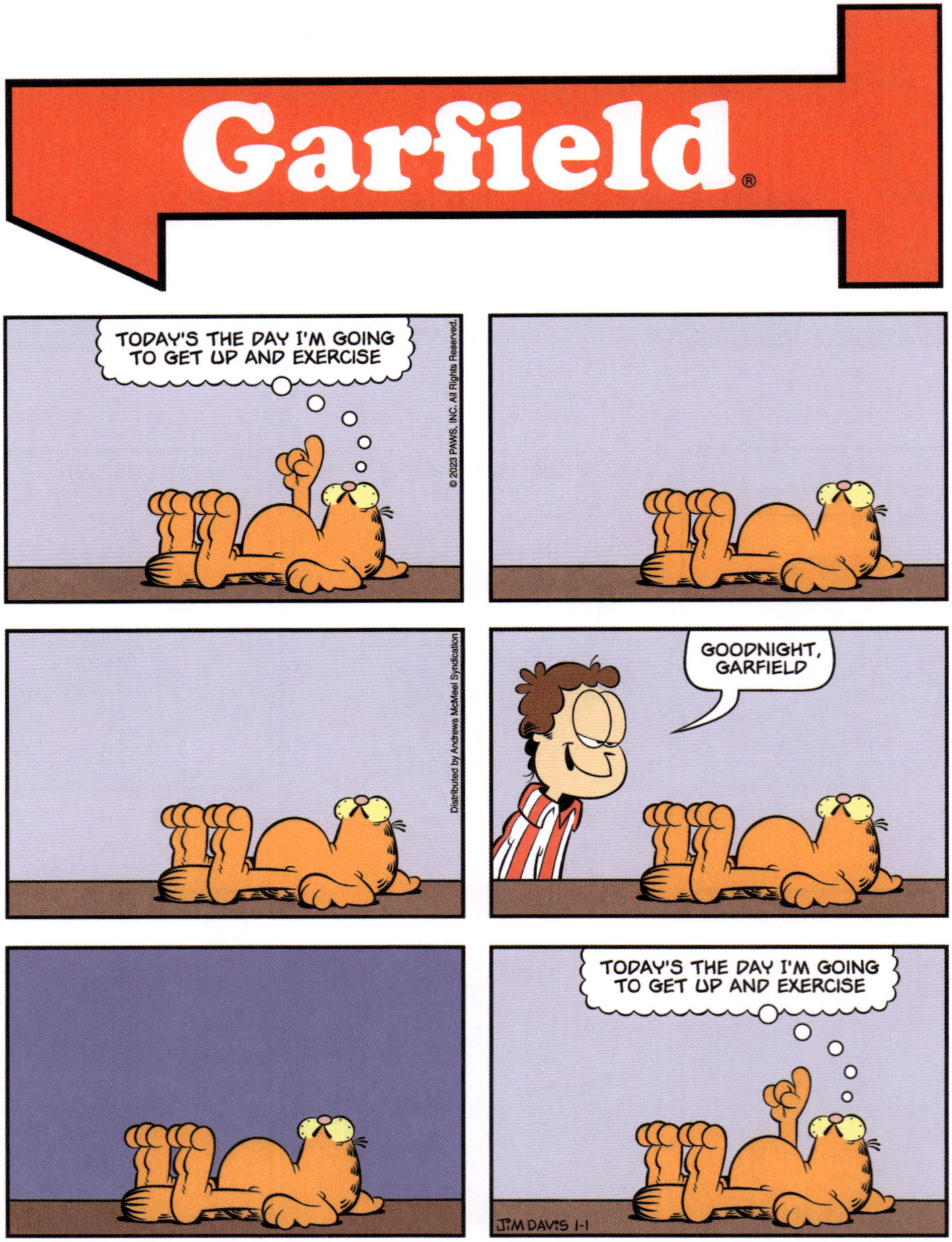
Garfield®
TODAY'S THE DAY I'M GOING TO GET UP AND EXERCISE
© 2023 PAWS, INC. All Rights Reserved.
Distributed by Andrews McMeel Syndication
GOODNIGHT, GARFIELD
TODAY'S THE DAY I'M GOING TO GET UP AND EXERCISE
JIM DAVIS 1-1

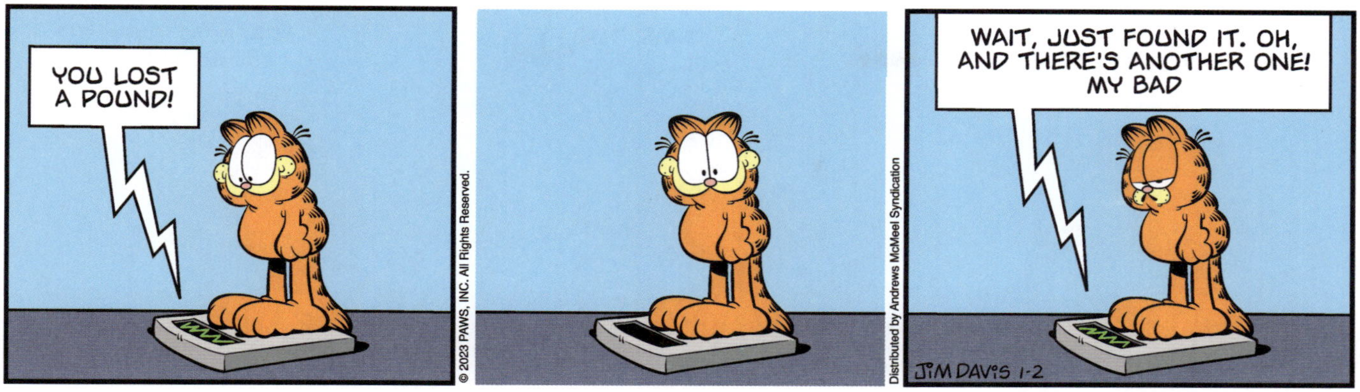
YOU LOST A POUND!
© 2023 PAWS, INC. All Rights Reserved.
Distributed by Andrews McMeel Syndication
WAIT, JUST FOUND IT. OH, AND THERE'S ANOTHER ONE! MY BAD
JIM DAVIS 1-2

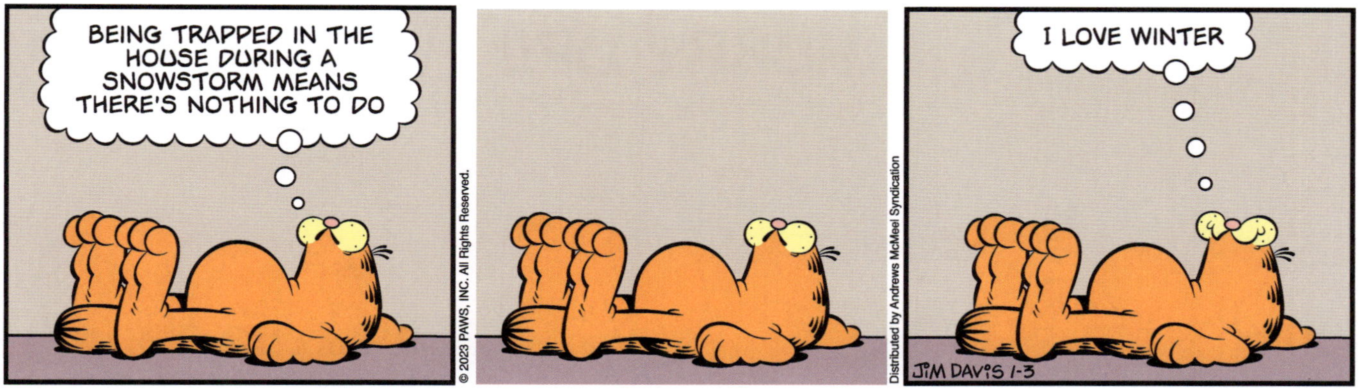
BEING TRAPPED IN THE HOUSE DURING A SNOWSTORM MEANS THERE'S NOTHING TO DO
© 2023 PAWS, INC. All Rights Reserved.
Distributed by Andrews McMeel Syndication
I LOVE WINTER
JIM DAVIS 1-3

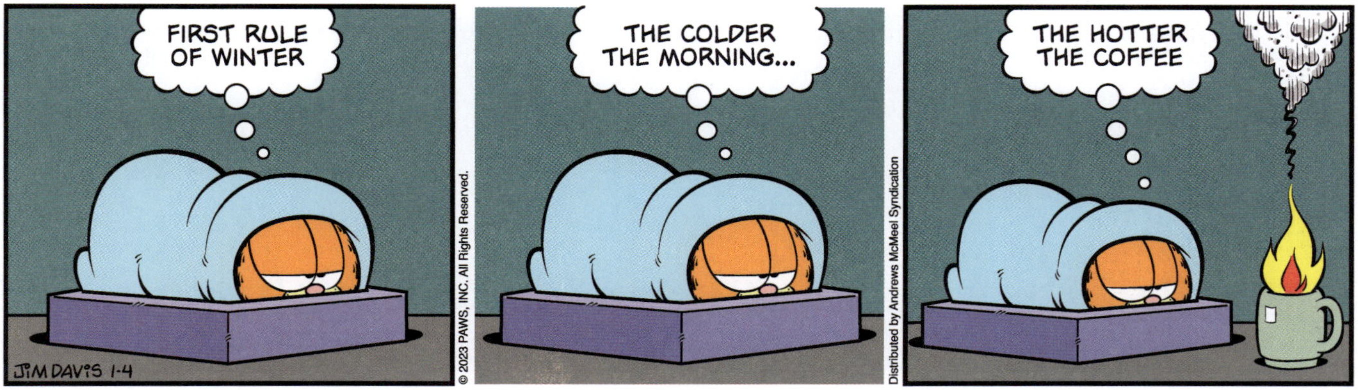
FIRST RULE OF WINTER
JIM DAVIS 1-4
© 2023 PAWS, INC. All Rights Reserved.
THE COLDER THE MORNING...
Distributed by Andrews McMeel Syndication
THE HOTTER THE COFFEE

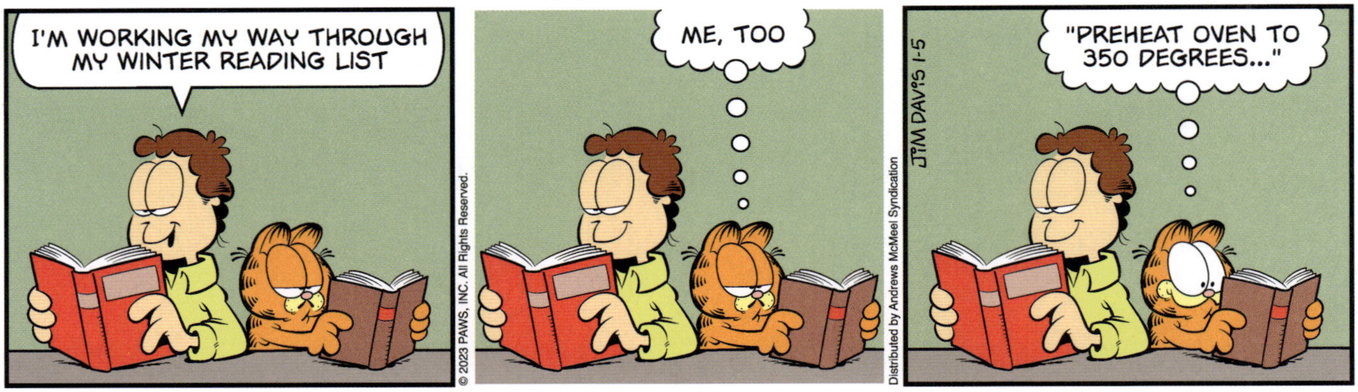
I'M WORKING MY WAY THROUGH MY WINTER READING LIST
ME, TOO
"PREHEAT OVEN TO 350 DEGREES..."
JIM DAVIS 1-5

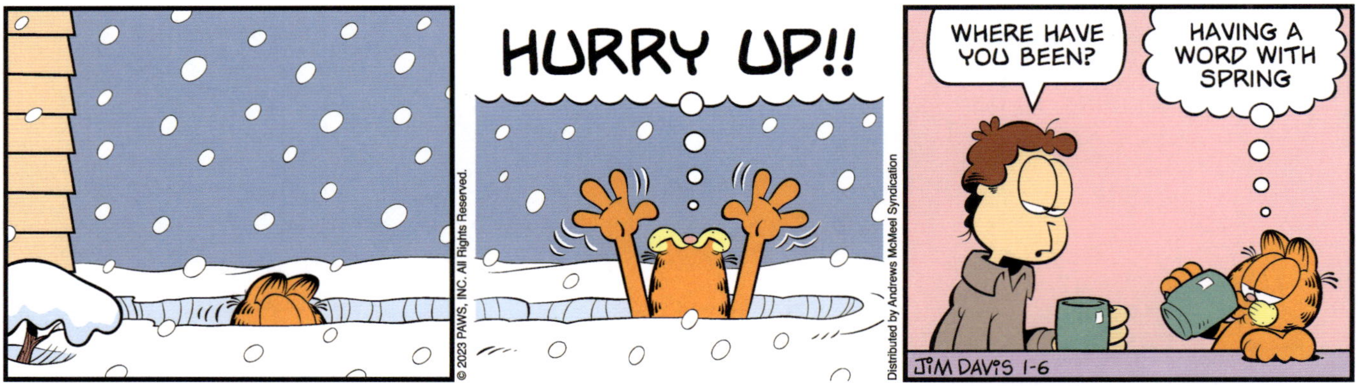
HURRY UP!!
WHERE HAVE YOU BEEN?
HAVING A WORD WITH SPRING
JIM DAVIS 1-6

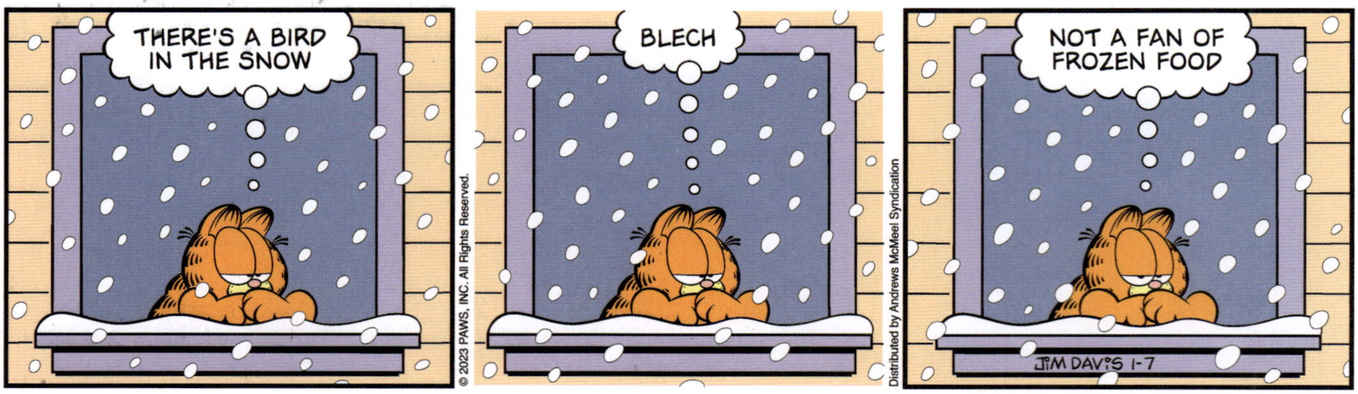
THERE'S A BIRD IN THE SNOW
BLECH
NOT A FAN OF FROZEN FOOD
JIM DAVIS 1-7

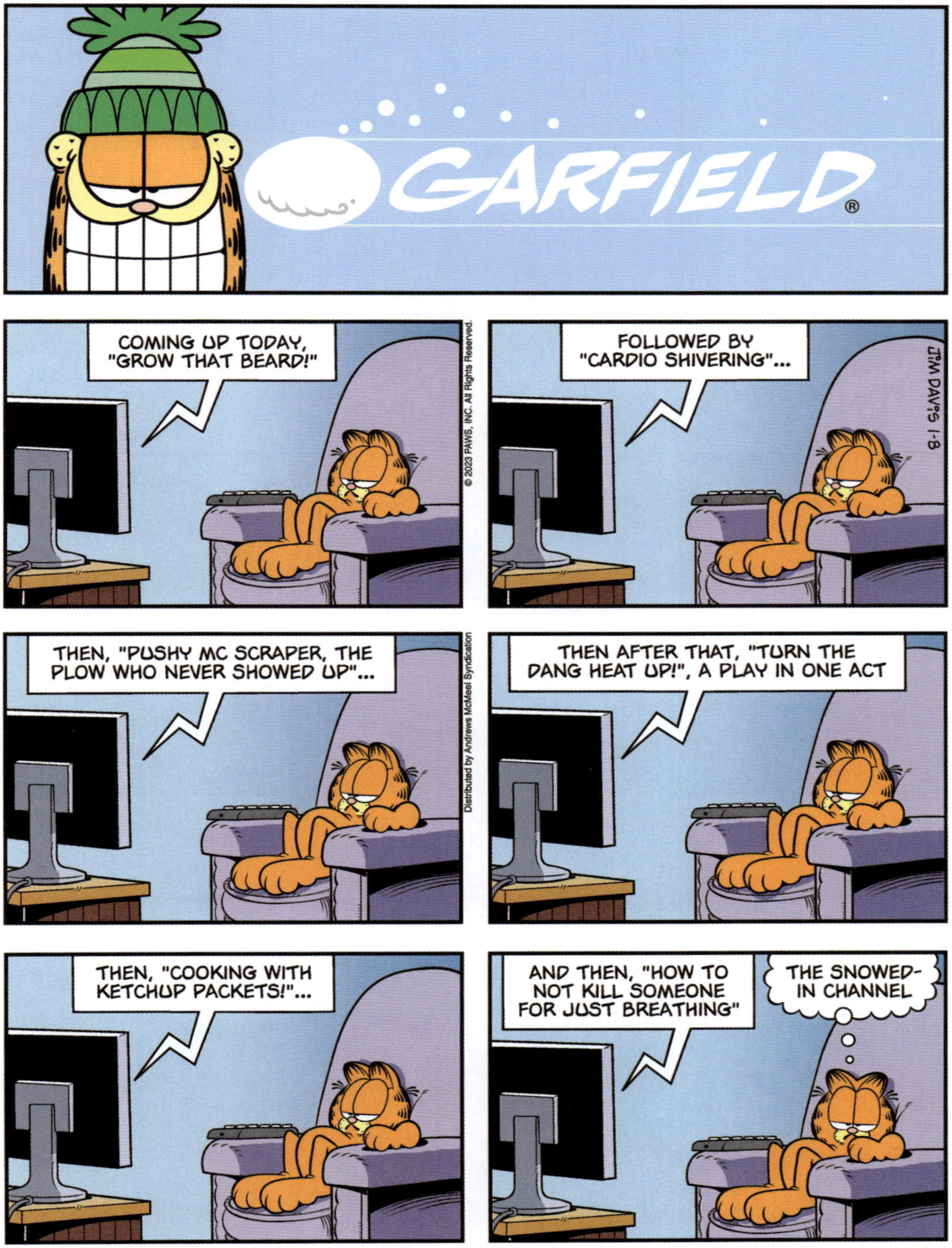
GARFIELD®
COMING UP TODAY, "GROW THAT BEARD!"
© 2023 PAWS, INC. All Rights Reserved.
FOLLOWED BY "CARDIO SHIVERING"...
JIM DAVIS 1-8
THEN, "PUSHY MC SCRAPER, THE PLOW WHO NEVER SHOWED UP"...
Distributed by Andrews McMeel Syndication
THEN AFTER THAT, "TURN THE DANG HEAT UP!", A PLAY IN ONE ACT
THEN, "COOKING WITH KETCHUP PACKETS!"...
AND THEN, "HOW TO NOT KILL SOMEONE FOR JUST BREATHING"
THE SNOWED-IN CHANNEL

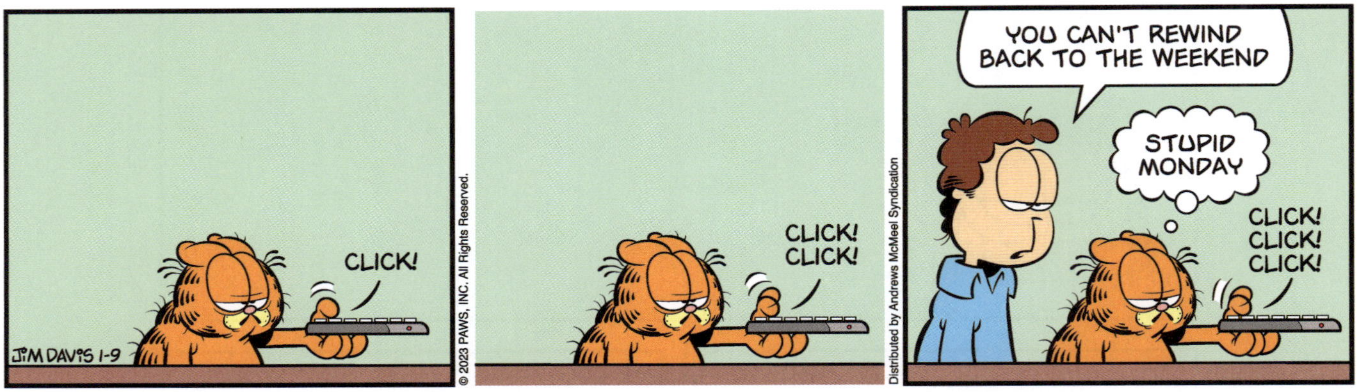
JIM DAVIS 1-9
CLICK!
© 2023 PAWS, INC. All Rights Reserved.
CLICK! CLICK!
Distributed by Andrews McMeel Syndication
YOU CAN'T REWIND BACK TO THE WEEKEND
STUPID MONDAY
CLICK! CLICK! CLICK!

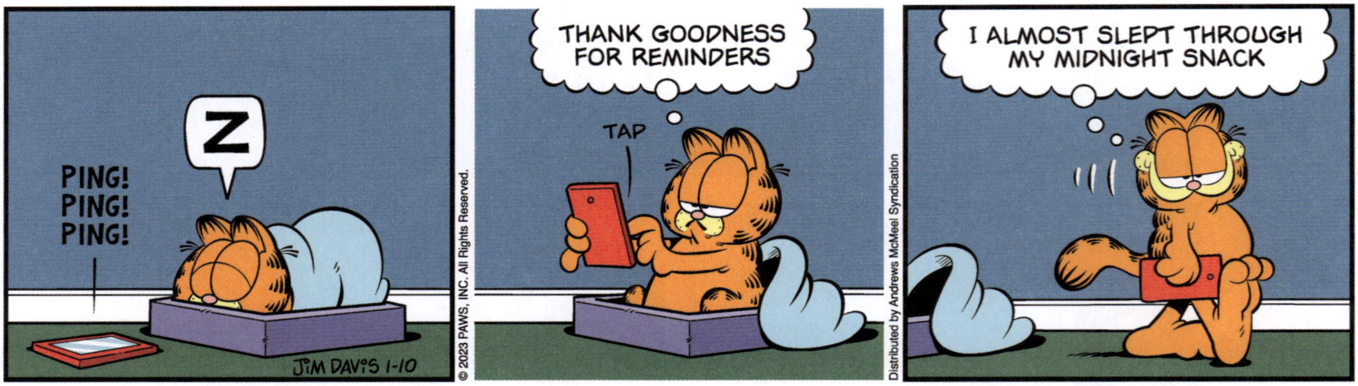
PING! PING! PING!
Z
JIM DAVIS 1-10
© 2023 PAWS, INC. All Rights Reserved.
THANK GOODNESS FOR REMINDERS
TAP
Distributed by Andrews McMeel Syndication
I ALMOST SLEPT THROUGH MY MIDNIGHT SNACK

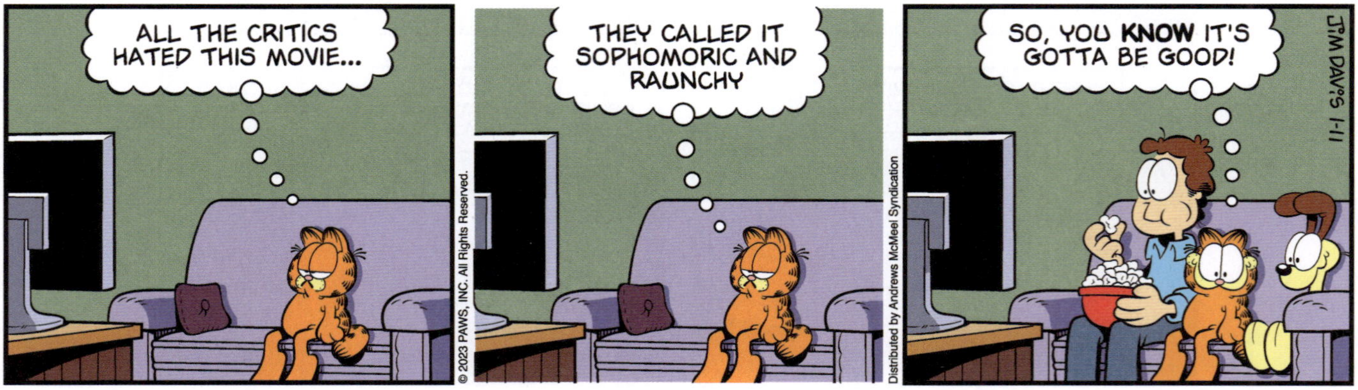
ALL THE CRITICS HATED THIS MOVIE...
© 2023 PAWS, INC. All Rights Reserved.
THEY CALLED IT SOPHOMORIC AND RAUNCHY
Distributed by Andrews McMeel Syndication
SO, YOU **KNOW** IT'S GOTTA BE GOOD!
JIM DAVIS 1-11

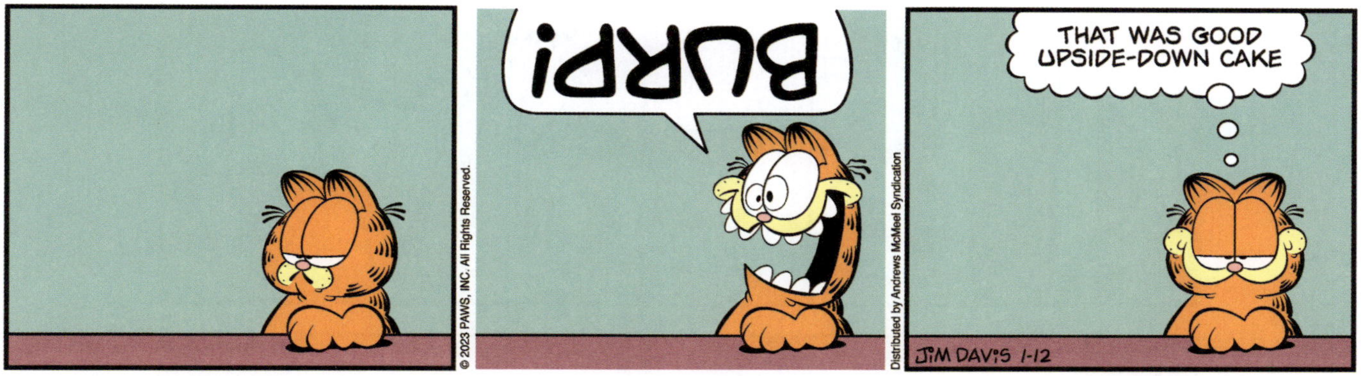
BURP!
THAT WAS GOOD UPSIDE-DOWN CAKE
© 2023 PAWS, INC. All Rights Reserved.
Distributed by Andrews McMeel Syndication
JIM DAVIS 1-12

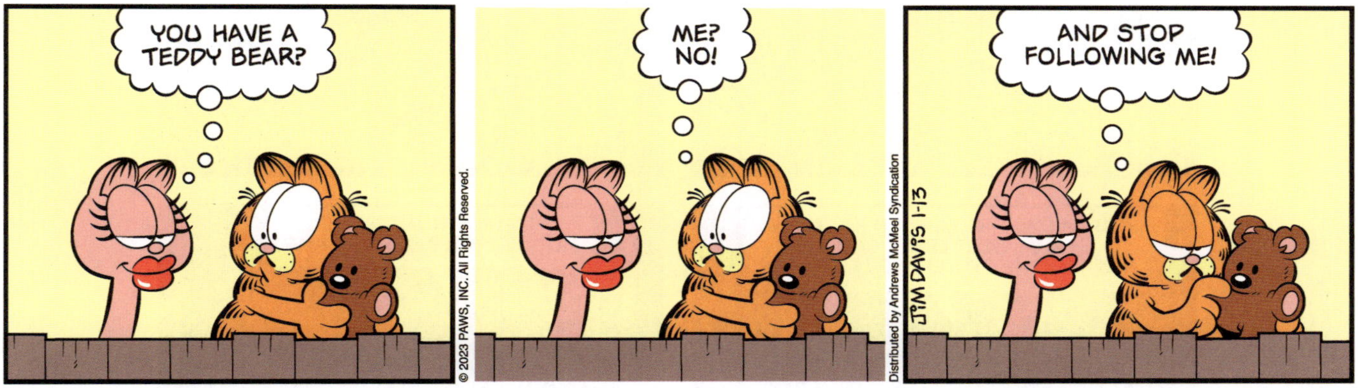
YOU HAVE A TEDDY BEAR?
ME? NO!
AND STOP FOLLOWING ME!
© 2023 PAWS, INC. All Rights Reserved.
Distributed by Andrews McMeel Syndication
JIM DAVIS 1-13

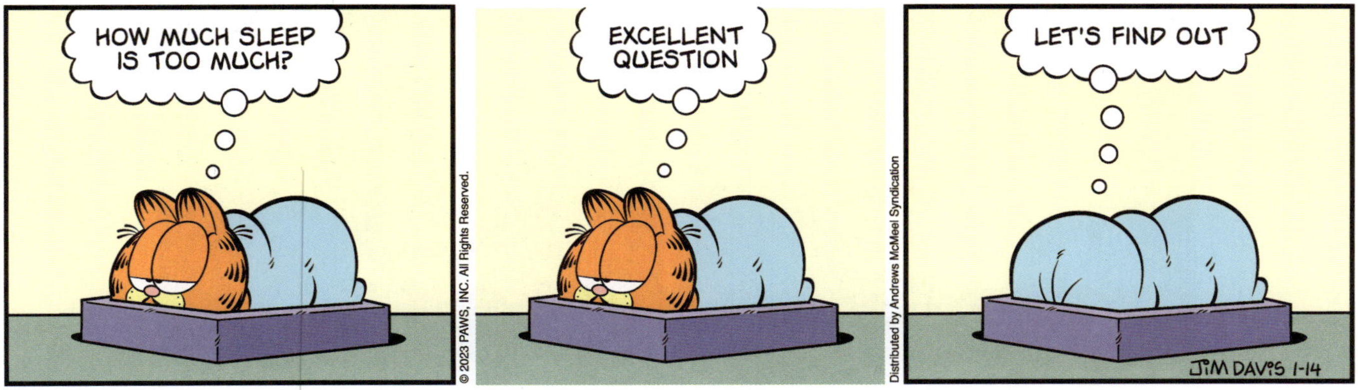
HOW MUCH SLEEP IS TOO MUCH?
EXCELLENT QUESTION
LET'S FIND OUT
© 2023 PAWS, INC. All Rights Reserved.
Distributed by Andrews McMeel Syndication
JIM DAVIS 1-14

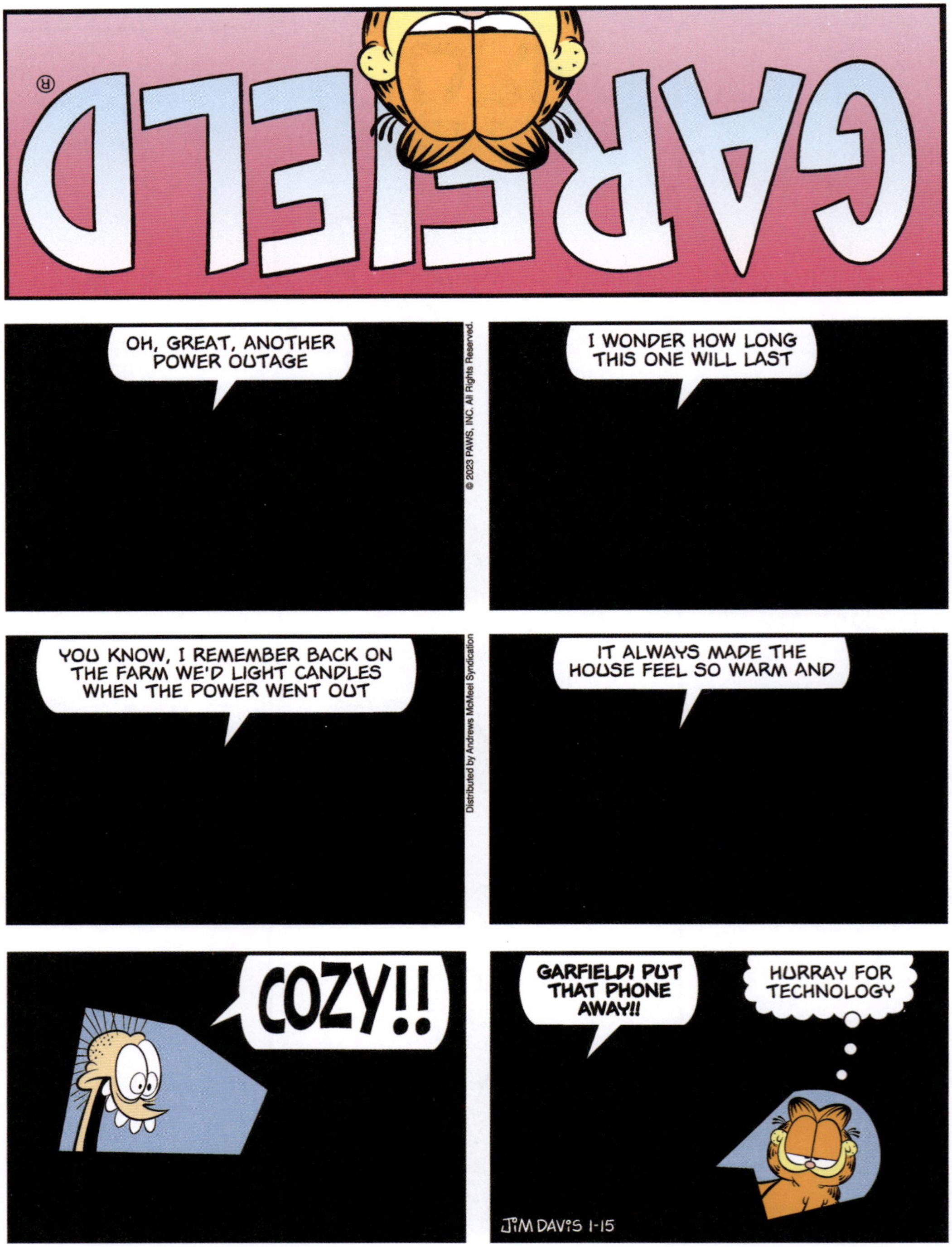
GARFIELD®
OH, GREAT, ANOTHER POWER OUTAGE
I WONDER HOW LONG THIS ONE WILL LAST
YOU KNOW, I REMEMBER BACK ON THE FARM WE'D LIGHT CANDLES WHEN THE POWER WENT OUT
IT ALWAYS MADE THE HOUSE FEEL SO WARM AND
COZY!!
GARFIELD! PUT THAT PHONE AWAY!!
HURRAY FOR TECHNOLOGY
JIM DAVIS 1-15
© 2023 PAWS, INC. All Rights Reserved.
Distributed by Andrews McMeel Syndication

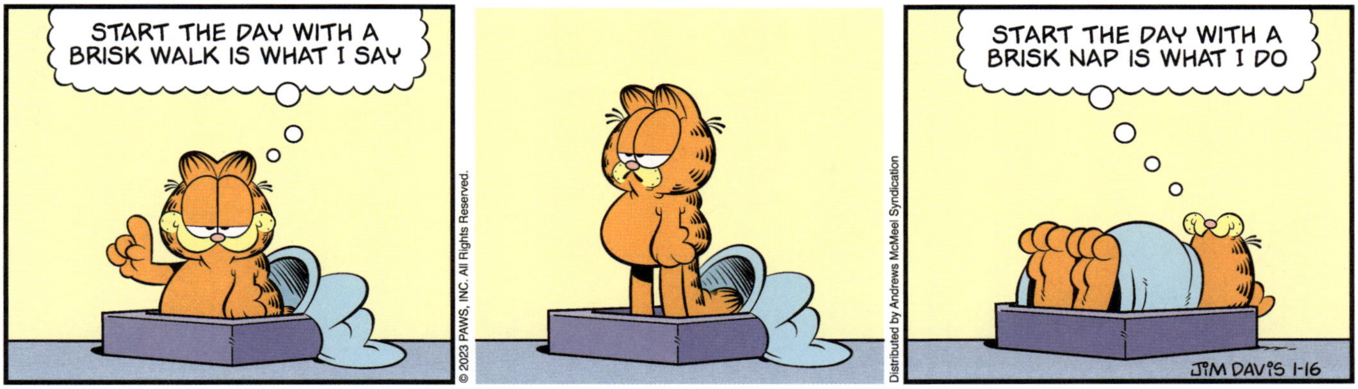
START THE DAY WITH A BRISK WALK IS WHAT I SAY
START THE DAY WITH A BRISK NAP IS WHAT I DO
JIM DAVIS 1-16

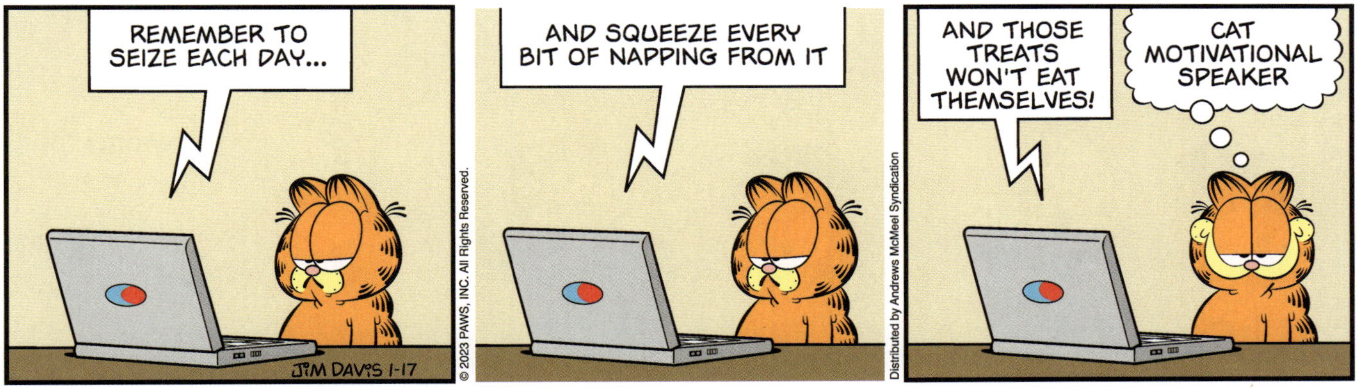
REMEMBER TO SEIZE EACH DAY...
AND SQUEEZE EVERY BIT OF NAPPING FROM IT
AND THOSE TREATS WON'T EAT THEMSELVES!
CAT MOTIVATIONAL SPEAKER
JIM DAVIS 1-17

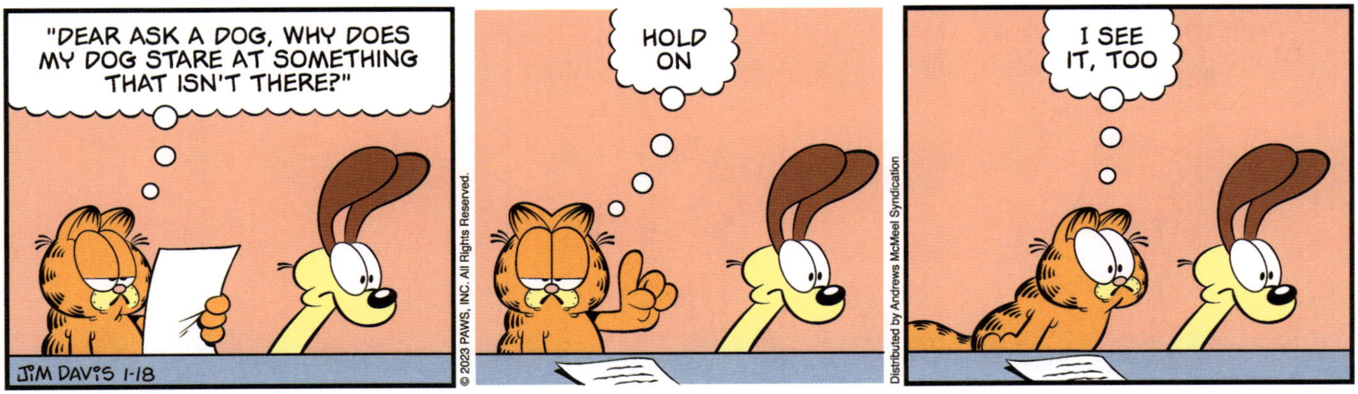
"DEAR ASK A DOG, WHY DOES MY DOG STARE AT SOMETHING THAT ISN'T THERE?"
HOLD ON
I SEE IT, TOO
JIM DAVIS 1-18

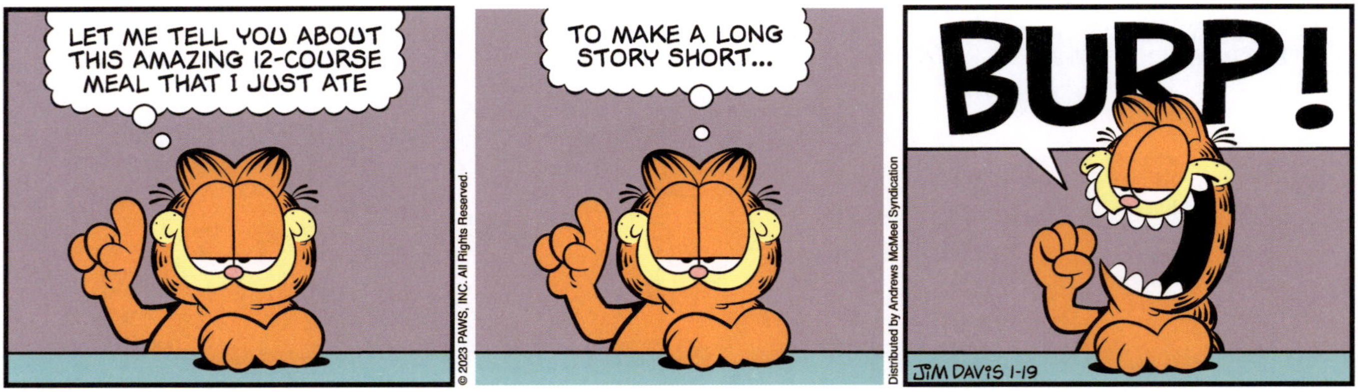
LET ME TELL YOU ABOUT THIS AMAZING 12-COURSE MEAL THAT I JUST ATE
TO MAKE A LONG STORY SHORT...
BURP!
© 2023 PAWS, INC. All Rights Reserved.
Distributed by Andrews McMeel Syndication
JIM DAVIS 1-19

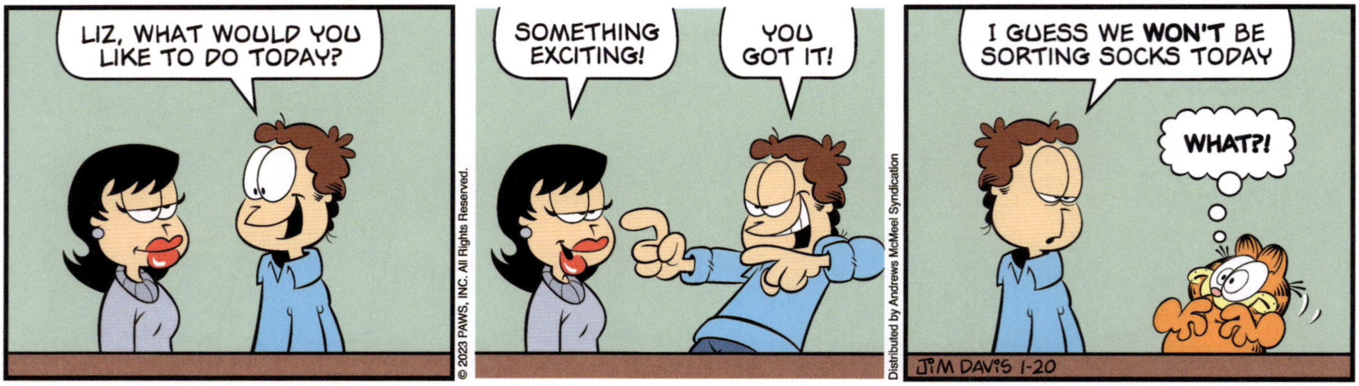
LIZ, WHAT WOULD YOU LIKE TO DO TODAY?
SOMETHING EXCITING!
YOU GOT IT!
I GUESS WE **WON'T** BE SORTING SOCKS TODAY
WHAT?!
© 2023 PAWS, INC. All Rights Reserved.
Distributed by Andrews McMeel Syndication
JIM DAVIS 1-20

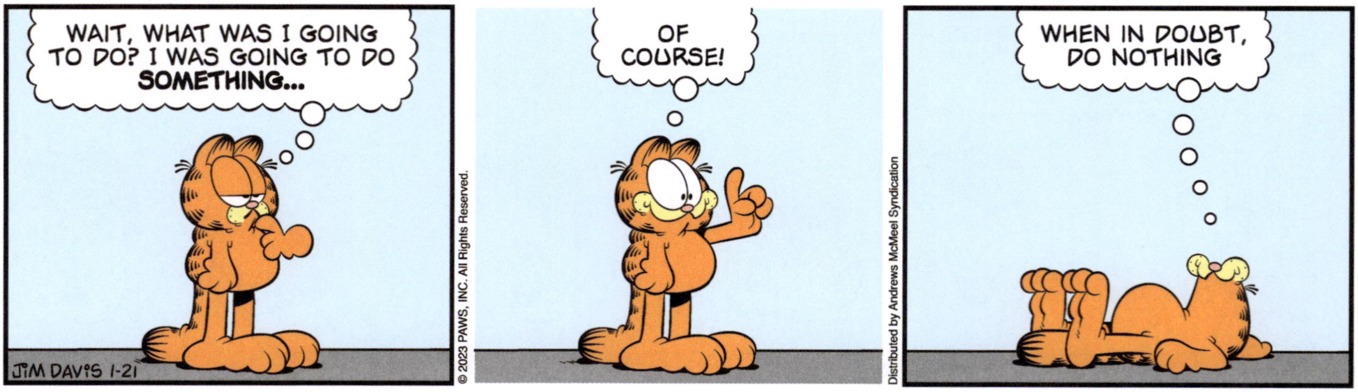
WAIT, WHAT WAS I GOING TO DO? I WAS GOING TO DO **SOMETHING...**
OF COURSE!
WHEN IN DOUBT, DO NOTHING
© 2023 PAWS, INC. All Rights Reserved.
Distributed by Andrews McMeel Syndication
JIM DAVIS 1-21

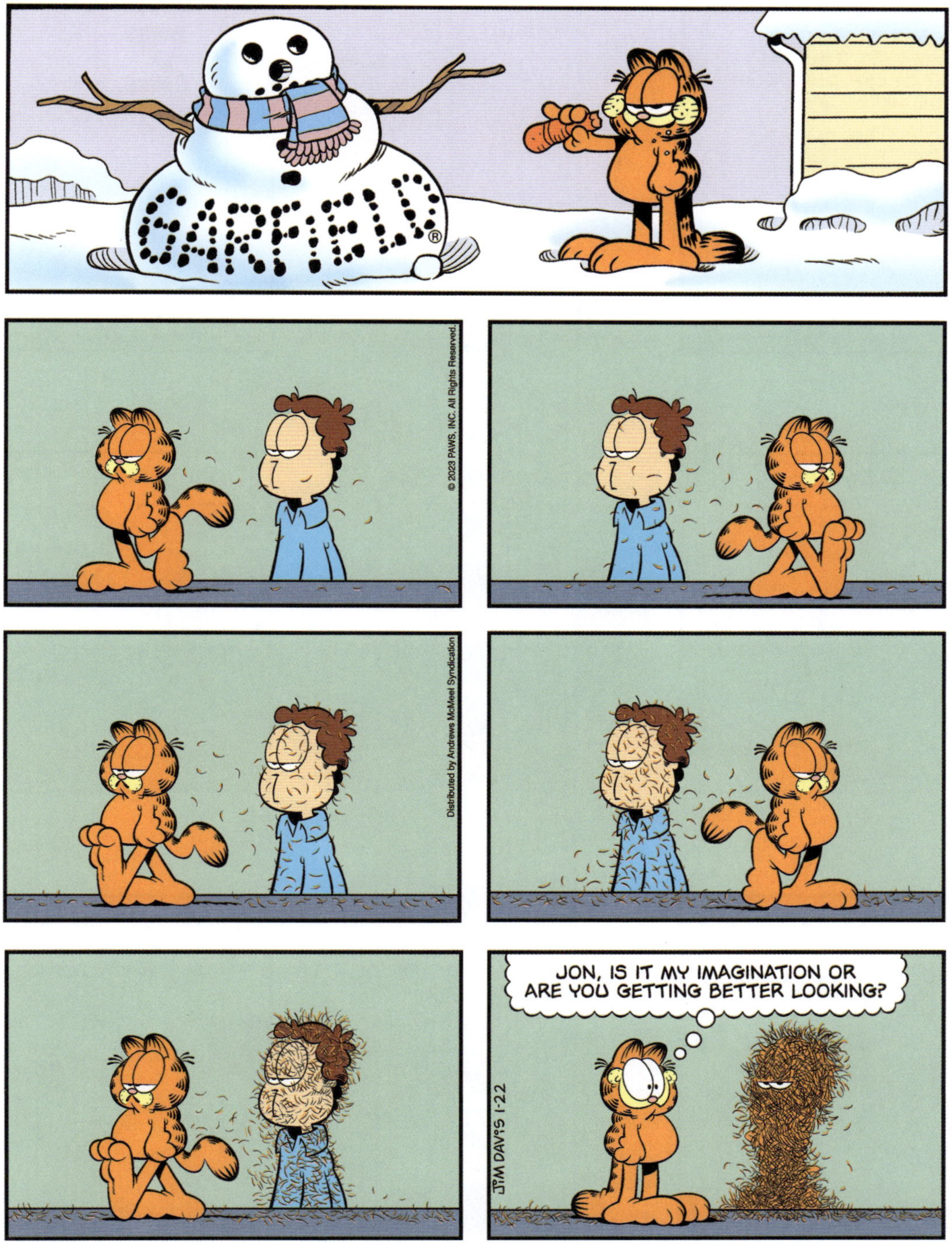
GARFIELD®
© 2023 PAWS, INC. All Rights Reserved.
Distributed by Andrews McMeel Syndication
JIM DAVIS 1-22
JON, IS IT MY IMAGINATION OR ARE YOU GETTING BETTER LOOKING?

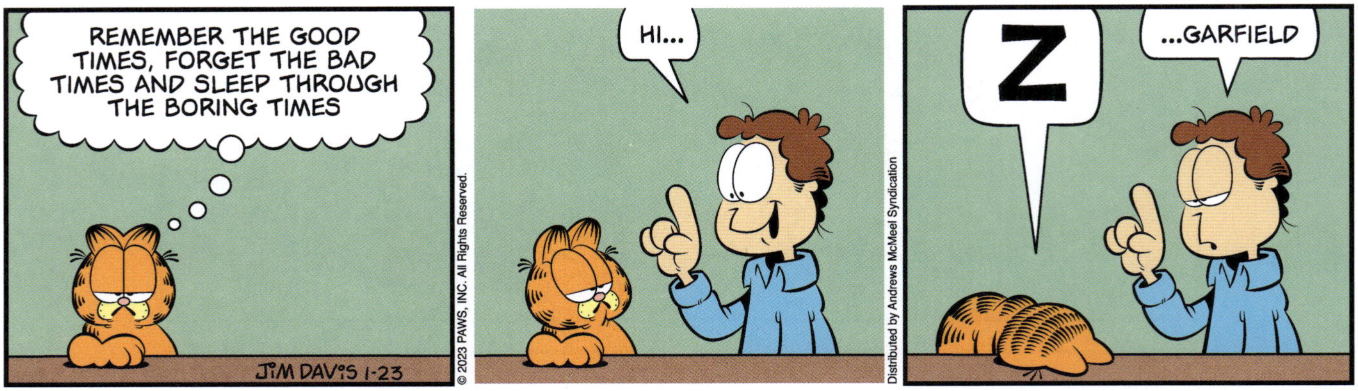
REMEMBER THE GOOD TIMES, FORGET THE BAD TIMES AND SLEEP THROUGH THE BORING TIMES
JIM DAVIS 1-23
© 2023 PAWS, INC. All Rights Reserved.
HI...
Distributed by Andrews McMeel Syndication
Z
...GARFIELD

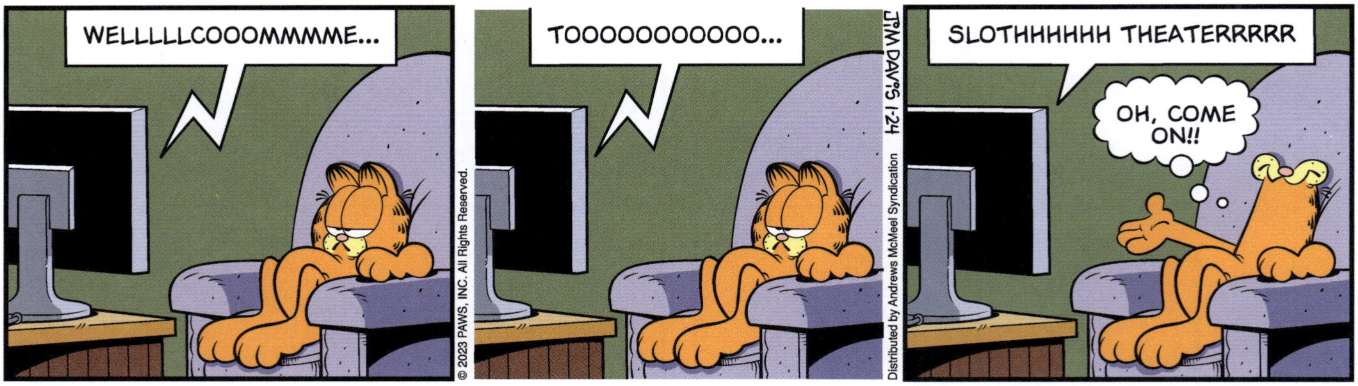
WELLLLLCOOOMMMME...
© 2023 PAWS, INC. All Rights Reserved.
TOOOOOOOOOOO...
JIM DAVIS 1-24
Distributed by Andrews McMeel Syndication
SLOTHHHHHH THEATERRRRR
OH, COME ON!!

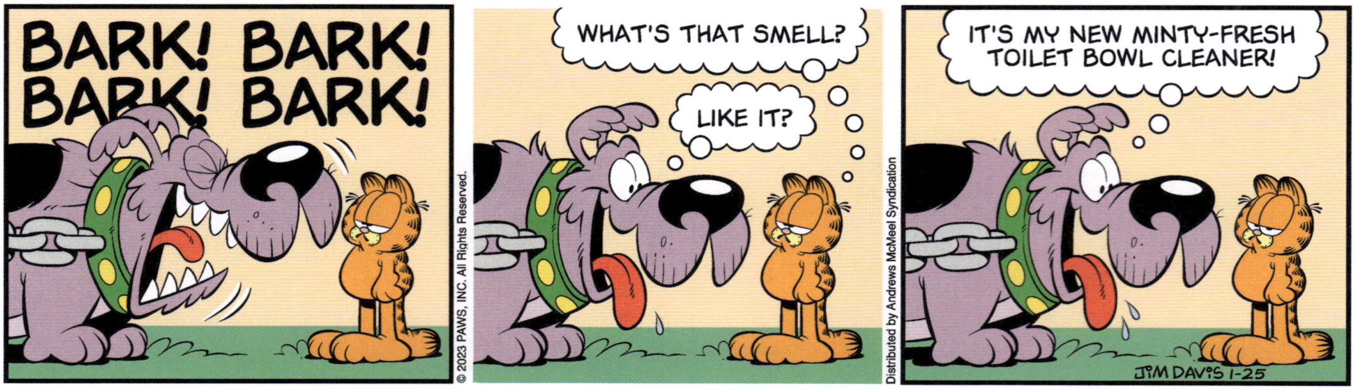
BARK! BARK! BARK! BARK!
© 2023 PAWS, INC. All Rights Reserved.
WHAT'S THAT SMELL?
LIKE IT?
Distributed by Andrews McMeel Syndication
IT'S MY NEW MINTY-FRESH TOILET BOWL CLEANER!
JIM DAVIS 1-25

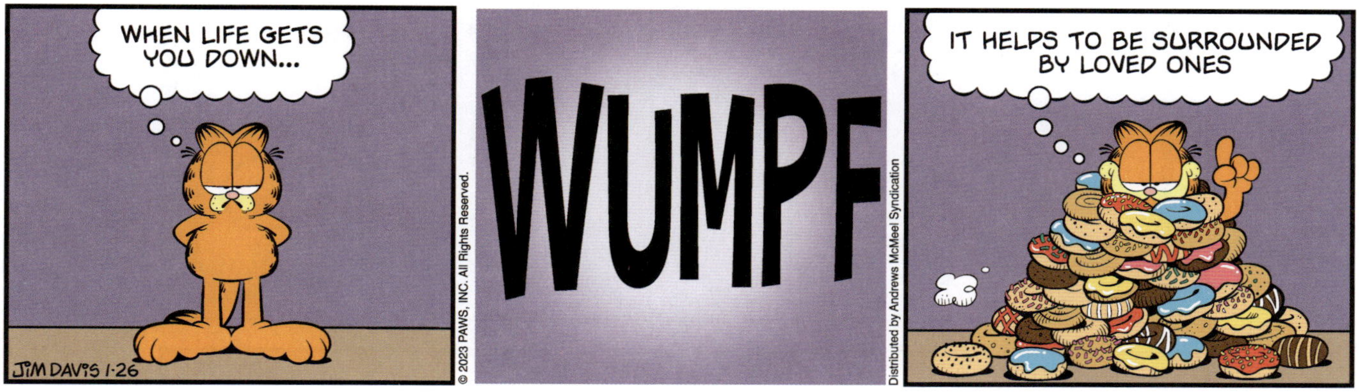
WHEN LIFE GETS YOU DOWN...
JIM DAVIS 1-26
© 2023 PAWS, INC. All Rights Reserved.
WUMPF
Distributed by Andrews McMeel Syndication
IT HELPS TO BE SURROUNDED BY LOVED ONES

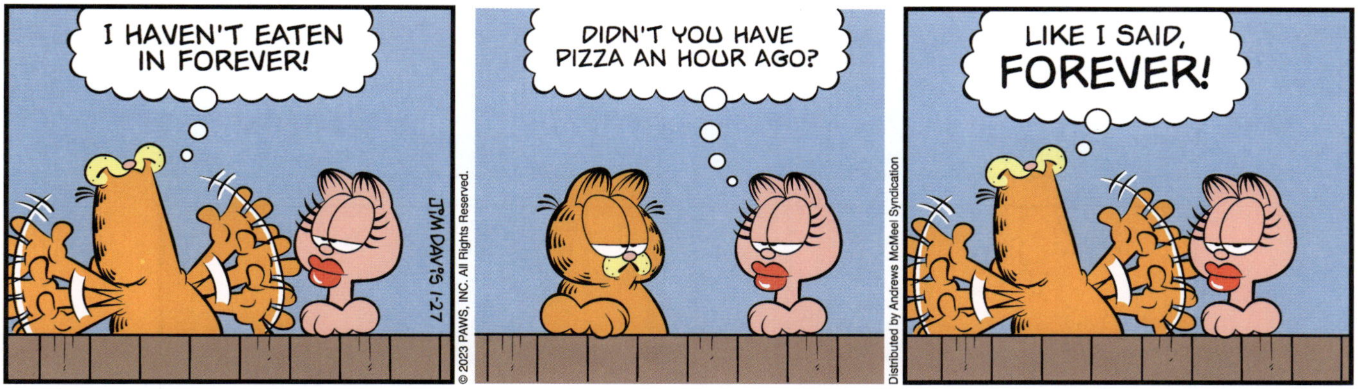
I HAVEN'T EATEN IN FOREVER!
JIM DAVIS 1-27
© 2023 PAWS, INC. All Rights Reserved.
DIDN'T YOU HAVE PIZZA AN HOUR AGO?
Distributed by Andrews McMeel Syndication
LIKE I SAID, FOREVER!

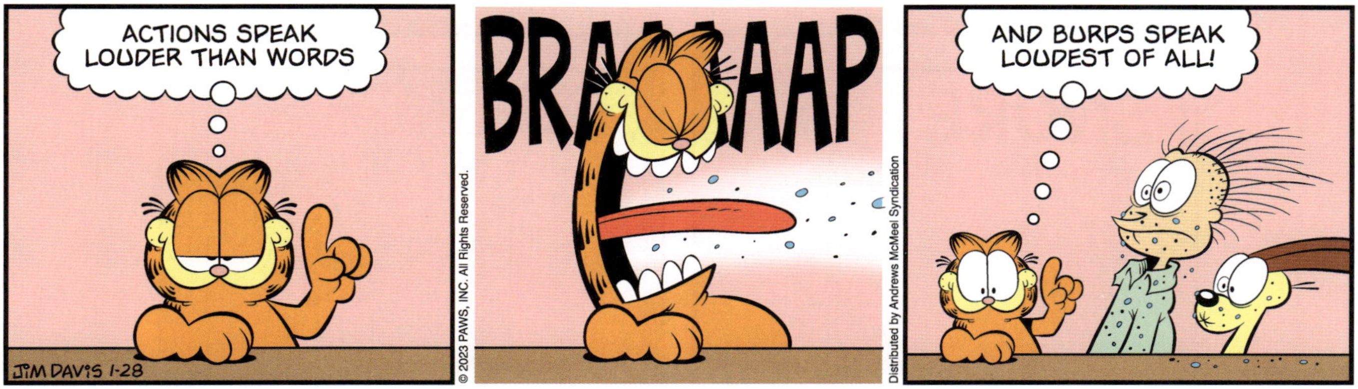
ACTIONS SPEAK LOUDER THAN WORDS
JIM DAVIS 1-28
© 2023 PAWS, INC. All Rights Reserved.
BRAAAAP
Distributed by Andrews McMeel Syndication
AND BURPS SPEAK LOUDEST OF ALL!

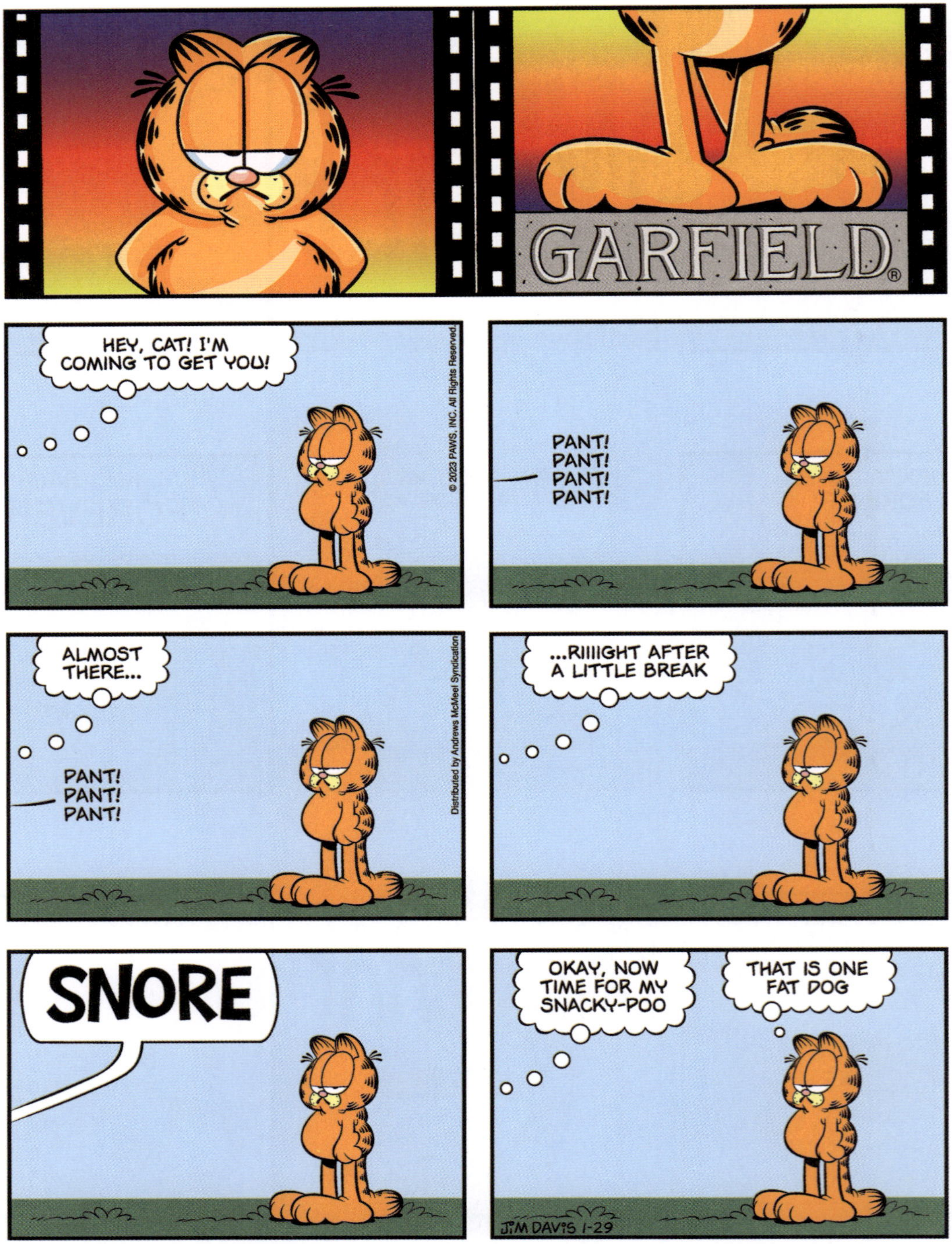
GARFIELD®
HEY, CAT! I'M COMING TO GET YOU!
© 2023 PAWS, INC. All Rights Reserved.
PANT! PANT! PANT! PANT!
ALMOST THERE...
PANT! PANT! PANT!
Distributed by Andrews McMeel Syndication
...RIIIIGHT AFTER A LITTLE BREAK
SNORE
OKAY, NOW TIME FOR MY SNACKY-POO
THAT IS ONE FAT DOG
JIM DAVIS 1-29

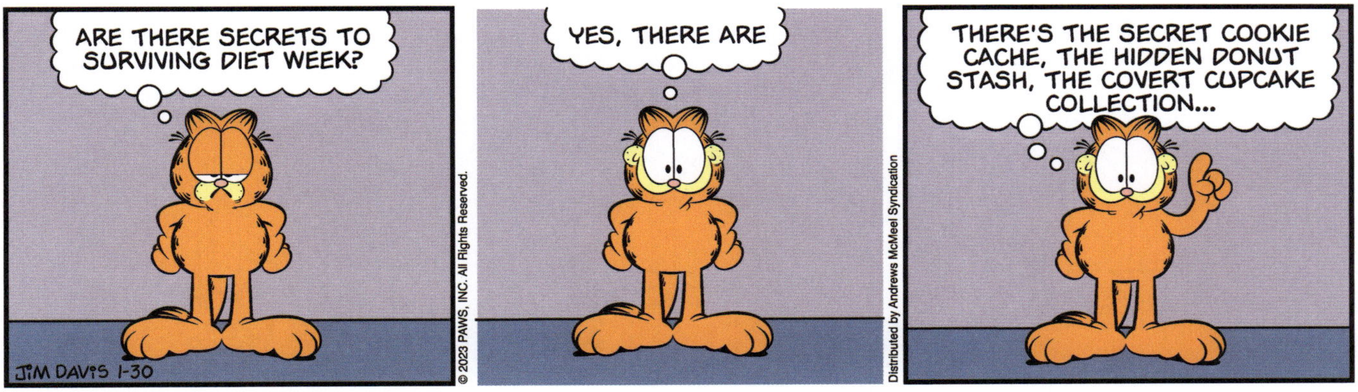
ARE THERE SECRETS TO SURVIVING DIET WEEK?
JIM DAVIS 1-30
YES, THERE ARE
© 2023 PAWS, INC. All Rights Reserved.
THERE'S THE SECRET COOKIE CACHE, THE HIDDEN DONUT STASH, THE COVERT CUPCAKE COLLECTION...
Distributed by Andrews McMeel Syndication

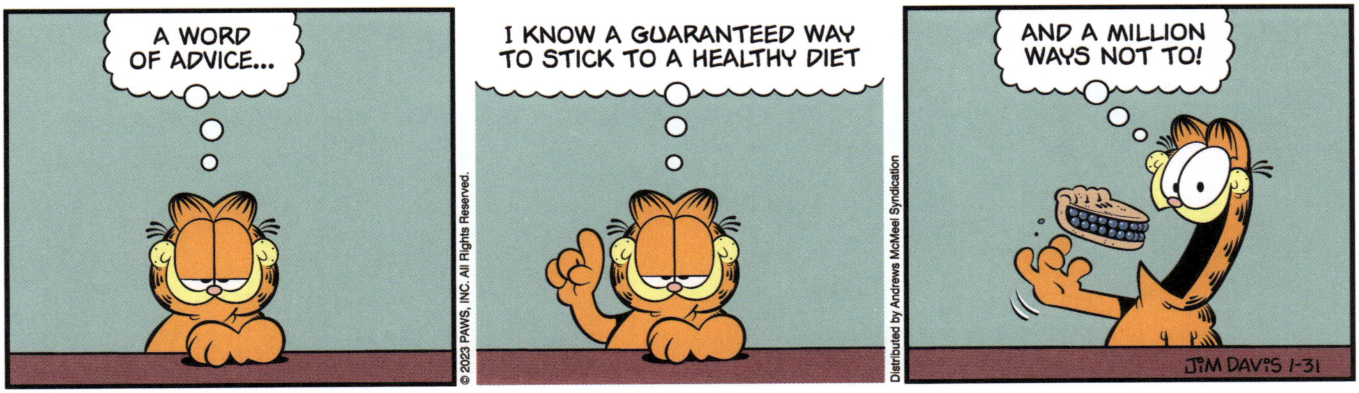
A WORD OF ADVICE...
I KNOW A GUARANTEED WAY TO STICK TO A HEALTHY DIET
© 2023 PAWS, INC. All Rights Reserved.
AND A MILLION WAYS NOT TO!
JIM DAVIS 1-31
Distributed by Andrews McMeel Syndication

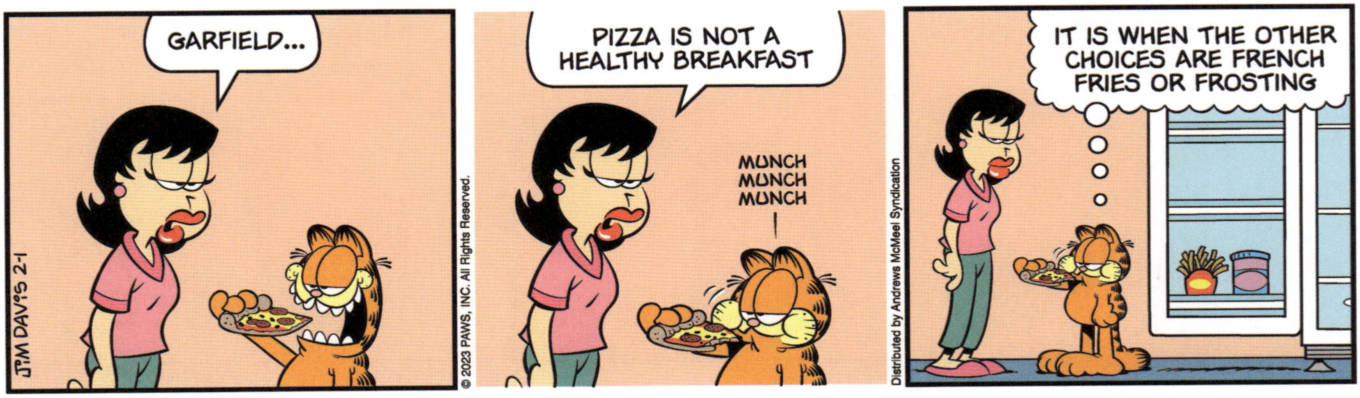
GARFIELD...
JIM DAVIS 2-1
PIZZA IS NOT A HEALTHY BREAKFAST
MUNCH MUNCH MUNCH
© 2023 PAWS, INC. All Rights Reserved.
IT IS WHEN THE OTHER CHOICES ARE FRENCH FRIES OR FROSTING
Distributed by Andrews McMeel Syndication

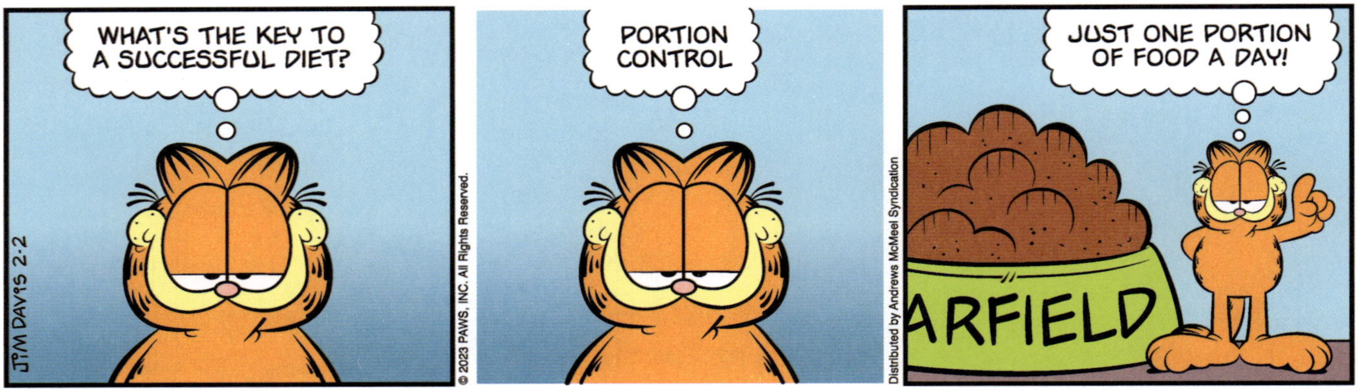
WHAT'S THE KEY TO A SUCCESSFUL DIET?
JIM DAVIS 2-2
PORTION CONTROL
© 2023 PAWS, INC. All Rights Reserved.
JUST ONE PORTION OF FOOD A DAY!
ARFIELD
Distributed by Andrews McMeel Syndication

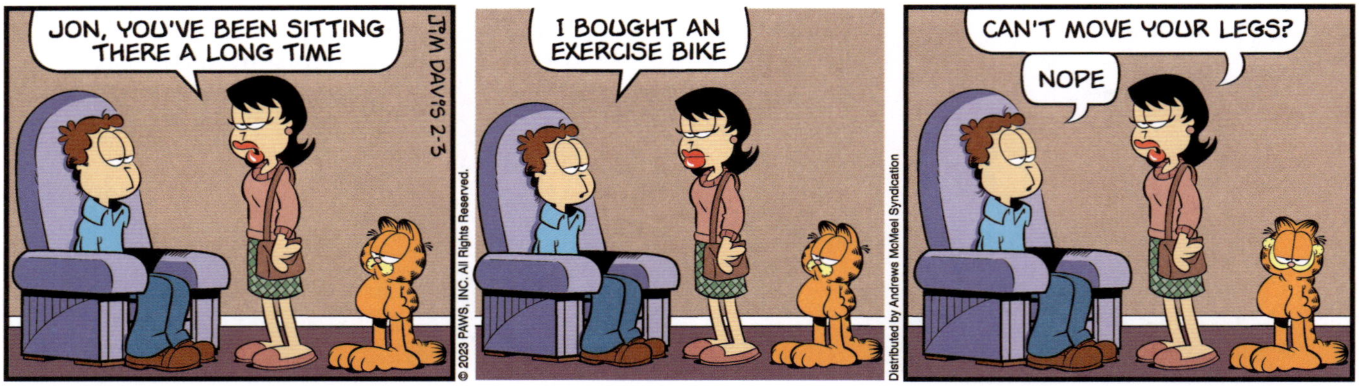
JON, YOU'VE BEEN SITTING THERE A LONG TIME
JIM DAVIS 2-3
I BOUGHT AN EXERCISE BIKE
© 2023 PAWS, INC. All Rights Reserved.
CAN'T MOVE YOUR LEGS?
NOPE
Distributed by Andrews McMeel Syndication

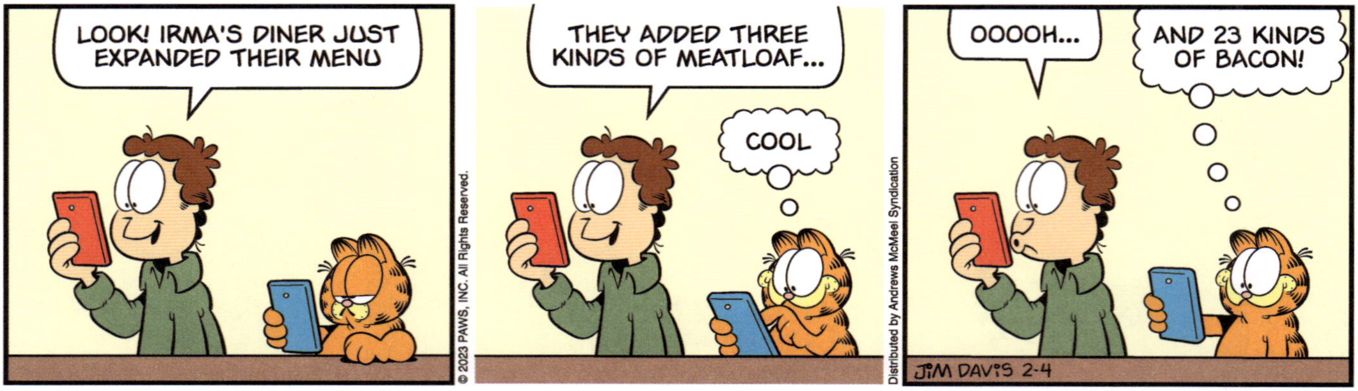
LOOK! IRMA'S DINER JUST EXPANDED THEIR MENU
THEY ADDED THREE KINDS OF MEATLOAF...
COOL
© 2023 PAWS, INC. All Rights Reserved.
OOOOH...
AND 23 KINDS OF BACON!
Distributed by Andrews McMeel Syndication
JIM DAVIS 2-4

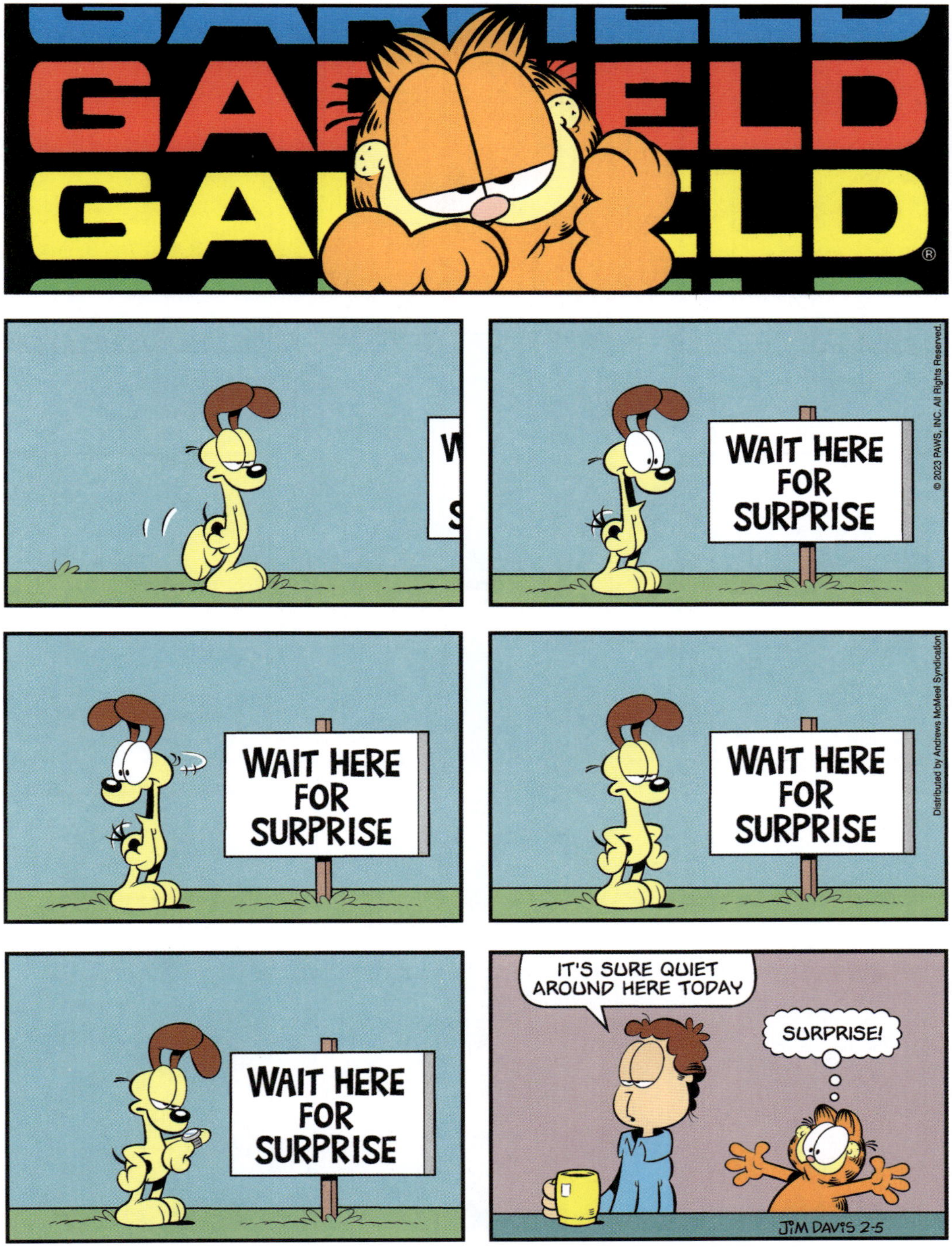
GARFIELD
GARFIELD
®
W
S
WAIT HERE FOR SURPRISE
© 2023 PAWS, INC. All Rights Reserved
WAIT HERE FOR SURPRISE
WAIT HERE FOR SURPRISE
Distributed by Andrews McMeel Syndication
WAIT HERE FOR SURPRISE
IT'S SURE QUIET AROUND HERE TODAY
SURPRISE!
JIM DAVIS 2-5

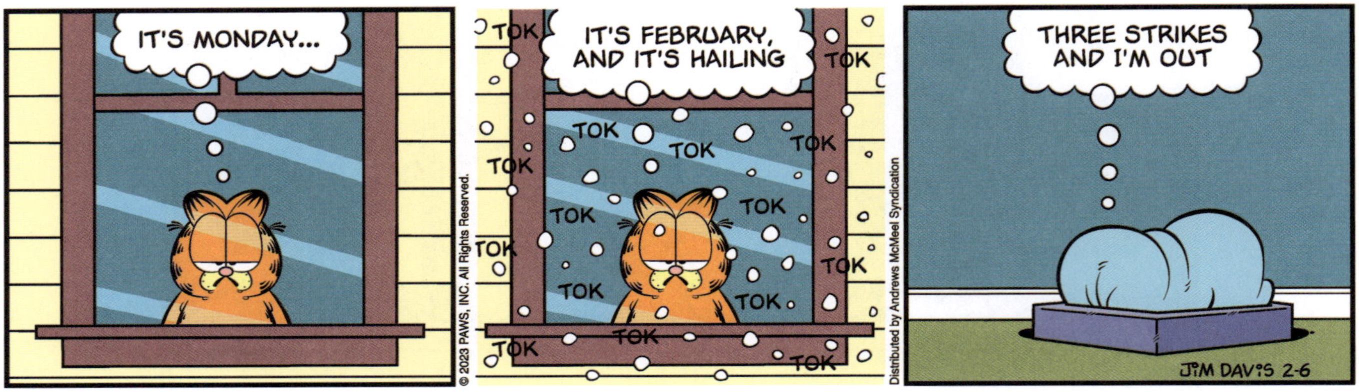
IT'S MONDAY...
TOK
IT'S FEBRUARY, AND IT'S HAILING
TOK TOK TOK TOK TOK TOK TOK TOK TOK TOK TOK TOK TOK
© 2023 PAWS, INC. All Rights Reserved.
THREE STRIKES AND I'M OUT
Distributed by Andrews McMeel Syndication
JIM DAVIS 2-6

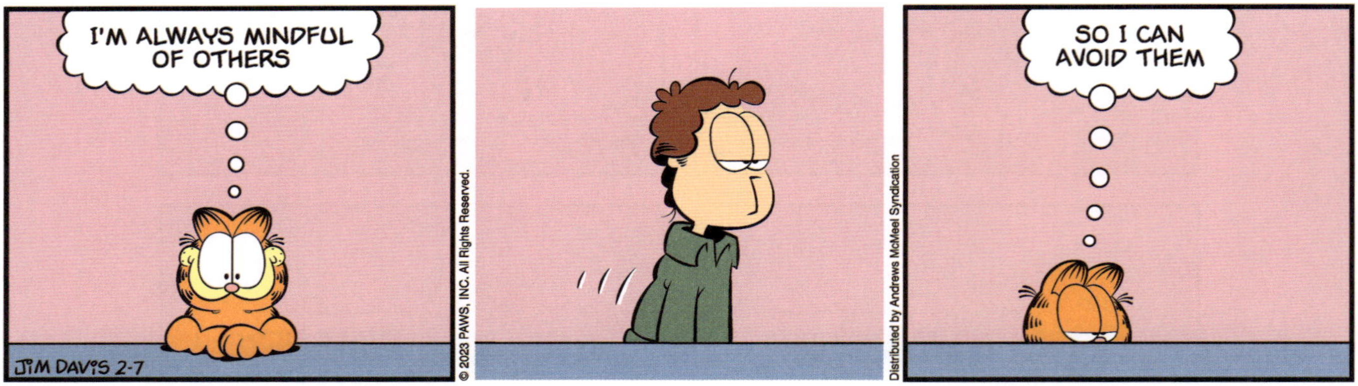
I'M ALWAYS MINDFUL OF OTHERS
JIM DAVIS 2-7
© 2023 PAWS, INC. All Rights Reserved.
SO I CAN AVOID THEM
Distributed by Andrews McMeel Syndication

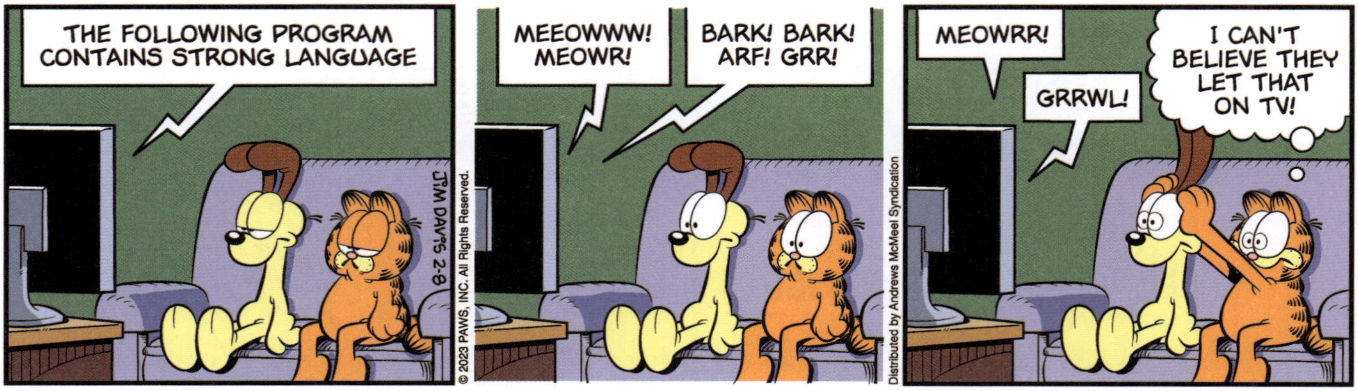
THE FOLLOWING PROGRAM CONTAINS STRONG LANGUAGE
JIM DAVIS 2-8
© 2023 PAWS, INC. All Rights Reserved.
MEEOWWW! MEOWR!
BARK! BARK! ARF! GRR!
Distributed by Andrews McMeel Syndication
MEOWRR!
GRRWL!
I CAN'T BELIEVE THEY LET THAT ON TV!

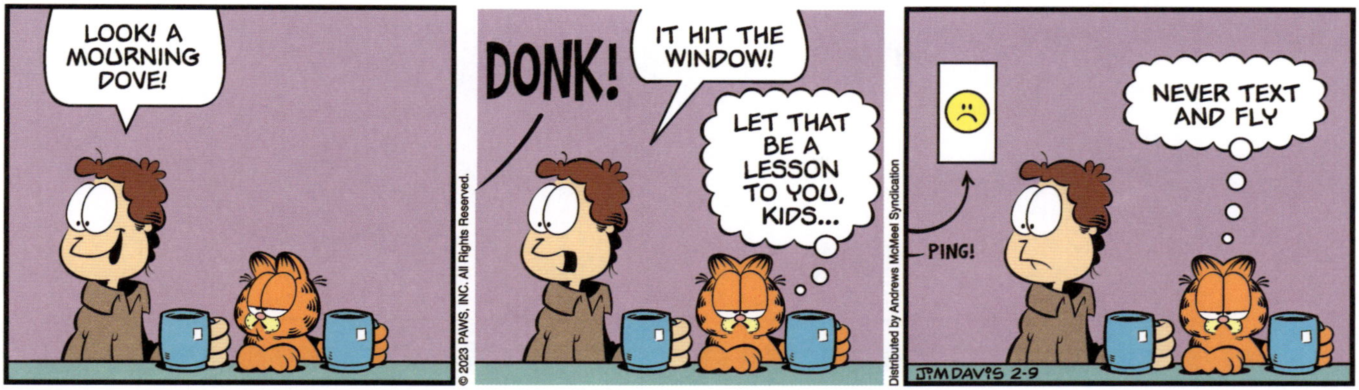
LOOK! A MOURNING DOVE!
DONK!
IT HIT THE WINDOW!
LET THAT BE A LESSON TO YOU, KIDS...
PING!
NEVER TEXT AND FLY
© 2023 PAWS, INC. All Rights Reserved.
Distributed by Andrews McMeel Syndication
JIM DAVIS 2-9

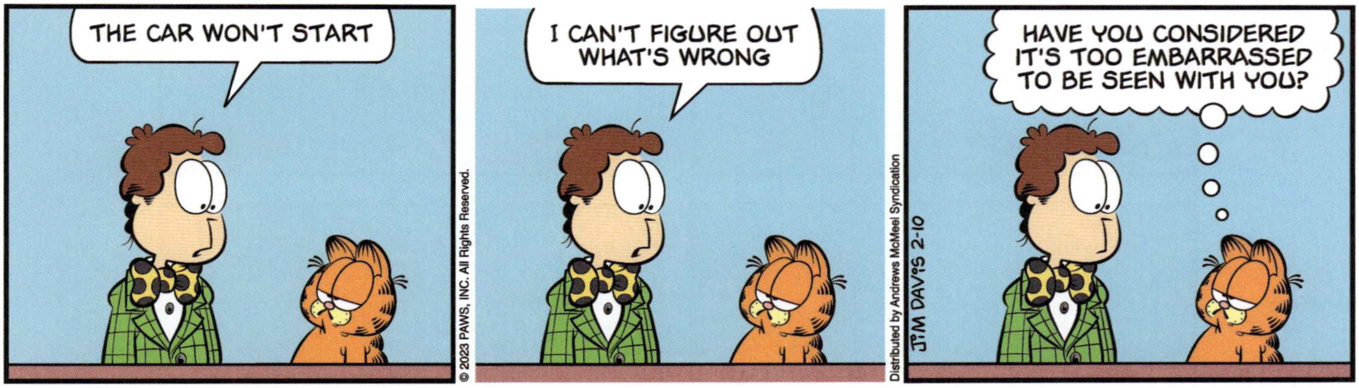
THE CAR WON'T START
I CAN'T FIGURE OUT WHAT'S WRONG
HAVE YOU CONSIDERED IT'S TOO EMBARRASSED TO BE SEEN WITH YOU?
© 2023 PAWS, INC. All Rights Reserved.
Distributed by Andrews McMeel Syndication
JIM DAVIS 2-10

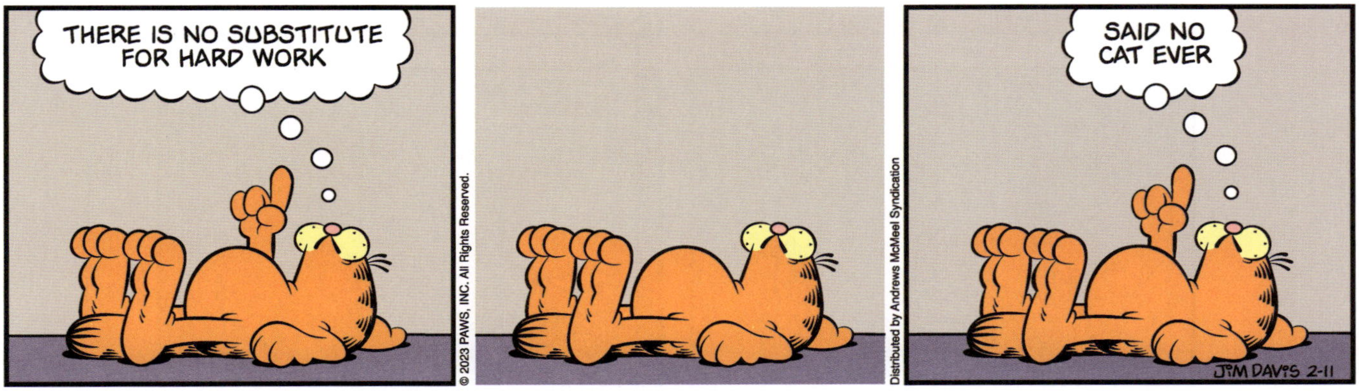
THERE IS NO SUBSTITUTE FOR HARD WORK
SAID NO CAT EVER
© 2023 PAWS, INC. All Rights Reserved.
Distributed by Andrews McMeel Syndication
JIM DAVIS 2-11

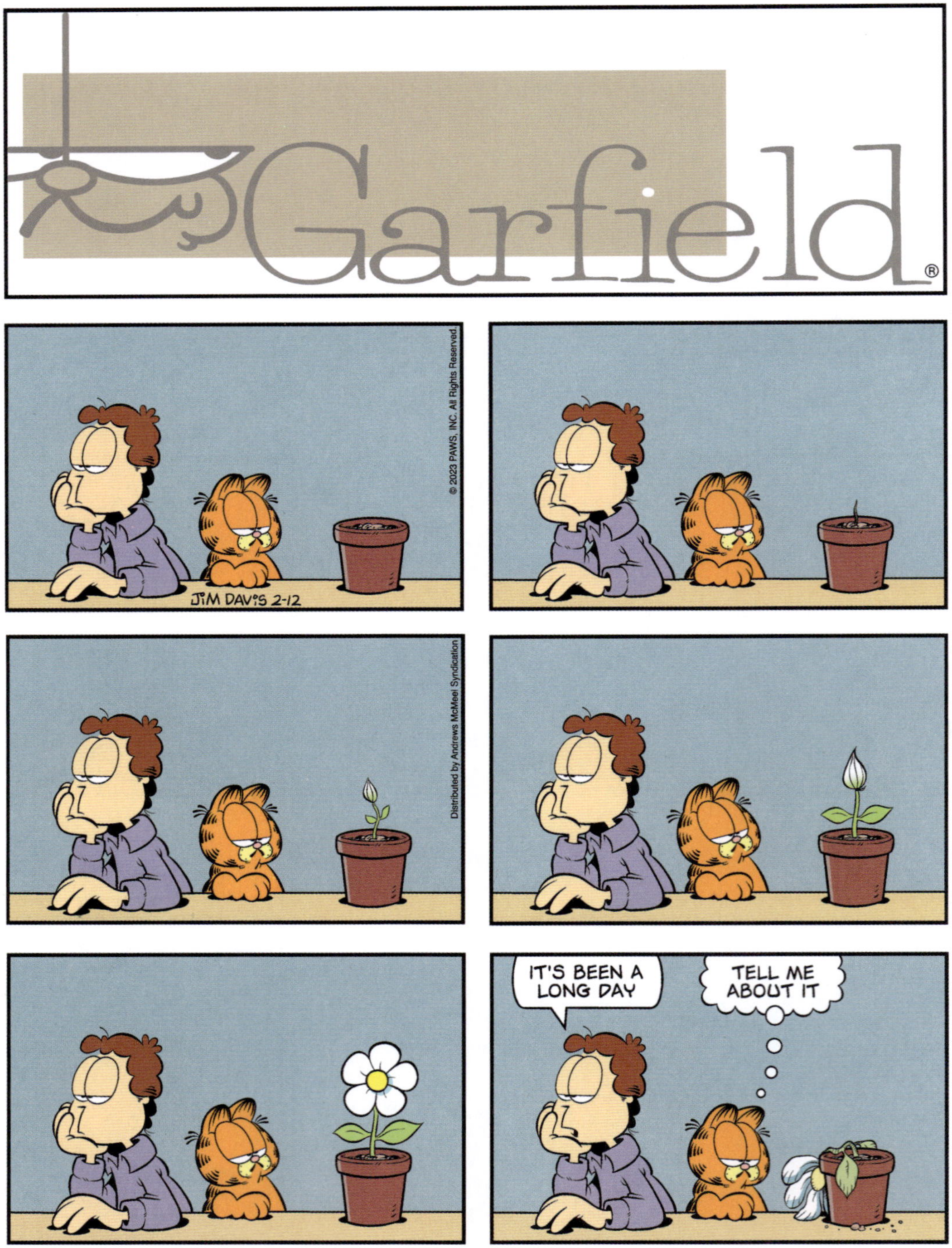
Garfield®
© 2023 PAWS, INC. All Rights Reserved.
JIM DAVIS 2-12
Distributed by Andrews McMeel Syndication
IT'S BEEN A LONG DAY
TELL ME ABOUT IT

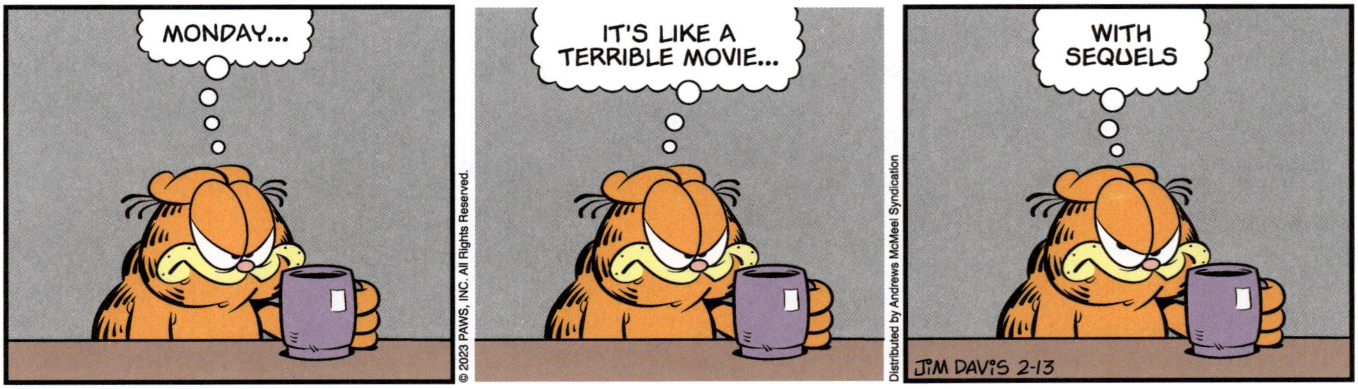
MONDAY...
IT'S LIKE A TERRIBLE MOVIE...
WITH SEQUELS
© 2023 PAWS, INC. All Rights Reserved.
Distributed by Andrews McMeel Syndication
JIM DAVIS 2-13

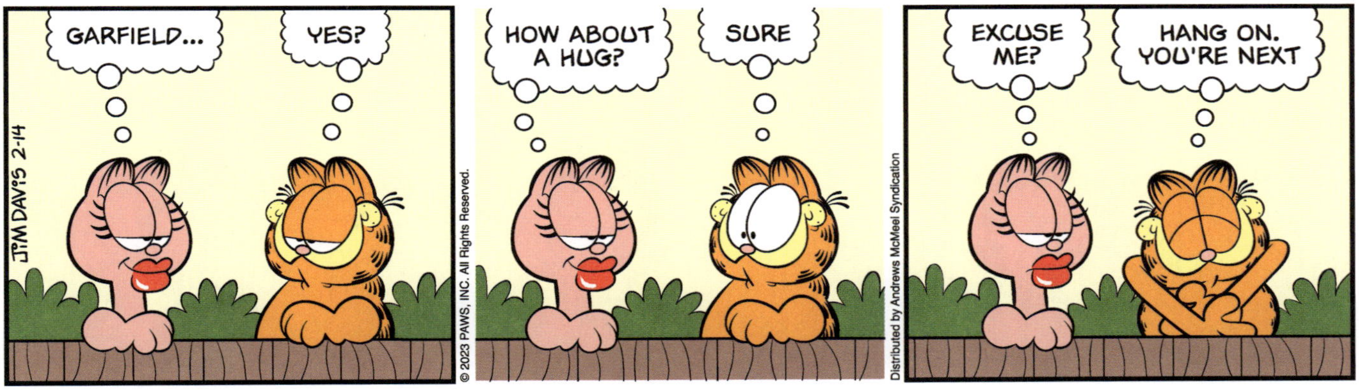
GARFIELD...
YES?
HOW ABOUT A HUG?
SURE
EXCUSE ME?
HANG ON. YOU'RE NEXT
JIM DAVIS 2-14
© 2023 PAWS, INC. All Rights Reserved.
Distributed by Andrews McMeel Syndication

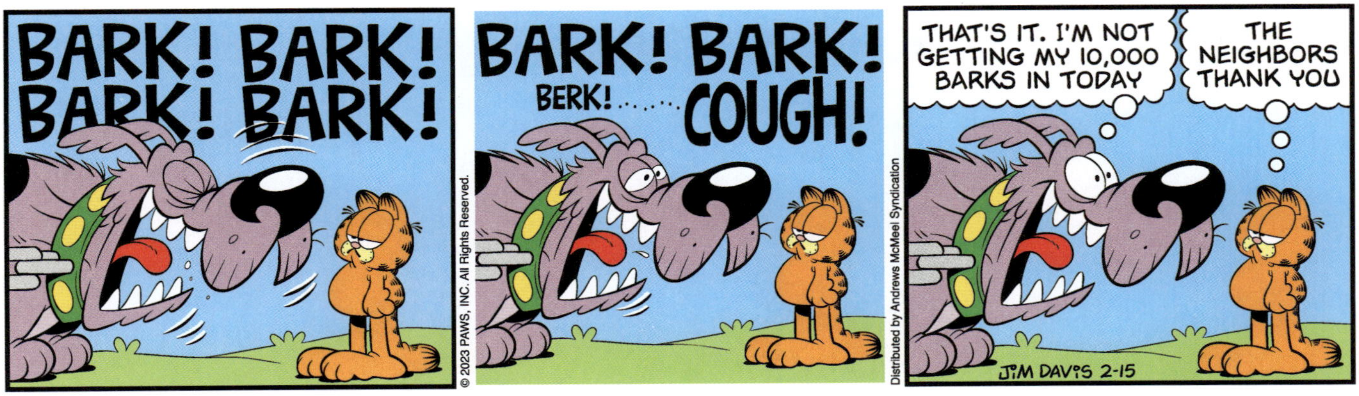
BARK! BARK! BARK! BARK!
BARK! BARK!
BERK! ...... COUGH!
THAT'S IT. I'M NOT GETTING MY 10,000 BARKS IN TODAY
THE NEIGHBORS THANK YOU
© 2023 PAWS, INC. All Rights Reserved.
Distributed by Andrews McMeel Syndication
JIM DAVIS 2-15

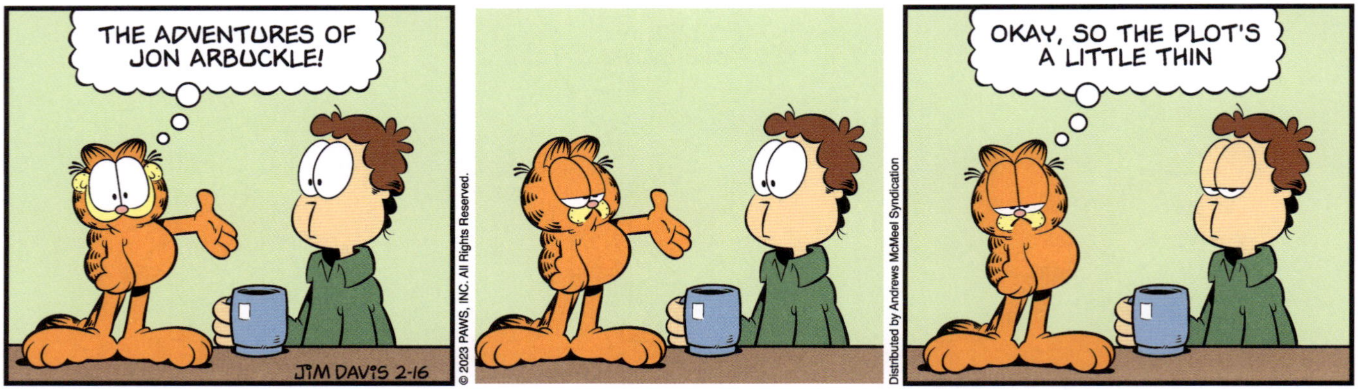
THE ADVENTURES OF JON ARBUCKLE!
JIM DAVIS 2-16
© 2023 PAWS, INC. All Rights Reserved.
Distributed by Andrews McMeel Syndication
OKAY, SO THE PLOT'S A LITTLE THIN

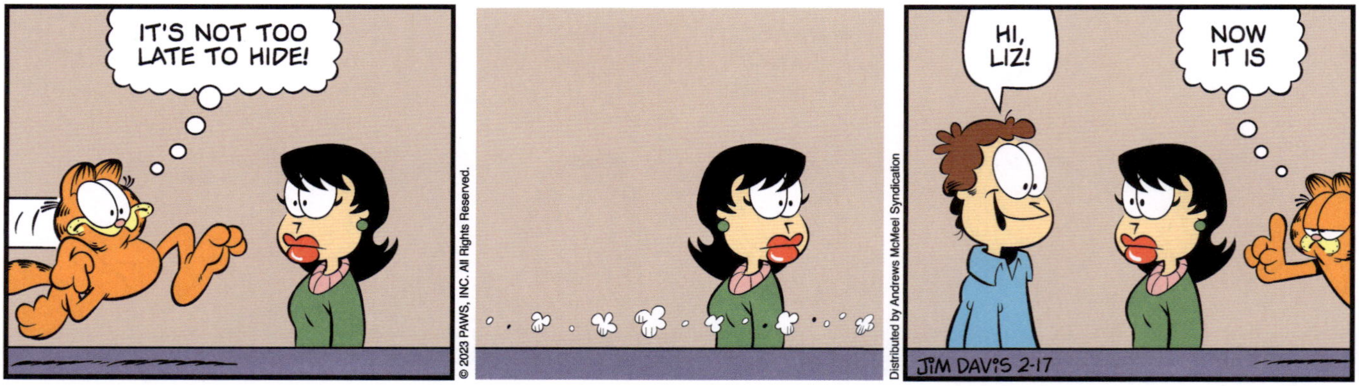
IT'S NOT TOO LATE TO HIDE!
© 2023 PAWS, INC. All Rights Reserved.
Distributed by Andrews McMeel Syndication
HI, LIZ!
NOW IT IS
JIM DAVIS 2-17

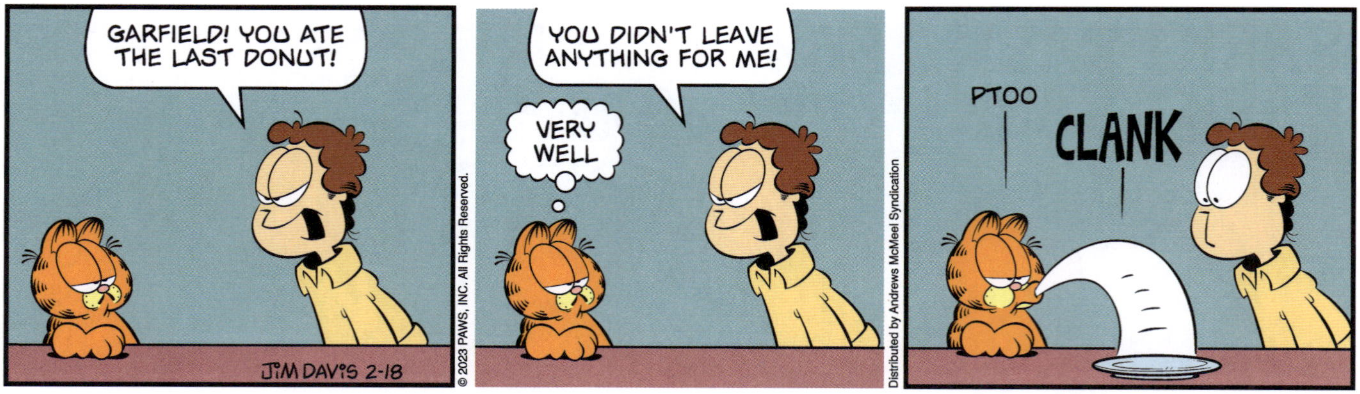
GARFIELD! YOU ATE THE LAST DONUT!
JIM DAVIS 2-18
© 2023 PAWS, INC. All Rights Reserved.
YOU DIDN'T LEAVE ANYTHING FOR ME!
VERY WELL
Distributed by Andrews McMeel Syndication
PTOO
CLANK

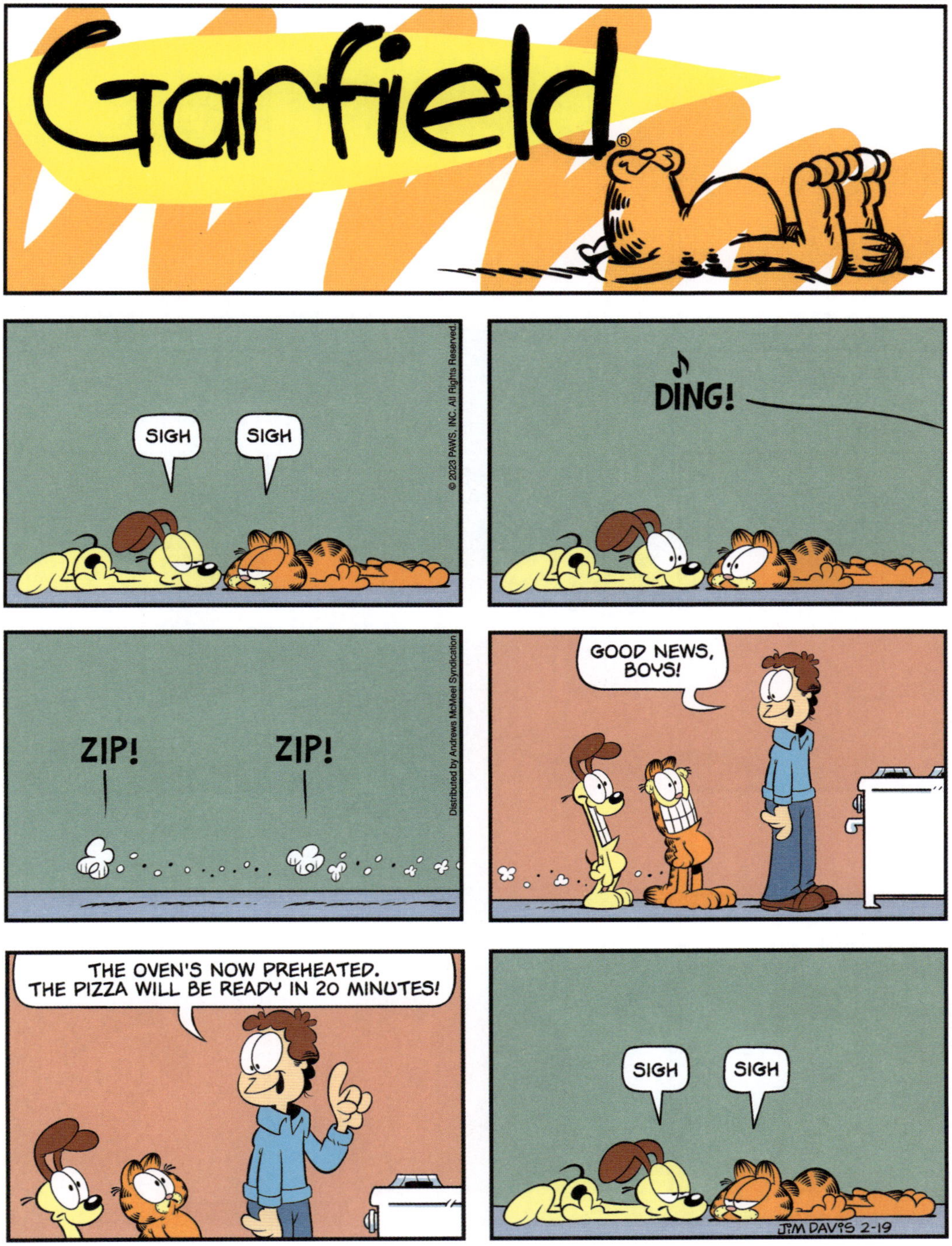
Garfield®
SIGH
SIGH
© 2023 PAWS, INC. All Rights Reserved.
DING!
ZIP!
ZIP!
Distributed by Andrews McMeel Syndication
GOOD NEWS, BOYS!
THE OVEN'S NOW PREHEATED. THE PIZZA WILL BE READY IN 20 MINUTES!
SIGH
SIGH
JIM DAVIS 2-19

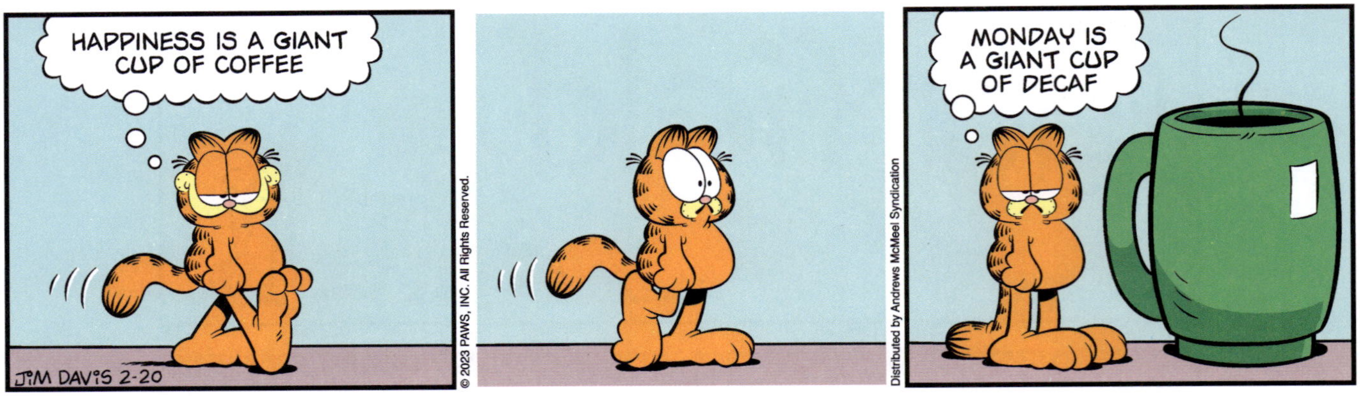
HAPPINESS IS A GIANT CUP OF COFFEE
JIM DAVIS 2-20
MONDAY IS A GIANT CUP OF DECAF

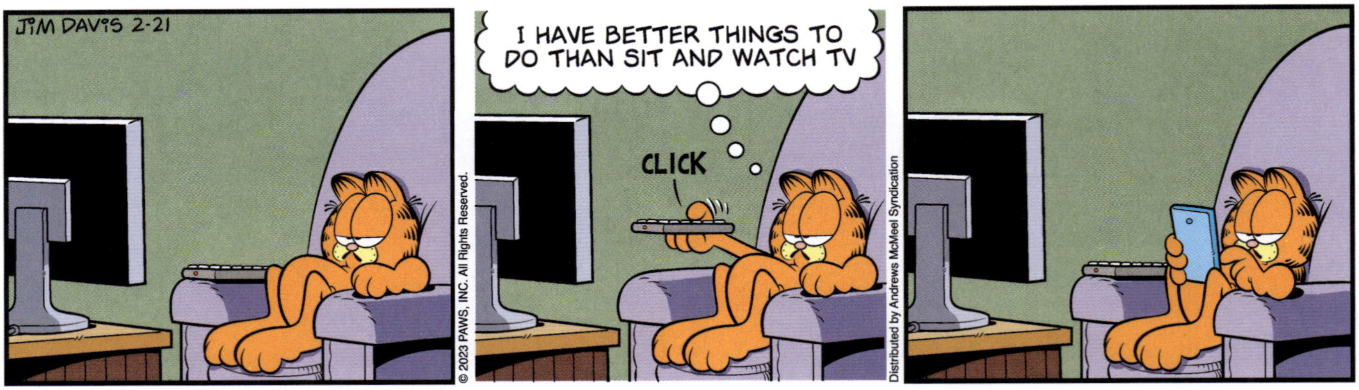
JIM DAVIS 2-21
I HAVE BETTER THINGS TO DO THAN SIT AND WATCH TV
CLICK

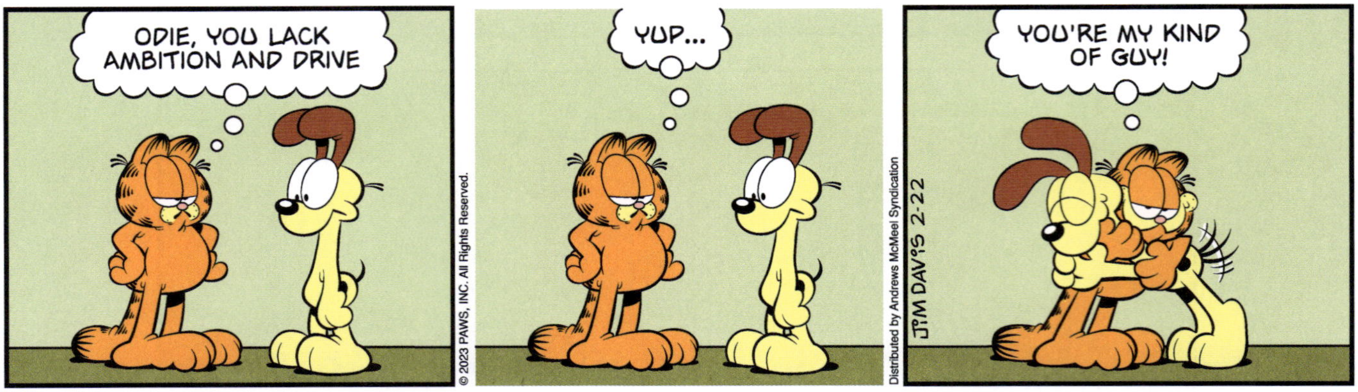
ODIE, YOU LACK AMBITION AND DRIVE
YUP...
YOU'RE MY KIND OF GUY!
JIM DAVIS 2-22

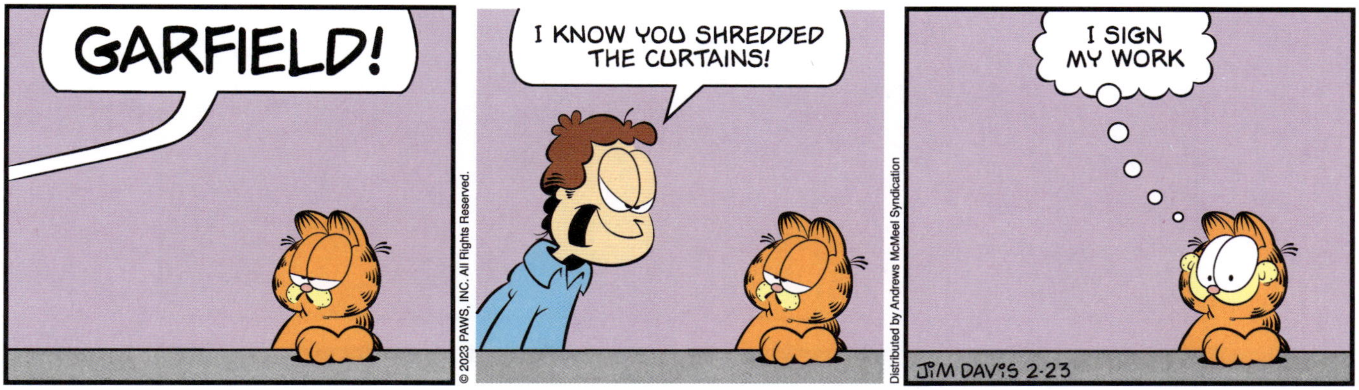
GARFIELD!
I KNOW YOU SHREDDED THE CURTAINS!
I SIGN MY WORK
JIM DAVIS 2-23
© 2023 PAWS, INC. All Rights Reserved.
Distributed by Andrews McMeel Syndication

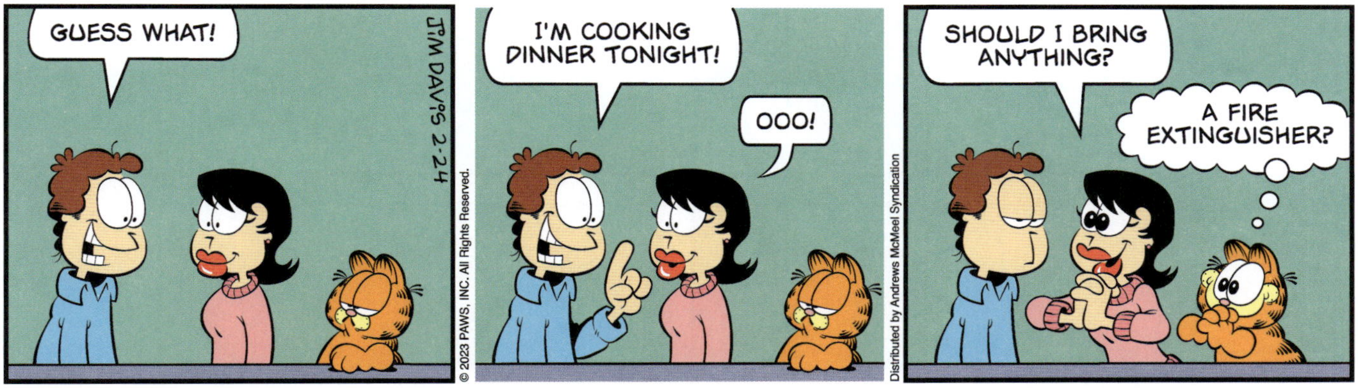
GUESS WHAT!
JIM DAVIS 2-24
I'M COOKING DINNER TONIGHT!
OOO!
SHOULD I BRING ANYTHING?
A FIRE EXTINGUISHER?
© 2023 PAWS, INC. All Rights Reserved.
Distributed by Andrews McMeel Syndication

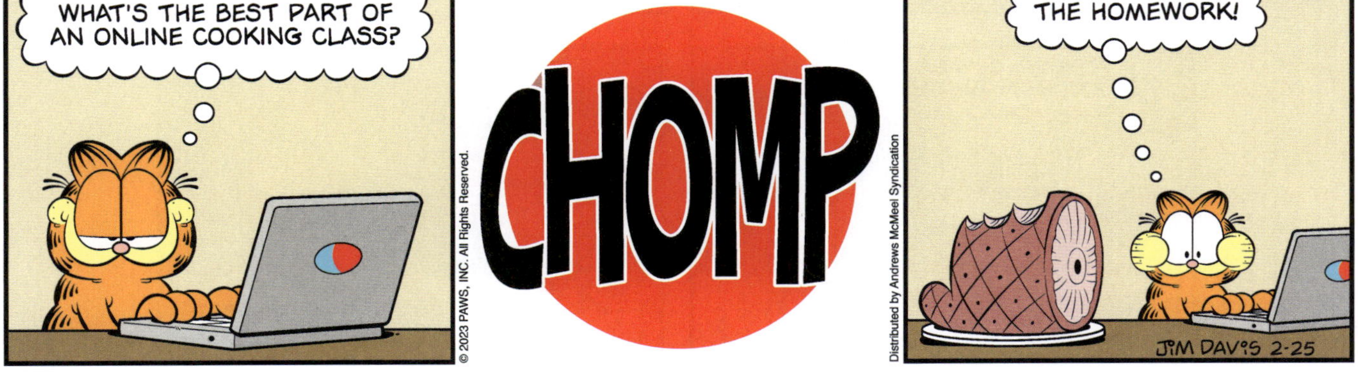
WHAT'S THE BEST PART OF AN ONLINE COOKING CLASS?
CHOMP
THE HOMEWORK!
JIM DAVIS 2-25
© 2023 PAWS, INC. All Rights Reserved.
Distributed by Andrews McMeel Syndication

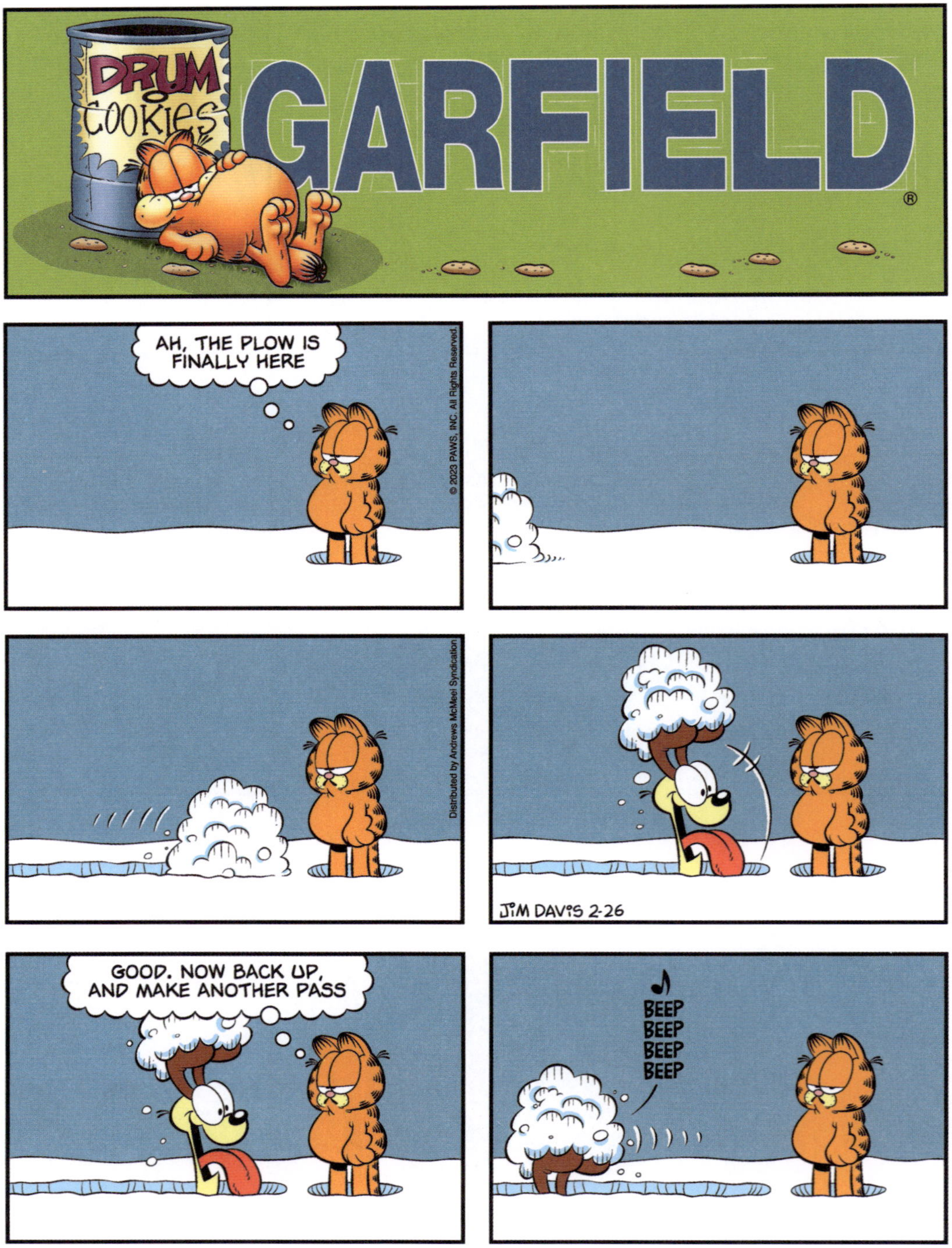
DRUM COOKIES
GARFIELD
AH, THE PLOW IS FINALLY HERE
© 2023 PAWS, INC. All Rights Reserved.
Distributed by Andrews McMeel Syndication
JIM DAVIS 2-26
GOOD. NOW BACK UP, AND MAKE ANOTHER PASS
BEEP BEEP BEEP BEEP

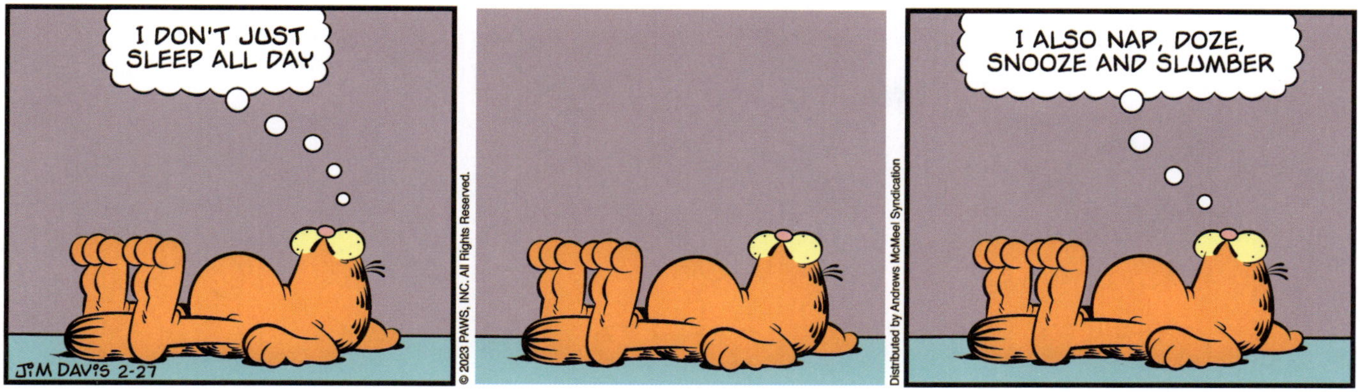
I DON'T JUST SLEEP ALL DAY
JIM DAVIS 2-27
© 2023 PAWS, INC. All Rights Reserved.
Distributed by Andrews McMeel Syndication
I ALSO NAP, DOZE, SNOOZE AND SLUMBER

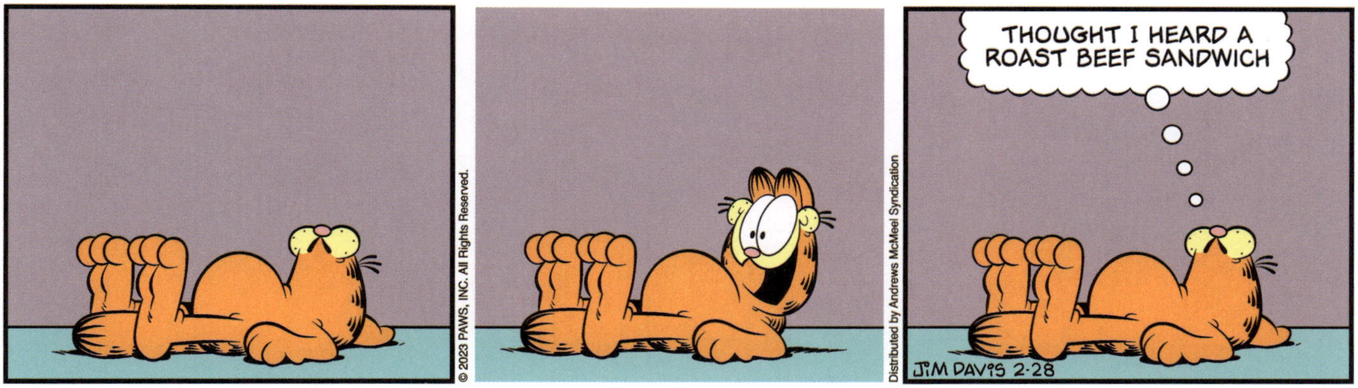
© 2023 PAWS, INC. All Rights Reserved.
Distributed by Andrews McMeel Syndication
THOUGHT I HEARD A ROAST BEEF SANDWICH
JIM DAVIS 2-28

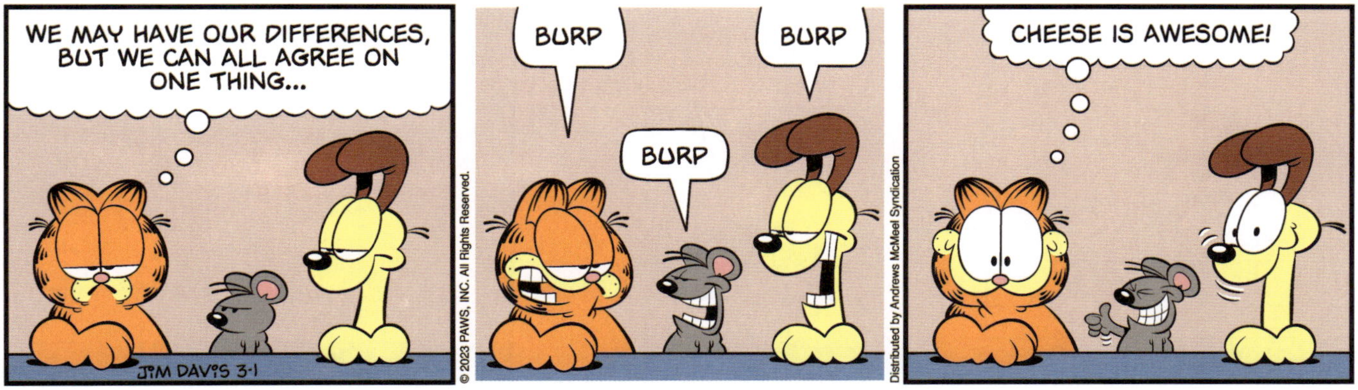
WE MAY HAVE OUR DIFFERENCES, BUT WE CAN ALL AGREE ON ONE THING...
JIM DAVIS 3-1
© 2023 PAWS, INC. All Rights Reserved.
BURP
BURP
BURP
Distributed by Andrews McMeel Syndication
CHEESE IS AWESOME!

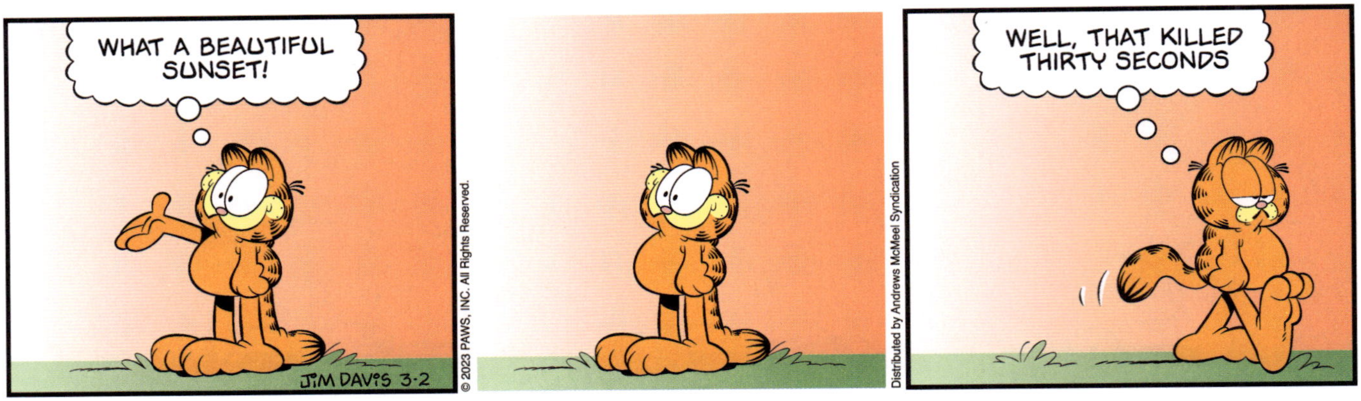
WHAT A BEAUTIFUL SUNSET!
JIM DAVIS 3-2
© 2023 PAWS, INC. All Rights Reserved.
Distributed by Andrews McMeel Syndication
WELL, THAT KILLED THIRTY SECONDS

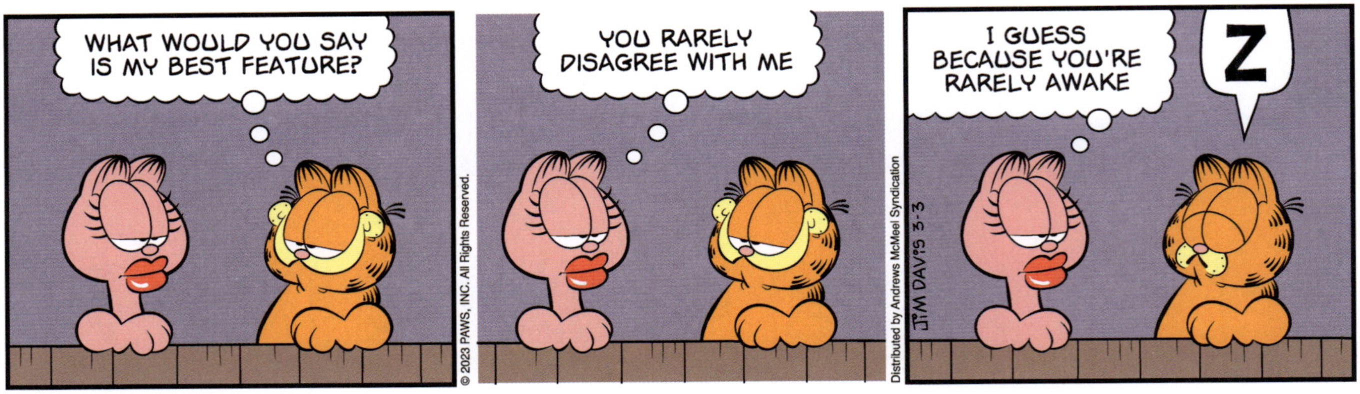
WHAT WOULD YOU SAY IS MY BEST FEATURE?
© 2023 PAWS, INC. All Rights Reserved.
YOU RARELY DISAGREE WITH ME
Distributed by Andrews McMeel Syndication
JIM DAVIS 3-3
I GUESS BECAUSE YOU'RE RARELY AWAKE
Z

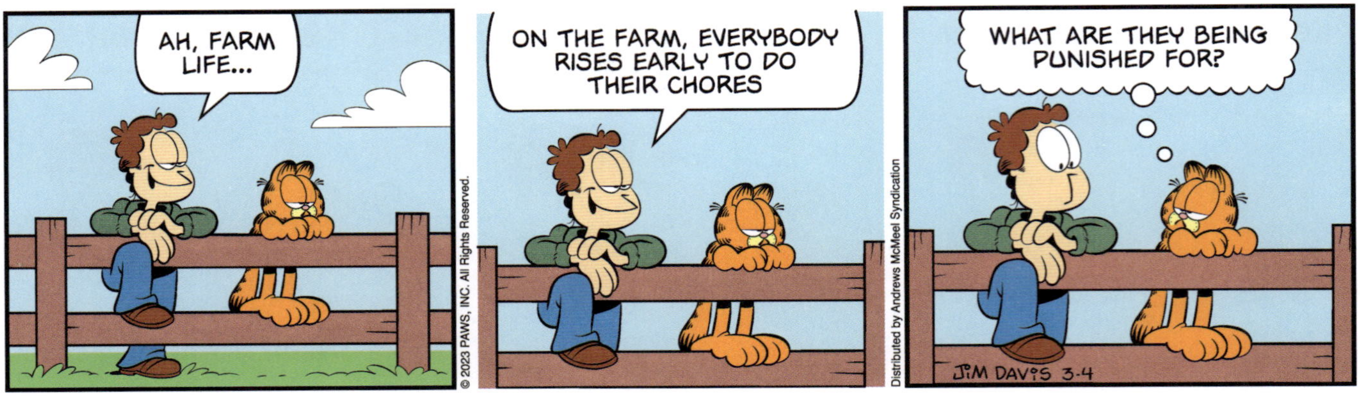
AH, FARM LIFE...
© 2023 PAWS, INC. All Rights Reserved.
ON THE FARM, EVERYBODY RISES EARLY TO DO THEIR CHORES
Distributed by Andrews McMeel Syndication
WHAT ARE THEY BEING PUNISHED FOR?
JIM DAVIS 3-4

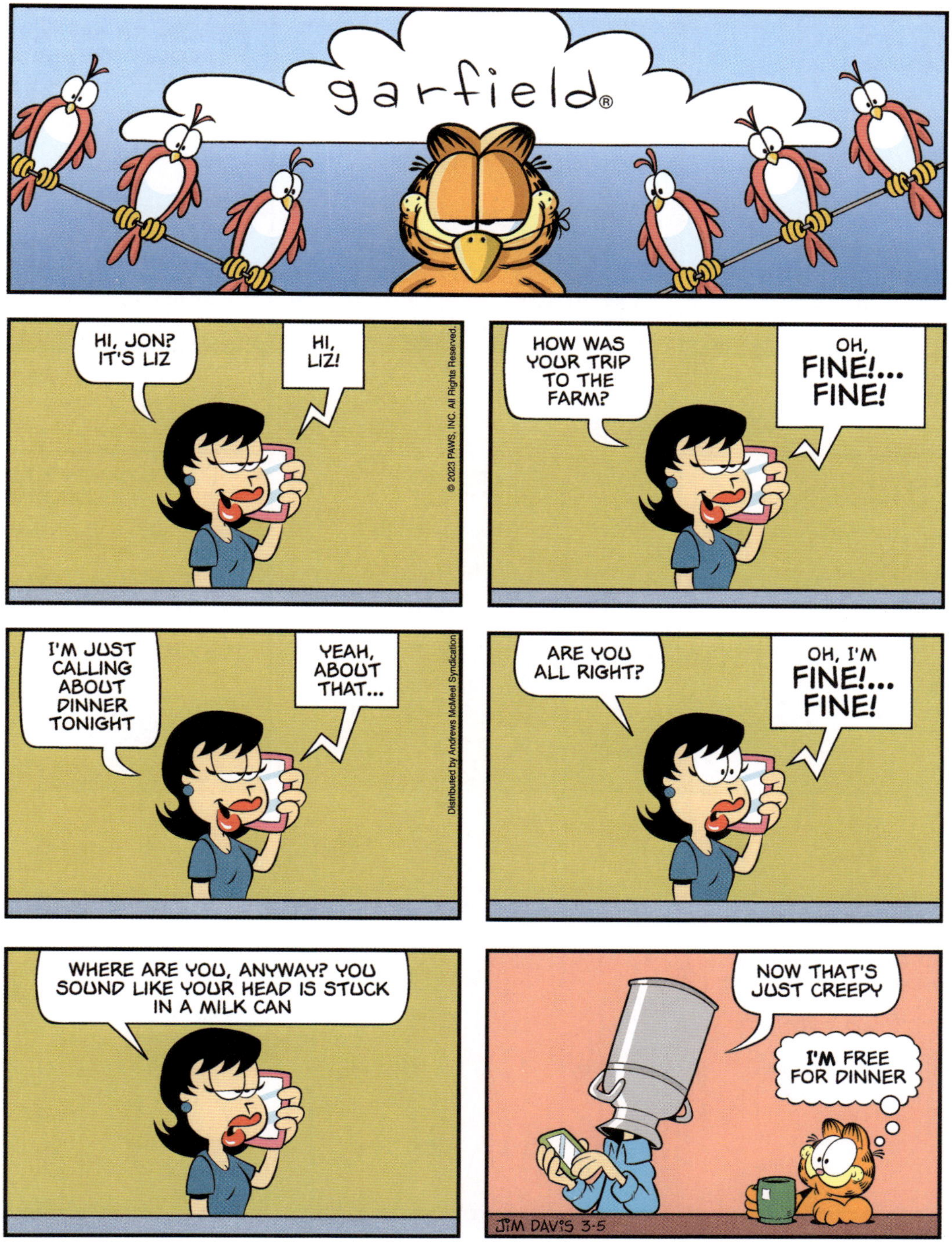

garfield®
HI, JON? IT'S LIZ
HI, LIZ!
© 2023 PAWS, INC. All Rights Reserved.
HOW WAS YOUR TRIP TO THE FARM?
OH, FINE!... FINE!
I'M JUST CALLING ABOUT DINNER TONIGHT
YEAH, ABOUT THAT...
Distributed by Andrews McMeel Syndication
ARE YOU ALL RIGHT?
OH, I'M FINE!... FINE!
WHERE ARE YOU, ANYWAY? YOU SOUND LIKE YOUR HEAD IS STUCK IN A MILK CAN
NOW THAT'S JUST CREEPY
I'M FREE FOR DINNER
JIM DAVIS 3-5

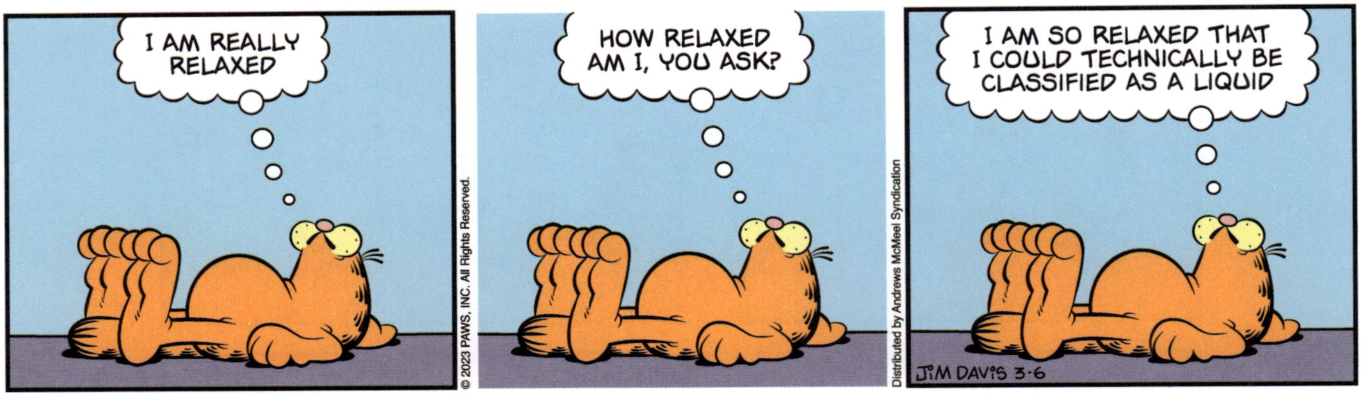
I AM REALLY RELAXED
HOW RELAXED AM I, YOU ASK?
I AM SO RELAXED THAT I COULD TECHNICALLY BE CLASSIFIED AS A LIQUID
© 2023 PAWS, INC. All Rights Reserved.
Distributed by Andrews McMeel Syndication
JIM DAVIS 3-6

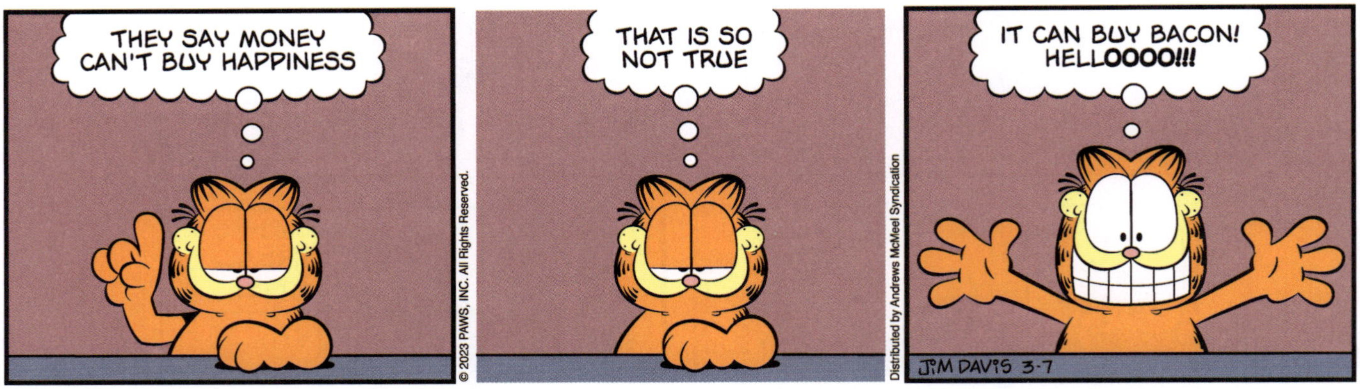
THEY SAY MONEY CAN'T BUY HAPPINESS
THAT IS SO NOT TRUE
IT CAN BUY BACON! HELLOOOO!!!
© 2023 PAWS, INC. All Rights Reserved.
Distributed by Andrews McMeel Syndication
JIM DAVIS 3-7

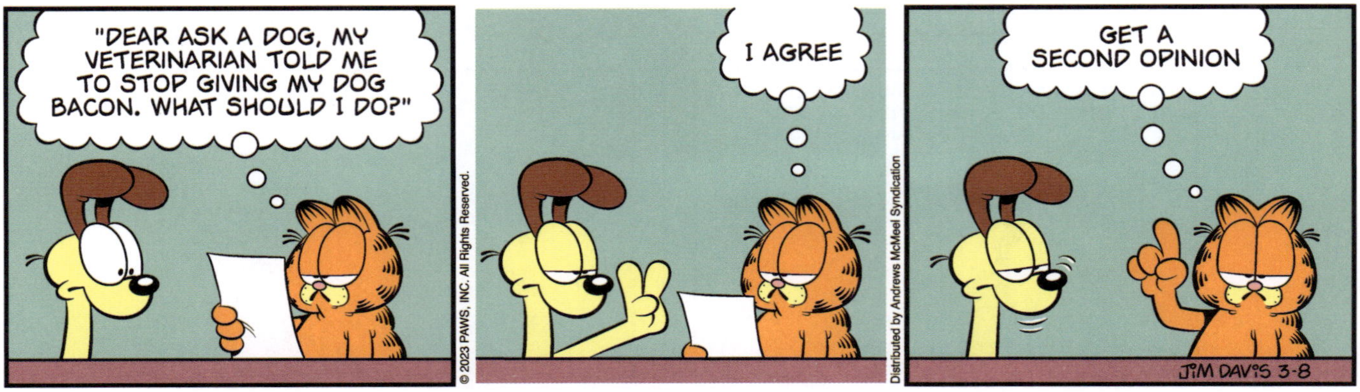
"DEAR ASK A DOG, MY VETERINARIAN TOLD ME TO STOP GIVING MY DOG BACON. WHAT SHOULD I DO?"
I AGREE
GET A SECOND OPINION
© 2023 PAWS, INC. All Rights Reserved.
Distributed by Andrews McMeel Syndication
JIM DAVIS 3-8

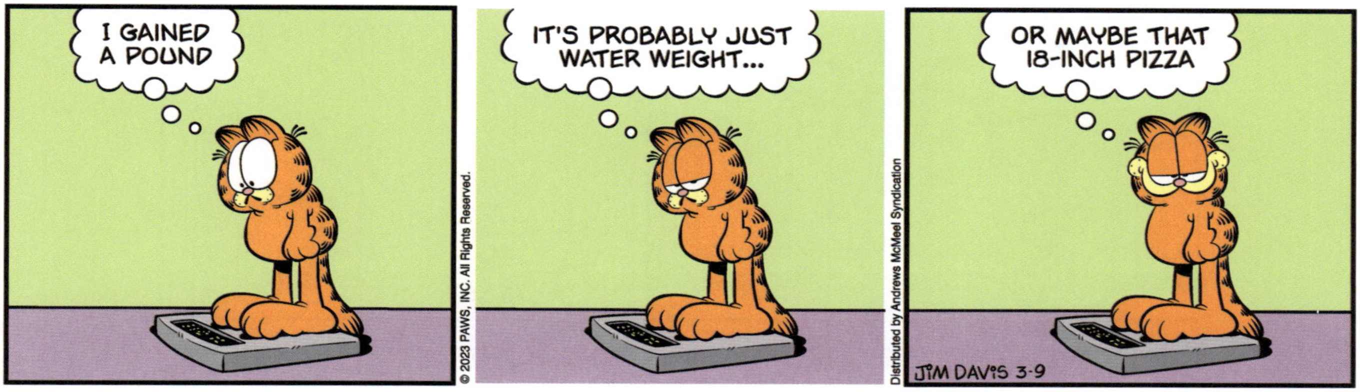
I GAINED A POUND
© 2023 PAWS, INC. All Rights Reserved.
IT'S PROBABLY JUST WATER WEIGHT...
Distributed by Andrews McMeel Syndication
OR MAYBE THAT 18-INCH PIZZA
JIM DAVIS 3-9

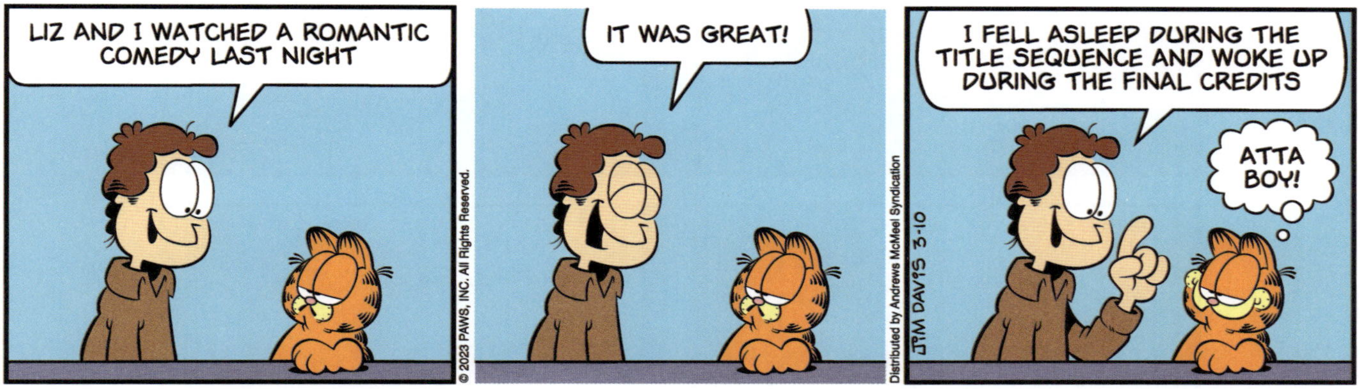
LIZ AND I WATCHED A ROMANTIC COMEDY LAST NIGHT
© 2023 PAWS, INC. All Rights Reserved.
IT WAS GREAT!
Distributed by Andrews McMeel Syndication
JIM DAVIS 3-10
I FELL ASLEEP DURING THE TITLE SEQUENCE AND WOKE UP DURING THE FINAL CREDITS
ATTA BOY!

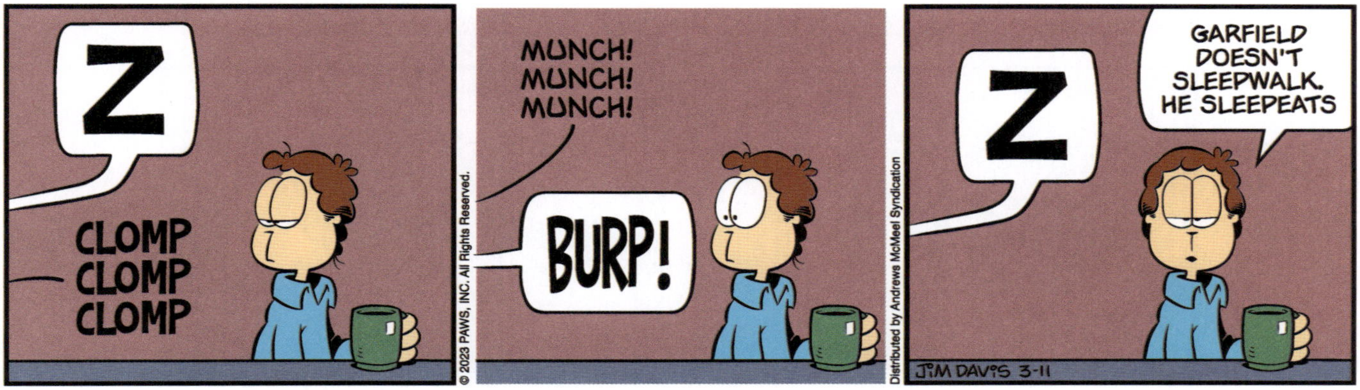
Z
CLOMP CLOMP CLOMP
© 2023 PAWS, INC. All Rights Reserved.
MUNCH! MUNCH! MUNCH!
BURP!
Distributed by Andrews McMeel Syndication
Z
GARFIELD DOESN'T SLEEPWALK. HE SLEEPEATS
JIM DAVIS 3-11

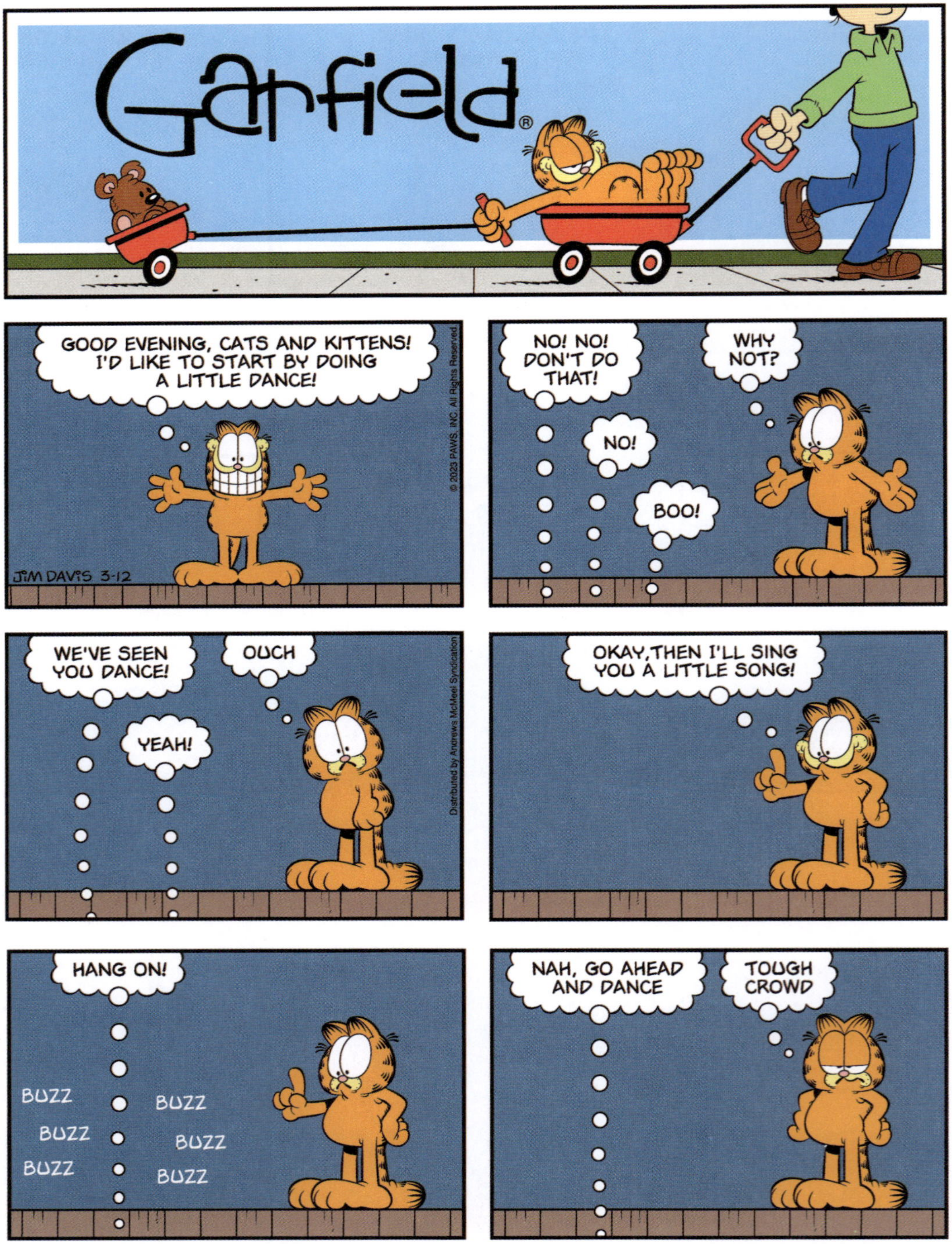
Garfield®
GOOD EVENING, CATS AND KITTENS! I'D LIKE TO START BY DOING A LITTLE DANCE!
JIM DAVIS 3-12
© 2023 PAWS, INC. All Rights Reserved
NO! NO! DON'T DO THAT!
NO!
BOO!
WHY NOT?
WE'VE SEEN YOU DANCE!
YEAH!
OUCH
Distributed by Andrews McMeel Syndication
OKAY, THEN I'LL SING YOU A LITTLE SONG!
HANG ON!
BUZZ
BUZZ
BUZZ
BUZZ
BUZZ
BUZZ
NAH, GO AHEAD AND DANCE
TOUGH CROWD

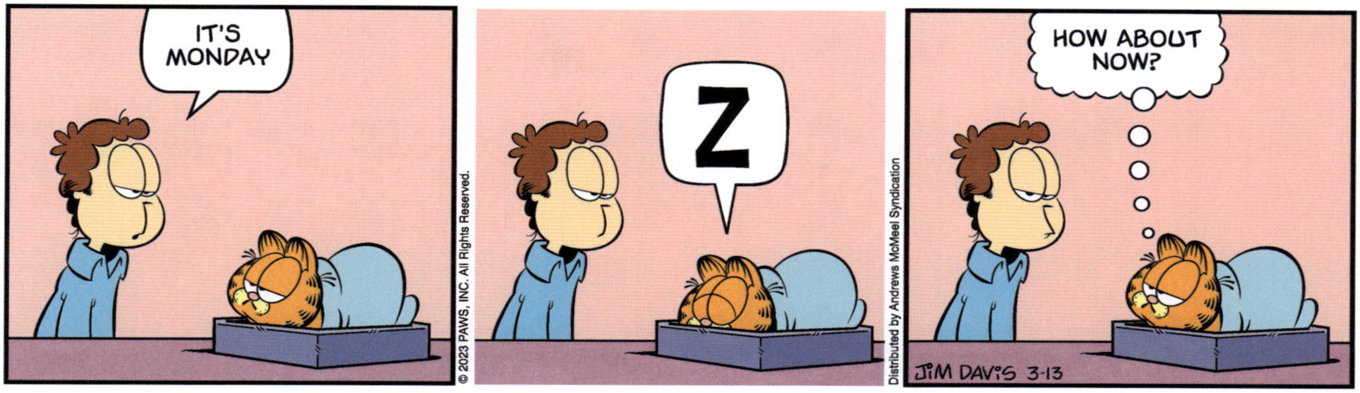
IT'S MONDAY
Z
HOW ABOUT NOW?
© 2023 PAWS, INC. All Rights Reserved.
Distributed by Andrews McMeel Syndication
JIM DAVIS 3-13

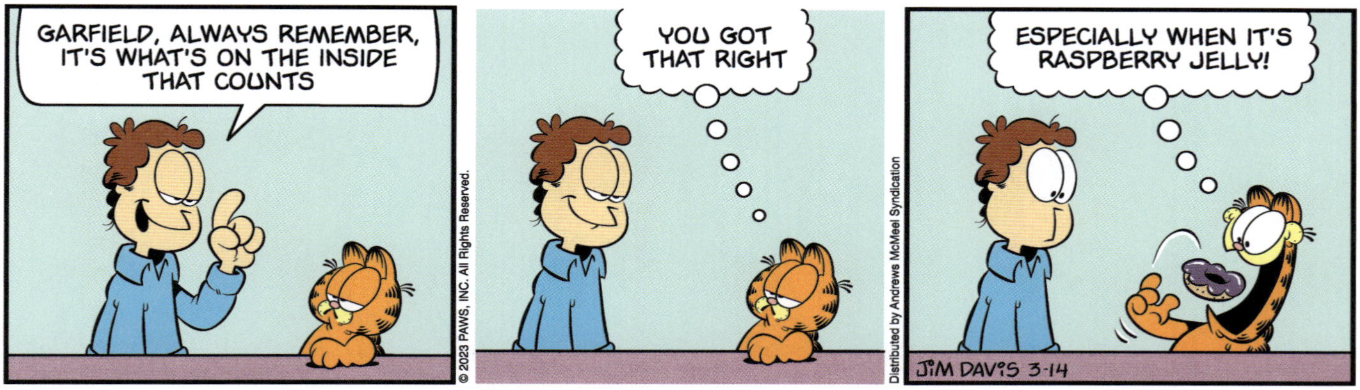
GARFIELD, ALWAYS REMEMBER, IT'S WHAT'S ON THE INSIDE THAT COUNTS
YOU GOT THAT RIGHT
ESPECIALLY WHEN IT'S RASPBERRY JELLY!
© 2023 PAWS, INC. All Rights Reserved.
Distributed by Andrews McMeel Syndication
JIM DAVIS 3-14

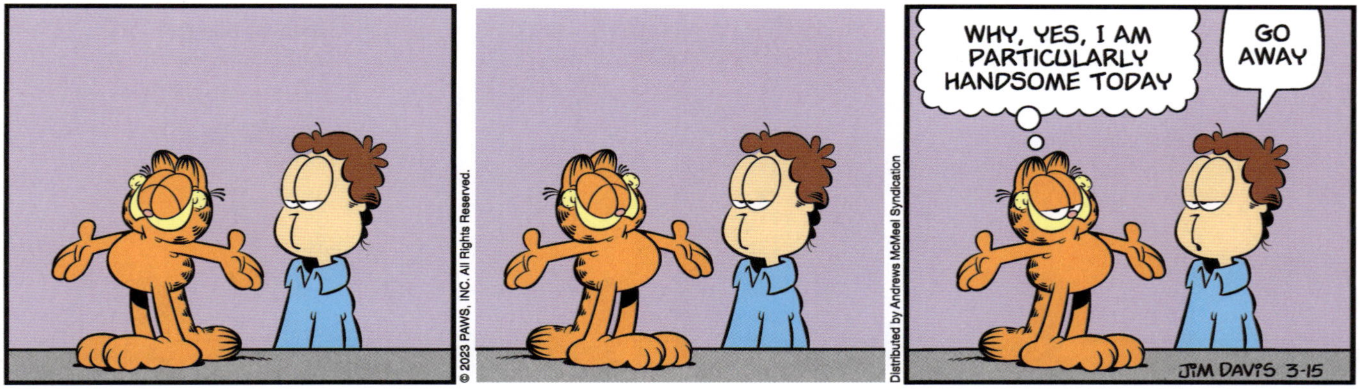
WHY, YES, I AM PARTICULARLY HANDSOME TODAY
GO AWAY
© 2023 PAWS, INC. All Rights Reserved.
Distributed by Andrews McMeel Syndication
JIM DAVIS 3-15

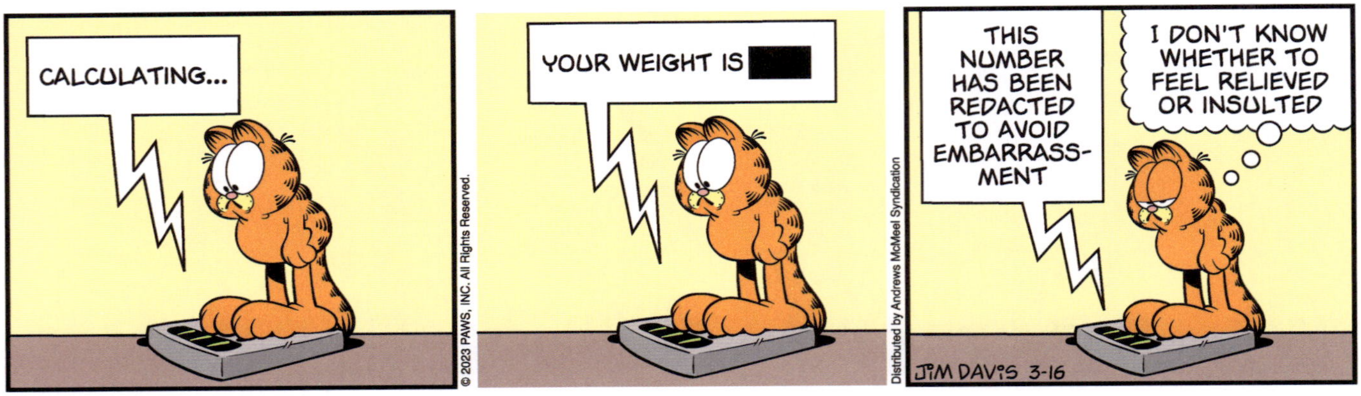
CALCULATING...
YOUR WEIGHT IS [redacted]
THIS NUMBER HAS BEEN REDACTED TO AVOID EMBARRASS-MENT
I DON'T KNOW WHETHER TO FEEL RELIEVED OR INSULTED
JIM DAVIS 3-16

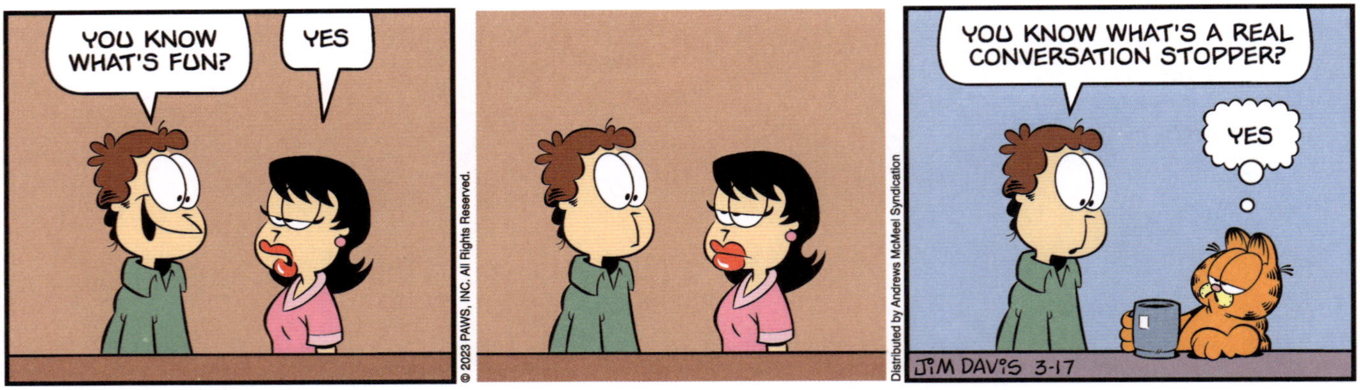
YOU KNOW WHAT'S FUN?
YES
YOU KNOW WHAT'S A REAL CONVERSATION STOPPER?
YES
JIM DAVIS 3-17

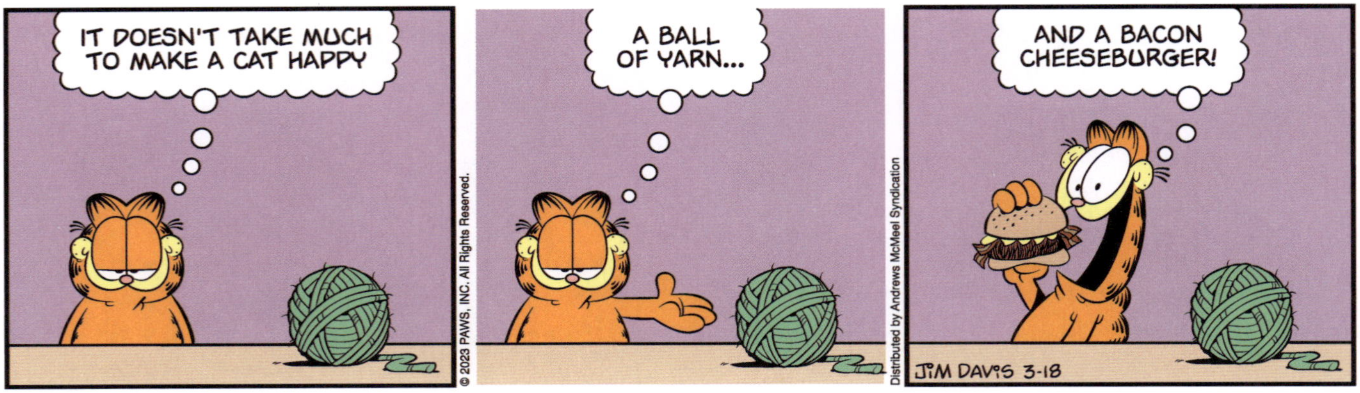
IT DOESN'T TAKE MUCH TO MAKE A CAT HAPPY
A BALL OF YARN...
AND A BACON CHEESEBURGER!
JIM DAVIS 3-18

Garfield®
© 2023 PAWS, INC. All Rights Reserved.
BARK!
JIM DAVIS 3-19
Distributed by Andrews McMeel Syndication
CREEEEEAK
WHEN DID WE GET A CHANDELIER?

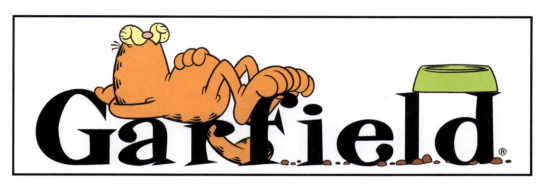

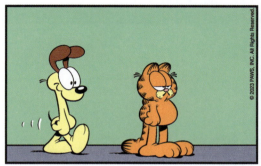

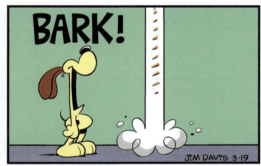

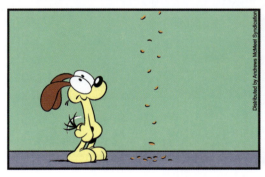

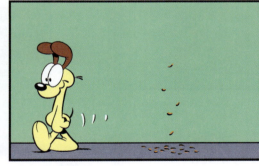

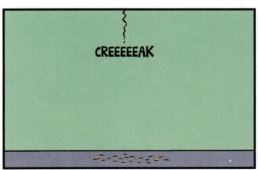

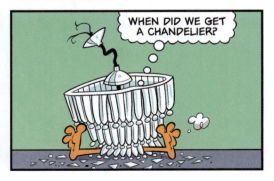

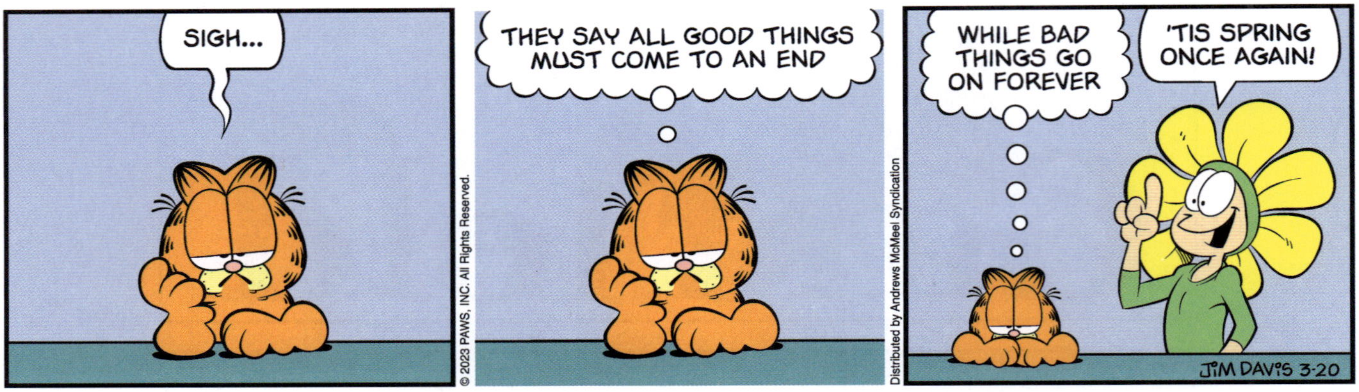
SIGH...
THEY SAY ALL GOOD THINGS MUST COME TO AN END
WHILE BAD THINGS GO ON FOREVER
'TIS SPRING ONCE AGAIN!
JIM DAVIS 3-20
© 2023 PAWS, INC. All Rights Reserved.
Distributed by Andrews McMeel Syndication

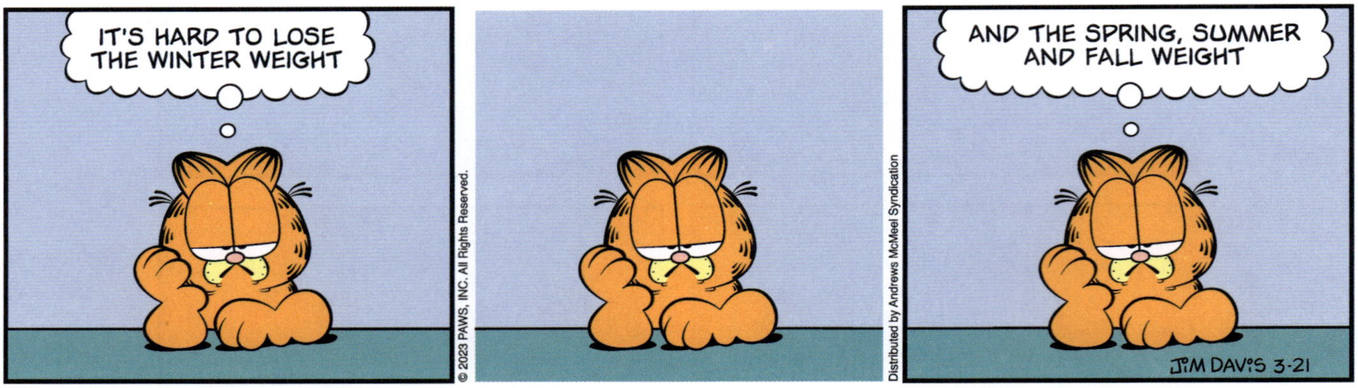
IT'S HARD TO LOSE THE WINTER WEIGHT
AND THE SPRING, SUMMER AND FALL WEIGHT
JIM DAVIS 3-21
© 2023 PAWS, INC. All Rights Reserved.
Distributed by Andrews McMeel Syndication

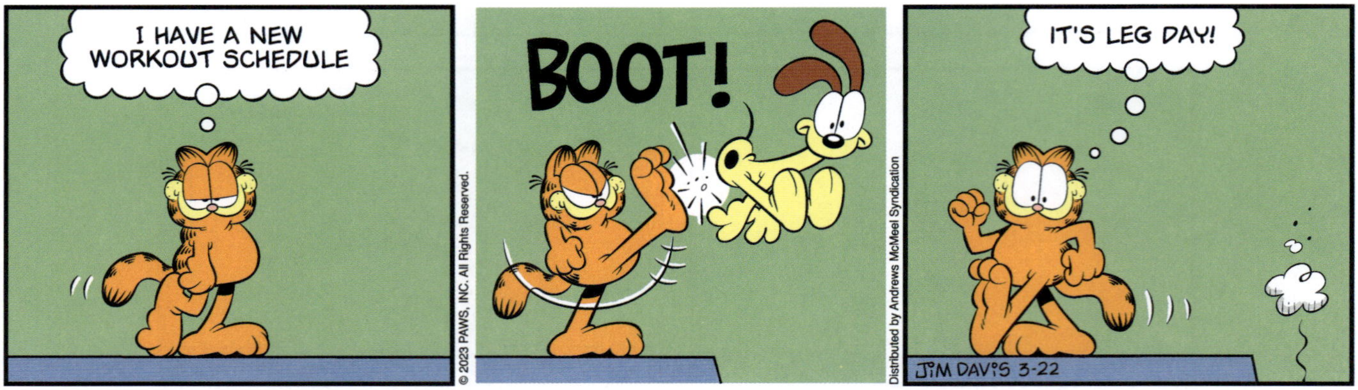
I HAVE A NEW WORKOUT SCHEDULE
BOOT!
IT'S LEG DAY!
JIM DAVIS 3-22
© 2023 PAWS, INC. All Rights Reserved.
Distributed by Andrews McMeel Syndication

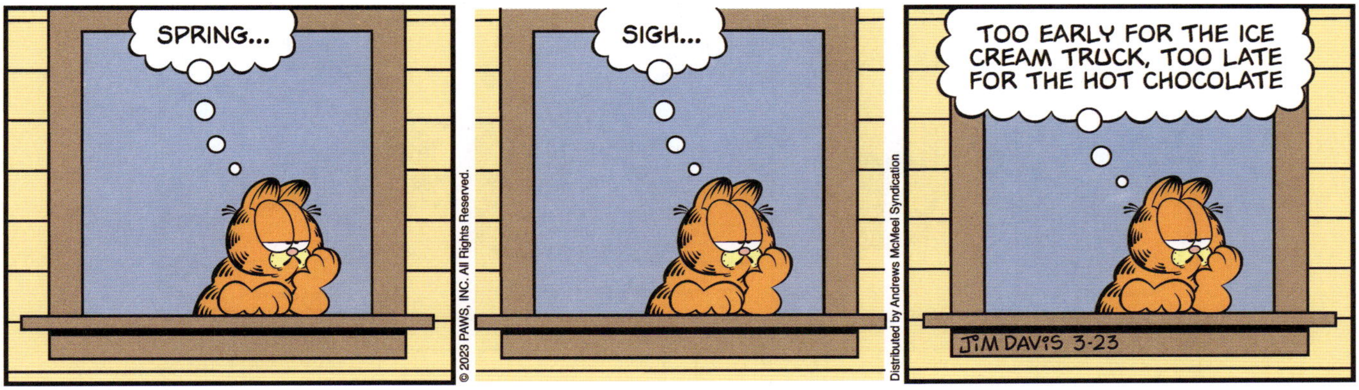
SPRING...
SIGH...
TOO EARLY FOR THE ICE CREAM TRUCK, TOO LATE FOR THE HOT CHOCOLATE
JIM DAVIS 3-23

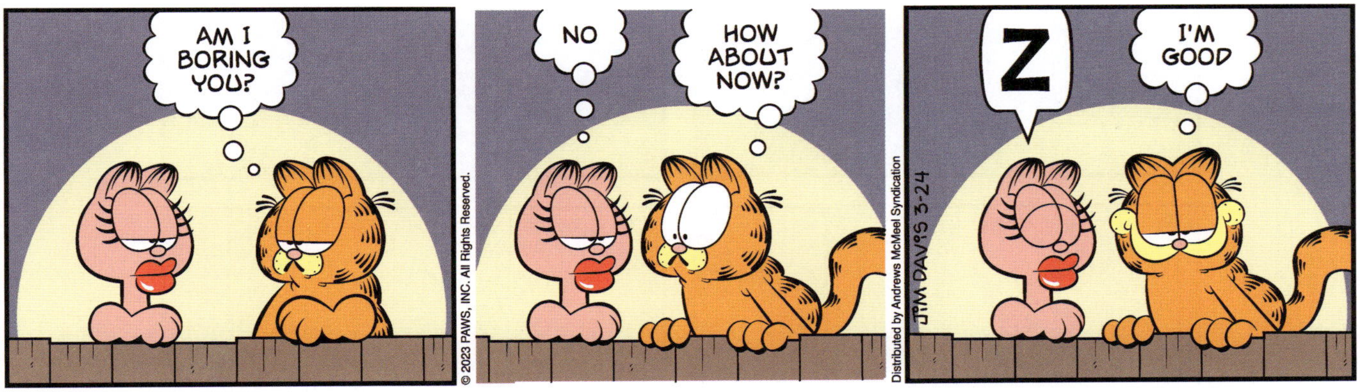
AM I BORING YOU?
NO
HOW ABOUT NOW?
Z
I'M GOOD
JIM DAVIS 3-24

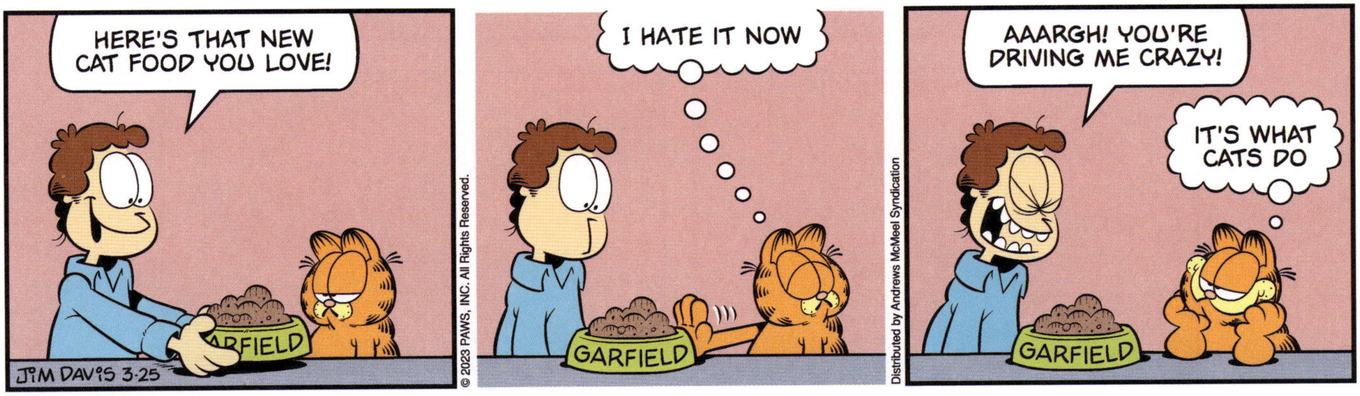
HERE'S THAT NEW CAT FOOD YOU LOVE!
GARFIELD
JIM DAVIS 3-25
I HATE IT NOW
GARFIELD
AAARGH! YOU'RE DRIVING ME CRAZY!
IT'S WHAT CATS DO
GARFIELD

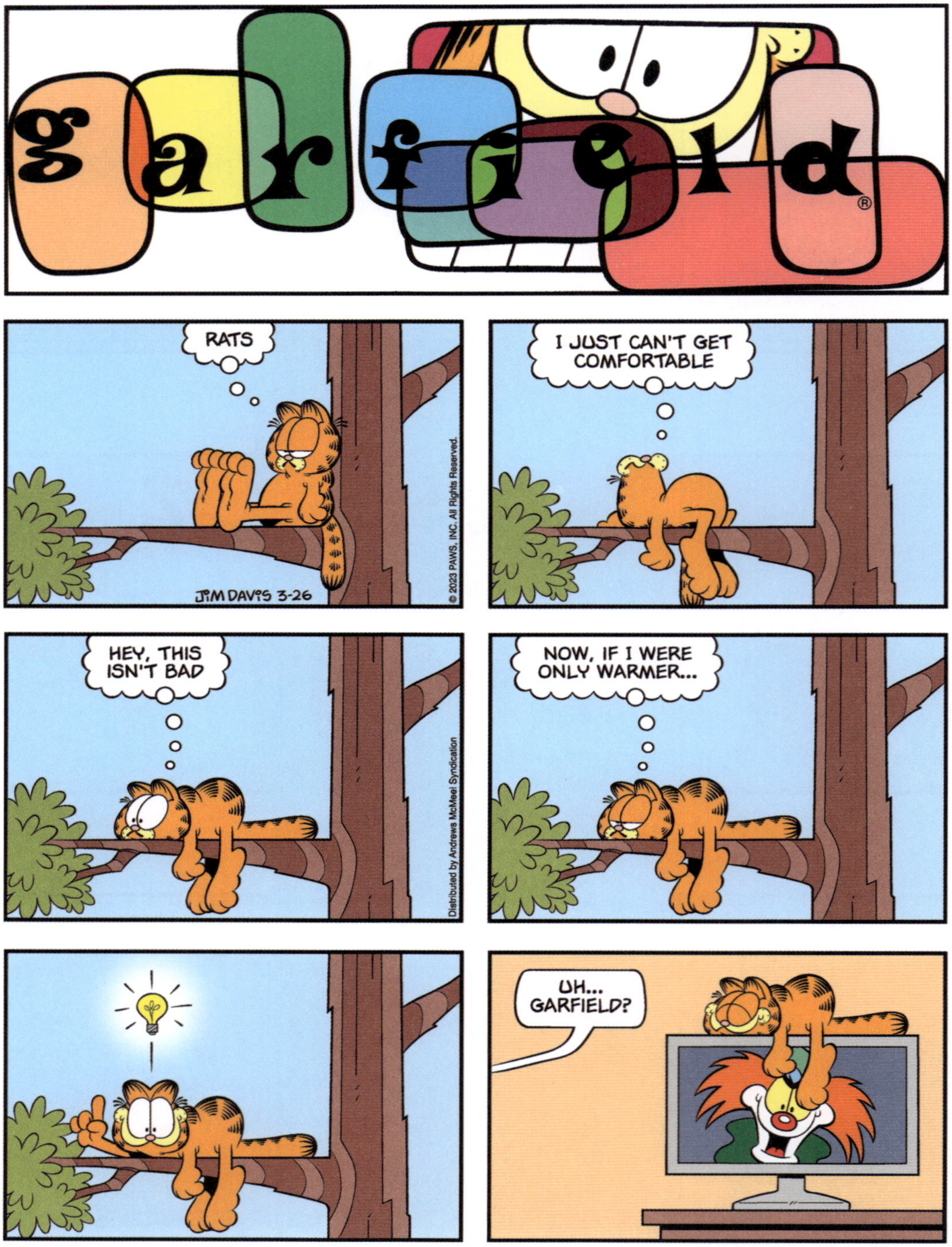
garfield
RATS
JIM DAVIS 3-26
© 2023 PAWS, INC. All Rights Reserved.
I JUST CAN'T GET COMFORTABLE
HEY, THIS ISN'T BAD
Distributed by Andrews McMeel Syndication
NOW, IF I WERE ONLY WARMER...
UH... GARFIELD?

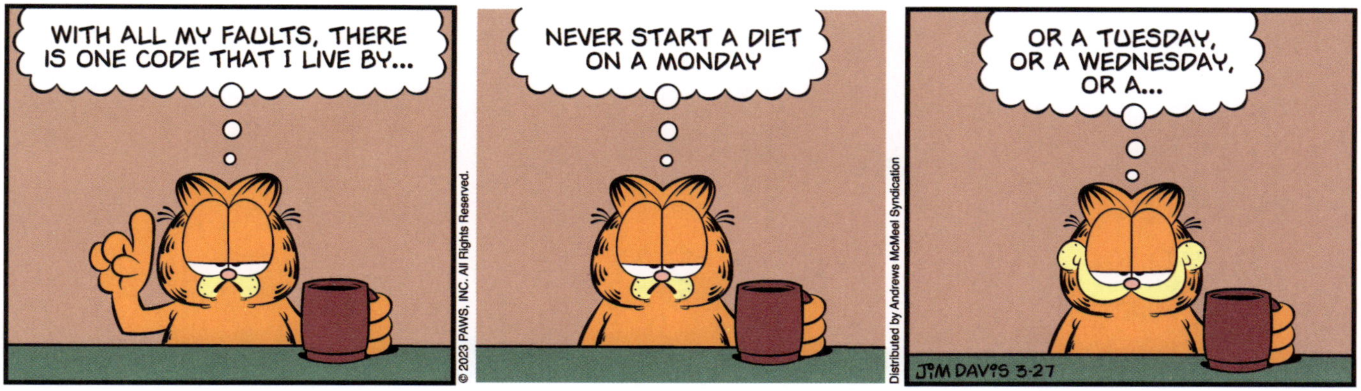
WITH ALL MY FAULTS, THERE IS ONE CODE THAT I LIVE BY...
© 2023 PAWS, INC. All Rights Reserved.
NEVER START A DIET ON A MONDAY
Distributed by Andrews McMeel Syndication
OR A TUESDAY, OR A WEDNESDAY, OR A...
JIM DAVIS 3-27

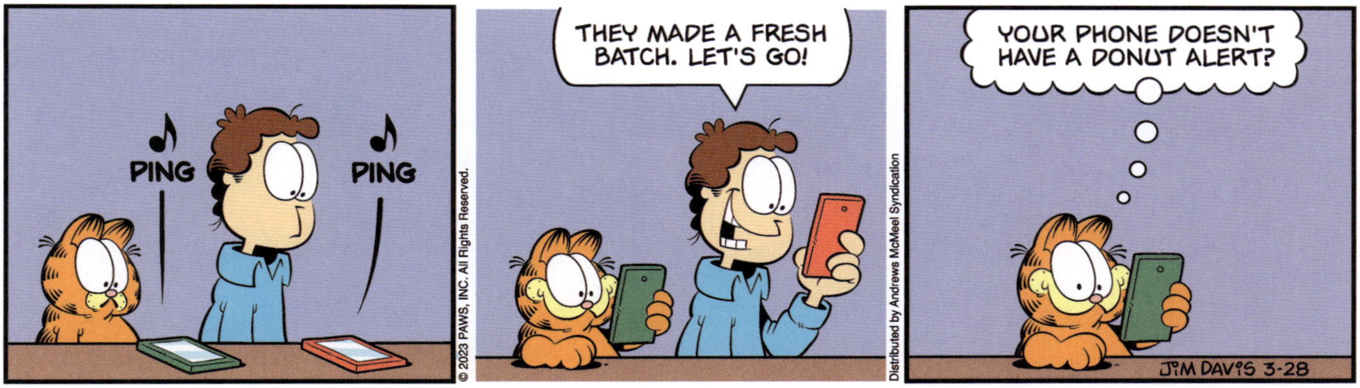
PING
PING
© 2023 PAWS, INC. All Rights Reserved.
THEY MADE A FRESH BATCH. LET'S GO!
Distributed by Andrews McMeel Syndication
YOUR PHONE DOESN'T HAVE A DONUT ALERT?
JIM DAVIS 3-28

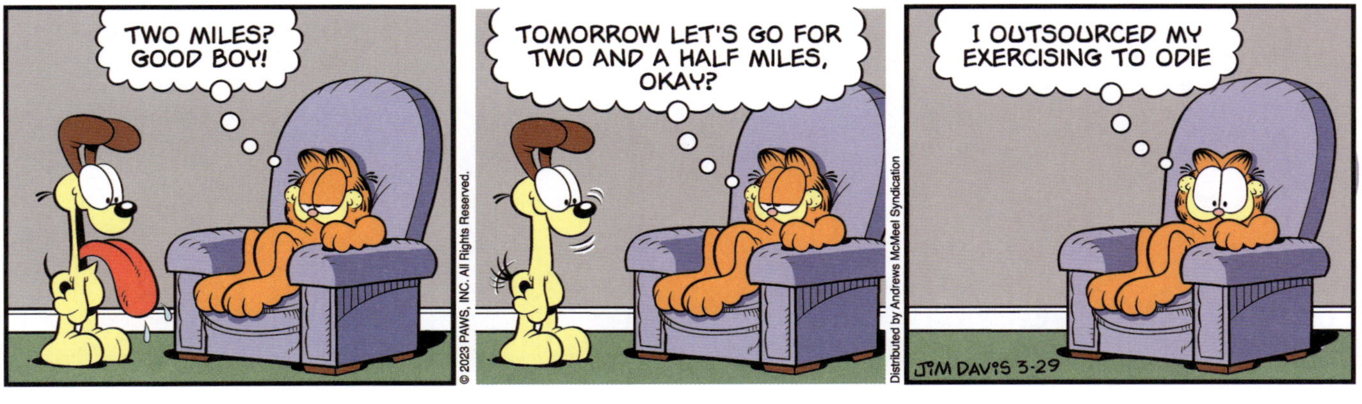
TWO MILES? GOOD BOY!
© 2023 PAWS, INC. All Rights Reserved.
TOMORROW LET'S GO FOR TWO AND A HALF MILES, OKAY?
Distributed by Andrews McMeel Syndication
I OUTSOURCED MY EXERCISING TO ODIE
JIM DAVIS 3-29

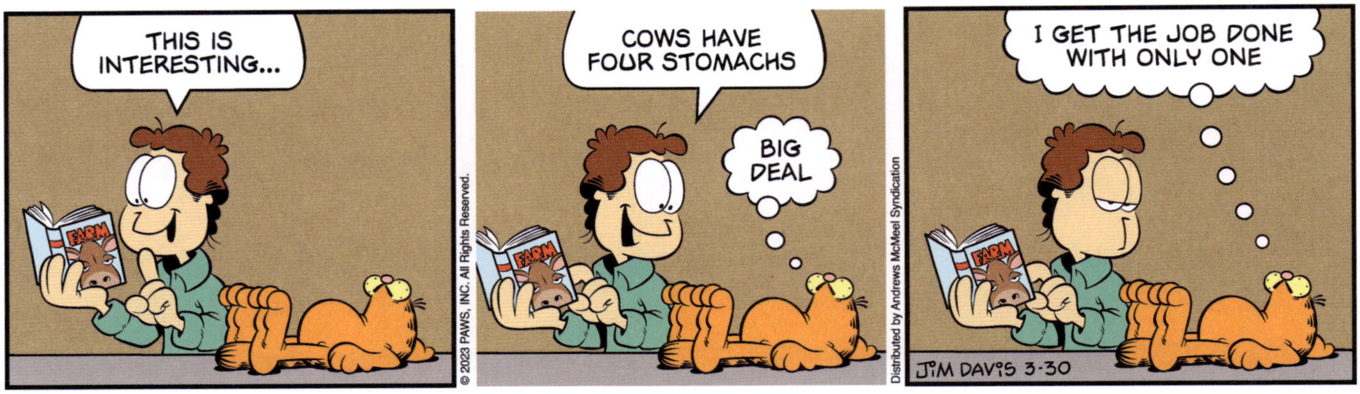
THIS IS INTERESTING...
FARM
COWS HAVE FOUR STOMACHS
BIG DEAL
I GET THE JOB DONE WITH ONLY ONE
JIM DAVIS 3-30
© 2023 PAWS, INC. All Rights Reserved.
Distributed by Andrews McMeel Syndication

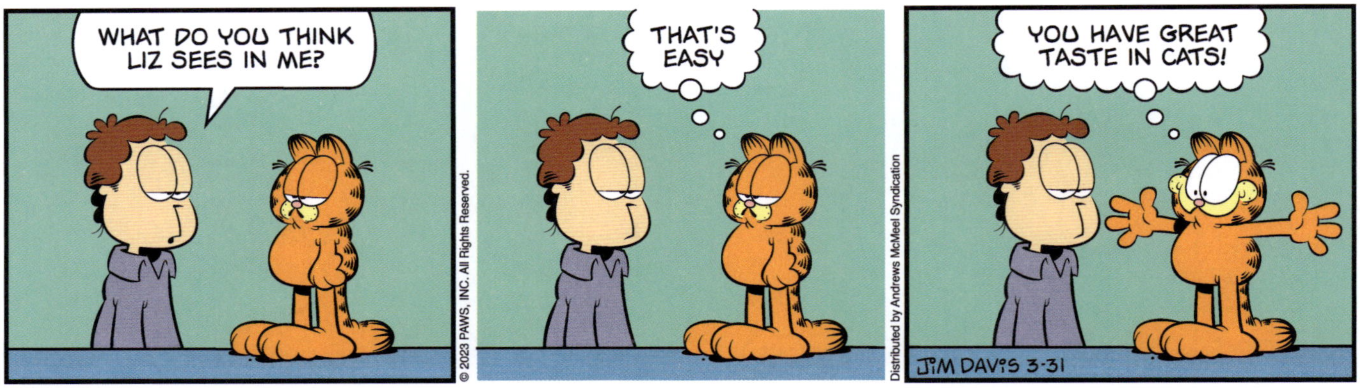
WHAT DO YOU THINK LIZ SEES IN ME?
THAT'S EASY
YOU HAVE GREAT TASTE IN CATS!
JIM DAVIS 3-31
© 2023 PAWS, INC. All Rights Reserved.
Distributed by Andrews McMeel Syndication

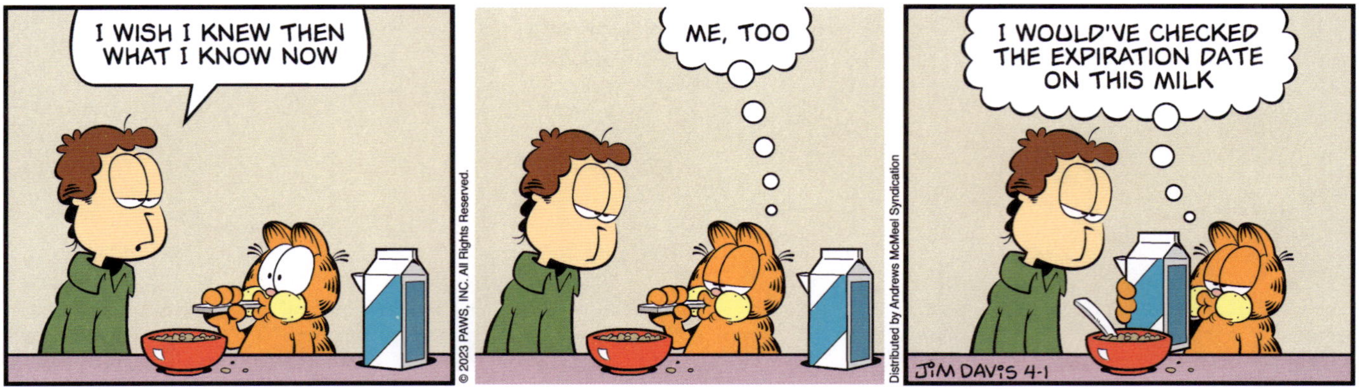
I WISH I KNEW THEN WHAT I KNOW NOW
ME, TOO
I WOULD'VE CHECKED THE EXPIRATION DATE ON THIS MILK
JIM DAVIS 4-1
© 2023 PAWS, INC. All Rights Reserved.
Distributed by Andrews McMeel Syndication

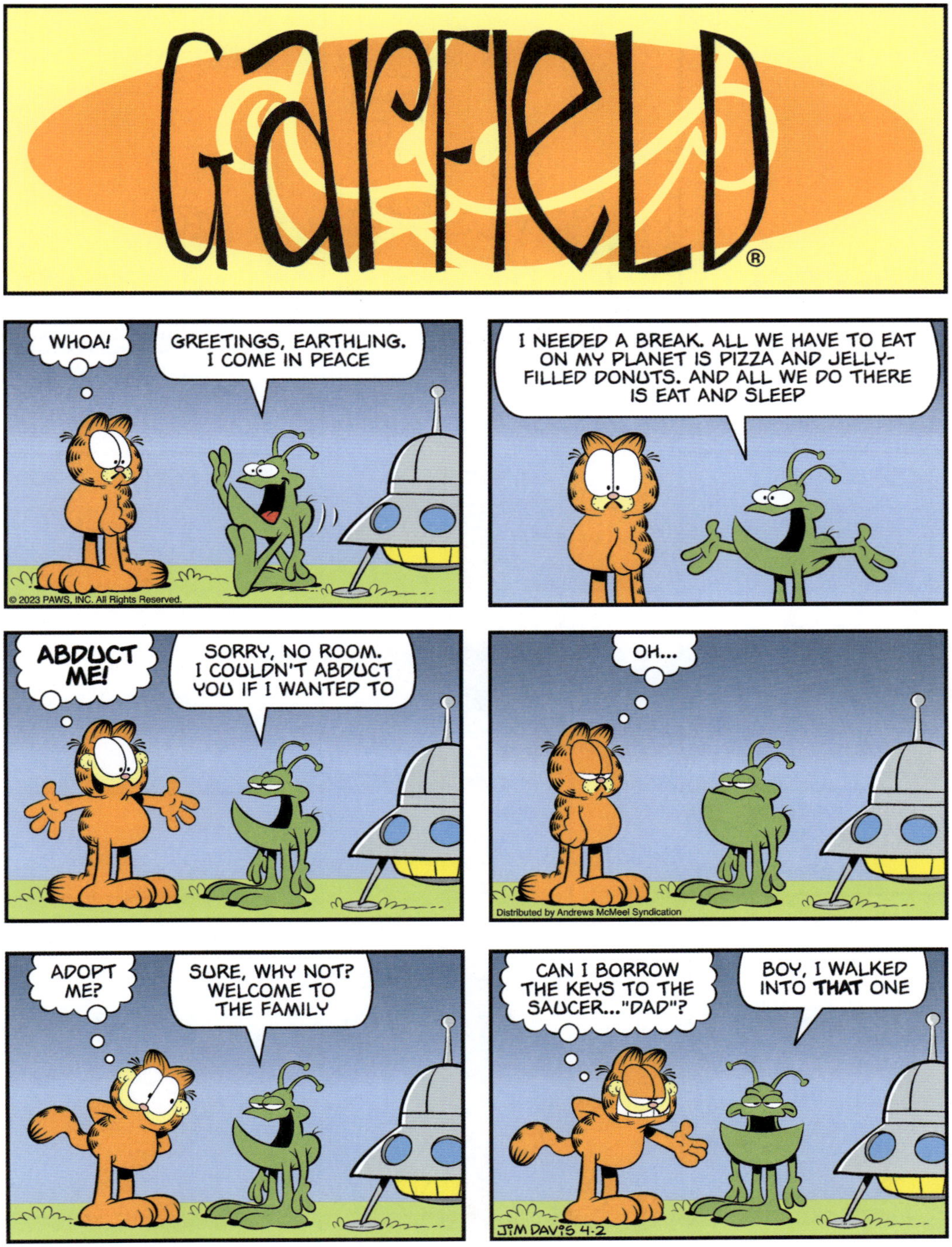
GARFIELD®
WHOA!
GREETINGS, EARTHLING. I COME IN PEACE
© 2023 PAWS, INC. All Rights Reserved.
I NEEDED A BREAK. ALL WE HAVE TO EAT ON MY PLANET IS PIZZA AND JELLY-FILLED DONUTS. AND ALL WE DO THERE IS EAT AND SLEEP
ABDUCT ME!
SORRY, NO ROOM. I COULDN'T ABDUCT YOU IF I WANTED TO
OH...
Distributed by Andrews McMeel Syndication
ADOPT ME?
SURE, WHY NOT? WELCOME TO THE FAMILY
CAN I BORROW THE KEYS TO THE SAUCER..."DAD"?
BOY, I WALKED INTO THAT ONE
JIM DAVIS 4-2

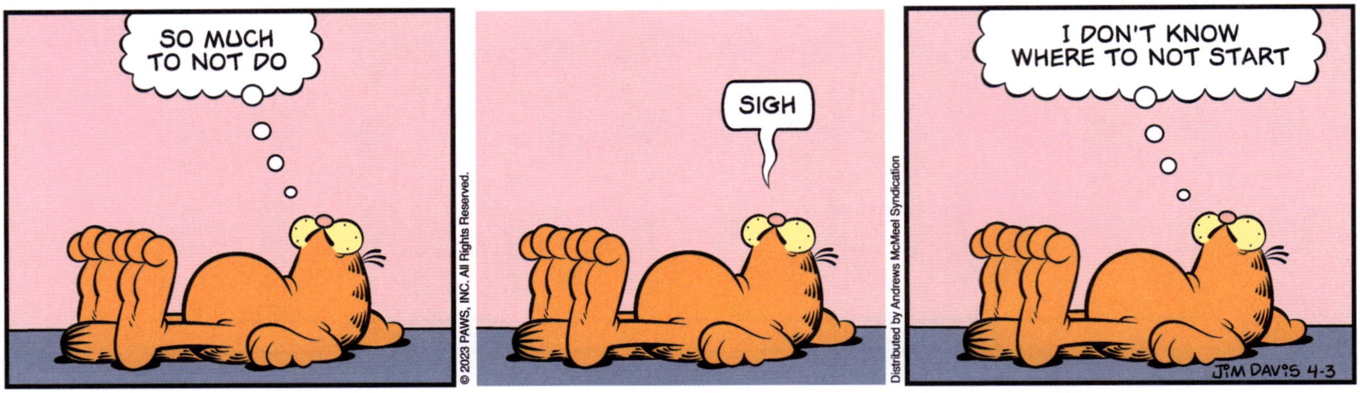
SO MUCH TO NOT DO
SIGH
I DON'T KNOW WHERE TO NOT START
JIM DAVIS 4-3
© 2023 PAWS, INC. All Rights Reserved.
Distributed by Andrews McMeel Syndication

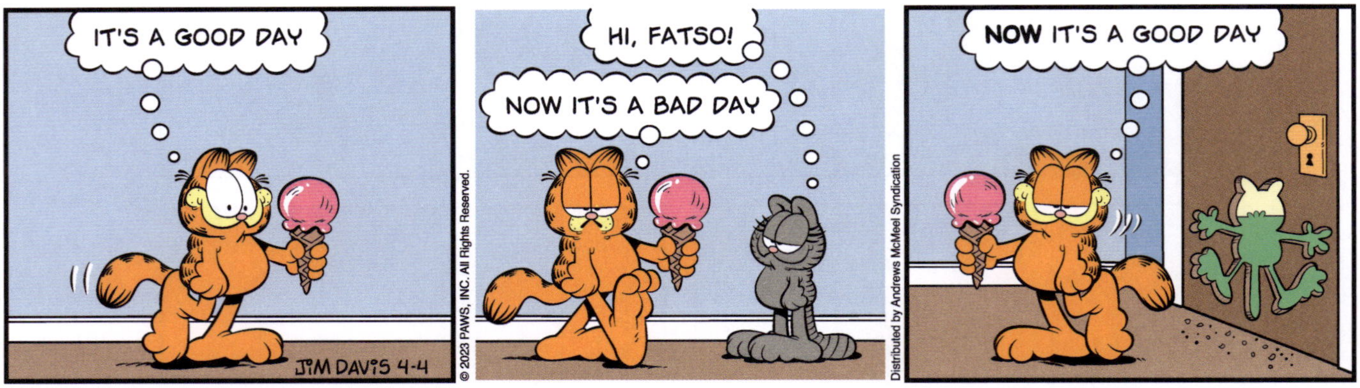
IT'S A GOOD DAY
JIM DAVIS 4-4
HI, FATSO!
NOW IT'S A BAD DAY
NOW IT'S A GOOD DAY
© 2023 PAWS, INC. All Rights Reserved.
Distributed by Andrews McMeel Syndication

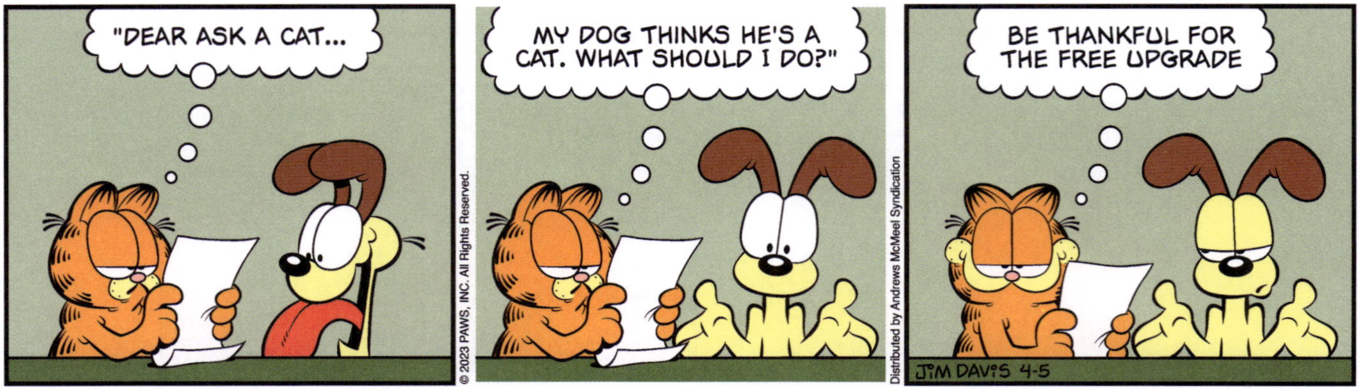
"DEAR ASK A CAT...
MY DOG THINKS HE'S A CAT. WHAT SHOULD I DO?"
BE THANKFUL FOR THE FREE UPGRADE
JIM DAVIS 4-5
© 2023 PAWS, INC. All Rights Reserved.
Distributed by Andrews McMeel Syndication

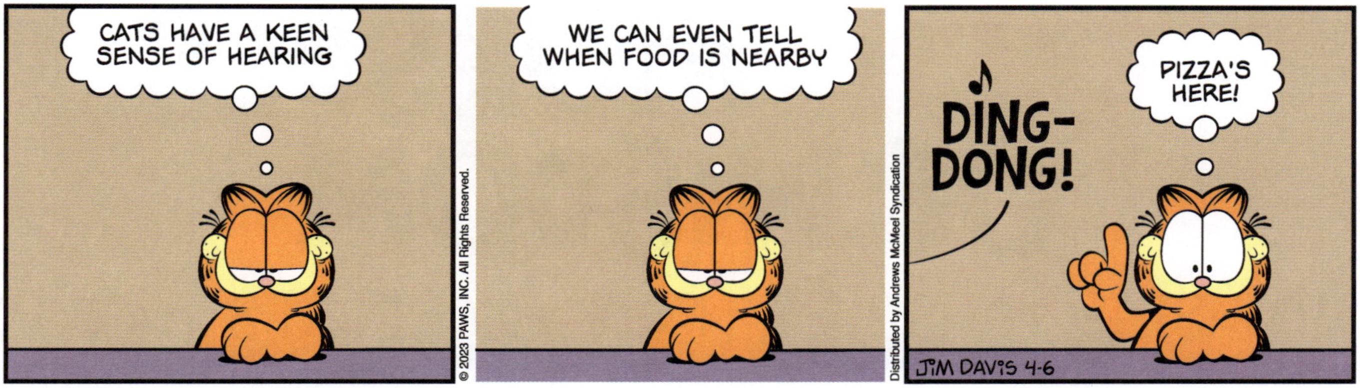
CATS HAVE A KEEN SENSE OF HEARING
WE CAN EVEN TELL WHEN FOOD IS NEARBY
DING-DONG!
PIZZA'S HERE!
© 2023 PAWS, INC. All Rights Reserved.
Distributed by Andrews McMeel Syndication
JIM DAVIS 4-6

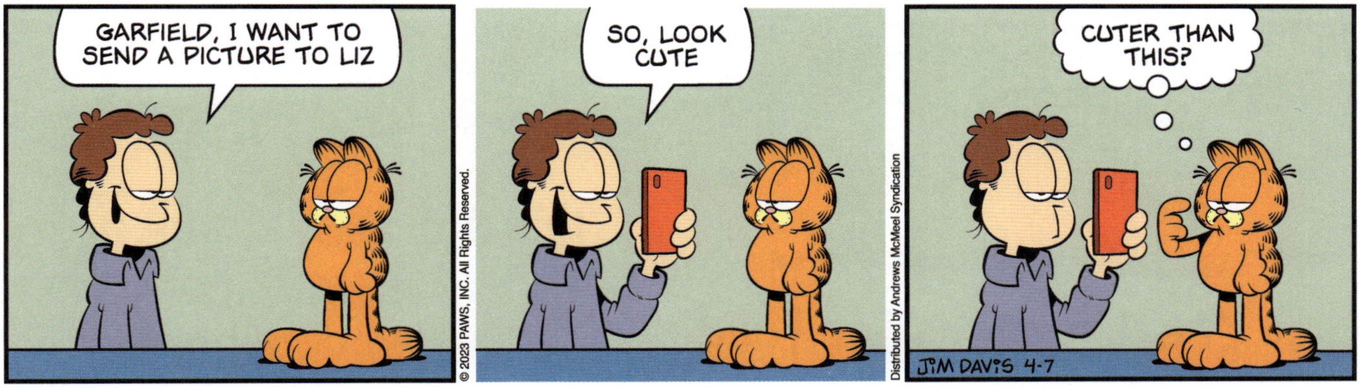
GARFIELD, I WANT TO SEND A PICTURE TO LIZ
SO, LOOK CUTE
CUTER THAN THIS?
© 2023 PAWS, INC. All Rights Reserved.
Distributed by Andrews McMeel Syndication
JIM DAVIS 4-7

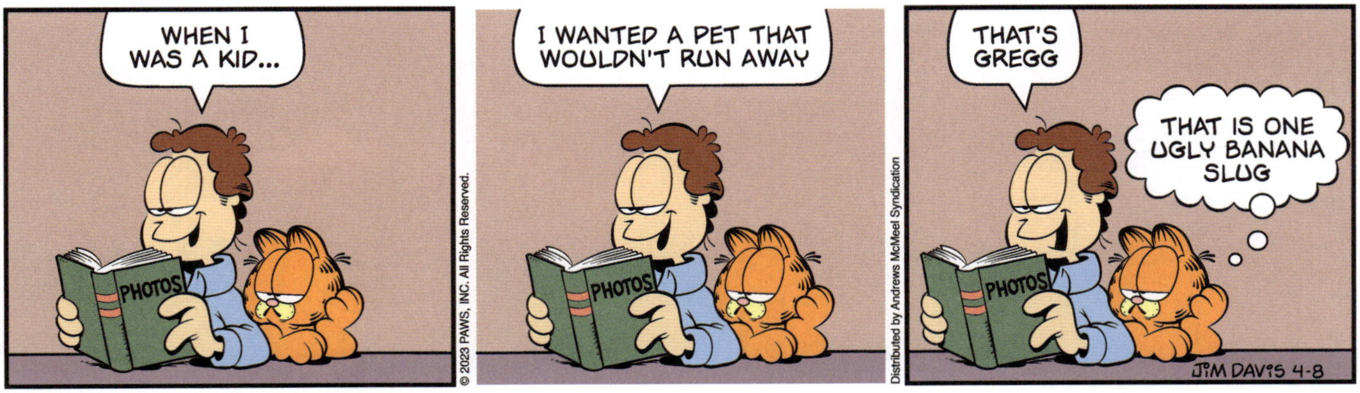
WHEN I WAS A KID...
I WANTED A PET THAT WOULDN'T RUN AWAY
THAT'S GREGG
THAT IS ONE UGLY BANANA SLUG
PHOTOS
© 2023 PAWS, INC. All Rights Reserved.
Distributed by Andrews McMeel Syndication
JIM DAVIS 4-8

MORE MORSELS OF WISDOM

Amusing musings from America's furriest philosopher

Go to great lengths for food.

It's not easy doing nothing. You never know when you're done.

The world doesn't run on money. It runs on coffee.

Love is taking the dog breath with the dog.

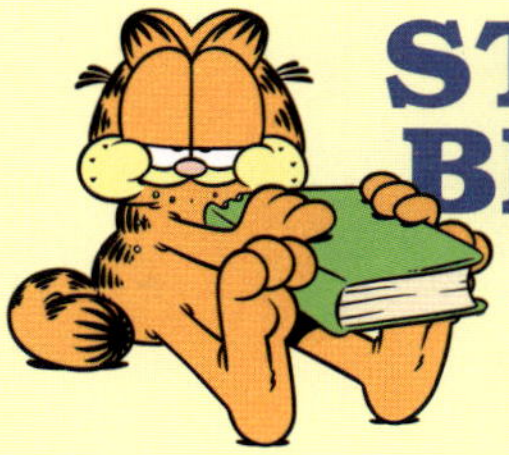

STRIPS, SPECIALS OR BESTSELLING BOOKS...

GARFIELD'S ON EVERYONE'S MENU.

Don't miss even one episode in the Tubby Tabby's hilarious series!

✿ GARFIELD AT LARGE . . . (#1) 978-0-345-44382-3
✿ GARFIELD GAINS WEIGHT . . . (#2) 978-0-345-44975-7
✿ GARFIELD BIGGER THAN LIFE . . . (#3) 978-0-345-45027-2
✿ GARFIELD WEIGHS IN . . . (#4) 978-0-345-45205-4
✿ GARFIELD TAKES THE CAKE . . . (#5) 978-0-345-44978-8
✿ GARFIELD EATS HIS HEART OUT . . . (#6) 978-0-345-46459-0
✿ GARFIELD SITS AROUND THE HOUSE . . . (#7) 978-0-345-46463-7
✿ GARFIELD TIPS THE SCALES . . . (#8) 978-0-345-46909-0
✿ GARFIELD LOSES HIS FEET . . . (#9) 978-0-345-46467-5
✿ GARFIELD MAKES IT BIG . . . (#10) 978-0-345-46468-2
✿ GARFIELD ROLLS ON . . . (#11) 978-0-345-47561-9
✿ GARFIELD OUT TO LUNCH . . . (#12) 978-0-345-47562-6
✿ GARFIELD FOOD FOR THOUGHT . . . (#13) 978-0-345-47563-3
✿ GARFIELD SWALLOWS HIS PRIDE . . . (#14) 978-0-345-91386-9
✿ GARFIELD WORLDWIDE . . . (#15) 978-0-345-91754-6
✿ GARFIELD ROUNDS OUT . . . (#16) 978-0-345-49169-5
✿ GARFIELD CHEWS THE FAT . . . (#17) 978-0-345-49170-1
✿ GARFIELD GOES TO WAIST . . . (#18) 978-0-345-49173-2
✿ GARFIELD HANGS OUT . . . (#19) 978-0-345-49174-9
✿ GARFIELD TAKES UP SPACE . . . (#20) 978-0-345-49178-7
✿ GARFIELD SAYS A MOUTHFUL . . . (#21) 978-0-345-49179-4
✿ GARFIELD BY THE POUND . . . (#22) 978-0-345-52558-1
✿ GARFIELD KEEPS HIS CHINS UP . . . (#23) 978-0-345-52559-8
✿ GARFIELD TAKES HIS LICKS . . . (#24) 978-0-345-52587-1
✿ GARFIELD HITS THE BIG TIME . . . (#25) 978-0-345-52589-5
✿ GARFIELD PULLS HIS WEIGHT . . . (#26) 978-0-345-52594-9
✿ GARFIELD DISHES IT OUT . . . (#27) 978-0-345-52595-6
✿ GARFIELD LIFE IN THE FAT LANE . . . (#28) 978-0-345-52600-7
✿ GARFIELD TONS OF FUN . . . (#29) 978-0-345-52601-4
✿ GARFIELD BIGGER AND BETTER . . . (#30) 978-0-345-52605-2
✿ GARFIELD HAMS IT UP . . . (#31) 978-0-345-52606-9
✿ GARFIELD THINKS BIG . . . (#32) 978-0-425-28516-9
✿ GARFIELD THROWS HIS WEIGHT AROUND . . . (#33) 978-0-425-28559-6
✿ GARFIELD LIFE TO THE FULLEST . . . (#34) 978-0-425-28564-0
✿ GARFIELD FEEDS THE KITTY . . . (#35) 978-0-425-28569-5
✿ GARFIELD HOGS THE SPOTLIGHT . . . (#36) 978-0-425-28574-9
✿ GARFIELD BEEFS UP . . . (#37) 978-0-345-44109-6
GARFIELD GETS COOKIN' . . . (#38) 978-0-345-44582-7
GARFIELD EATS CROW . . . (#39) 978-0-345-45201-6
GARFIELD SURVIVAL OF THE FATTEST . . . (#40) 978-0-345-46458-3
GARFIELD OLDER AND WIDER . . . (#41) 978-0-345-46462-0
GARFIELD PIGS OUT . . . (#42) 978-0-345-46466-8
GARFIELD BLOTS OUT THE SUN . . . (#43) 978-0-345-46615-0
GARFIELD GOES BANANAS . . . (#44) 978-0-345-91346-3
GARFIELD LARGE & IN CHARGE . . . (#45) 978-0-345-49172-5
GARFIELD SPILLS THE BEANS . . . (#46) 978-0-345-49177-0
GARFIELD GETS HIS JUST DESSERTS . . . (#47) 978-0-345-91387-6
GARFIELD WILL EAT FOR FOOD . . . (#48) 978-0-345-49176-3
GARFIELD WEIGHS HIS OPTIONS . . . (#49) 978-0-345-49181-7
GARFIELD POTBELLY OF GOLD . . . (#50) 978-0-345-52244-3
GARFIELD SHOVELS IT IN . . . (#51) 978-0-345-52419-5
GARFIELD LARD OF THE JUNGLE . . . (#52) 978-0-345-52584-0
GARFIELD BRINGS HOME THE BACON . . . (#53) 978-0-345-52586-4
GARFIELD GETS IN A PICKLE . . . (#54) 978-0-345-52590-1
GARFIELD SINGS FOR HIS SUPPER . . . (#55) 978-0-345-52593-2
GARFIELD CAUTION: WIDE LOAD . . . (#56) 978-0-345-52596-3
GARFIELD SOUPED UP . . . (#57) 978-0-345-52598-7
GARFIELD GOES TO HIS HAPPY PLACE . . . (#58) 978-0-345-52602-1
GARFIELD THE BIG CHEESE . . . (#59) 978-0-345-52604-5
GARFIELD CLEANS HIS PLATE . . . (#60) 978-0-345-52608-3
GARFIELD CHICKENS OUT . . . (#61) 978-0-425-28515-2
GARFIELD LISTENS TO HIS GUT . . . (#62) 978-0-425-28557-2
GARFIELD COOKS UP TROUBLE . . . (#63) 978-0-425-28562-6
GARFIELD FEEDS HIS FACE . . . (#64) 978-0-425-28567-1
GARFIELD EATS AND RUNS . . . (#65) 978-0-425-28572-5
GARFIELD NUTTY AS A FRUITCAKE . . . (#66) 978-0-425-28576-3
GARFIELD SLURPS AND BURPS . . . (#67) 978-1-9848-1773-0
GARFIELD BELLY LAUGHS . . . (#68) 978-1-9848-1777-8
GARFIELD EASY AS PIE . . . (#69) 978-0-593-15640-7
GARFIELD GOES HOG WILD . . . (#70) 978-0-593-15642-1
GARFIELD WHAT LEFTOVERS? . . . (#71) 978-0-593-15644-5
GARFIELD LIVIN' THE SWEET LIFE . . . (#72) 978-0-593-15646-9
GARFIELD ROAD PIZZA . . . (#73) 978-0-593-15648-3
GARFIELD HOME COOKIN' . . . (#74) 978-0-593-59919-8
GARFIELD FULLY CAFFEINATED . . . (#75) 978-0-593-59921-1
GARFIELD DONUT DISTURB . . . (#76) 978-0-593-87333-5

DVD TIE-INS

GARFIELD AS HIMSELF . . . 978-0-345-47805-4
GARFIELD HOLIDAY CELEBRATIONS . . . 978-0-345-47930-3
GARFIELD TRAVEL ADVENTURES . . . 978-0-345-48087-3

AND DON'T MISS . . .

GARFIELD AT 25: IN DOG YEARS I'D BE DEAD . . . 978-0-345-45204-7
GARFIELD'S JOKE ZONE/INSULTS . . . 978-0-345-46263-3
GARFIELD FAT CAT 3-PACK/ VOL. 1 . . . 978-0-345-46455-2
GARFIELD FAT CAT 3-PACK/ VOL. 2 . . . 978-0-345-46465-1
GARFIELD FAT CAT 3-PACK/ VOL. 3 . . . 978-0-345-48088-0
GARFIELD FAT CAT 3-PACK/ VOL. 4 . . . 978-0-345-49171-8
GARFIELD FAT CAT 3-PACK/ VOL. 5 . . . 978-0-345-49180-8
GARFIELD FAT CAT 3-PACK/ VOL. 6 . . . 978-0-345-52420-1
GARFIELD FAT CAT 3-PACK/ VOL. 7 . . . 978-0-345-52588-8
GARFIELD FAT CAT 3-PACK/ VOL. 8 . . . 978-0-345-52599-4
GARFIELD FAT CAT 3-PACK/ VOL. 9 . . . 978-0-345-52607-6
GARFIELD FAT CAT 3-PACK/ VOL. 10 . . . 978-0-425-28558-9
GARFIELD FAT CAT 3-PACK/ VOL. 11 . . . 978-0-425-28566-4
GARFIELD FAT CAT 3-PACK/ VOL. 12 . . . 978-0-425-28578-7
GARFIELD FAT CAT 3-PACK/ VOL. 13 . . . 978-0-345-46460-6
GARFIELD FAT CAT 3-PACK/ VOL. 14 . . . 978-0-345-49175-6
GARFIELD FAT CAT 3-PACK/ VOL. 15 . . . 978-0-345-52585-7
GARFIELD FAT CAT 3-PACK/ VOL. 16 . . . 978-0-345-52592-5
GARFIELD FAT CAT 3-PACK/ VOL. 17 . . . 978-0-345-52603-8
GARFIELD FAT CAT 3-PACK/ VOL. 18 . . . 978-0-399-59440-3
GARFIELD FAT CAT 3-PACK/ VOL. 19 . . . 978-0-425-28561-9
GARFIELD FAT CAT 3-PACK/ VOL. 20 . . . 978-0-425-28571-8
GARFIELD FAT CAT 3-PACK/ VOL. 21 . . . 978-1-9848-1775-4
GARFIELD FAT CAT 3-PACK/ VOL. 22 . . . 978-0-593-15638-4
GARFIELD FAT CAT 3-PACK/ VOL. 23 . . . 978-0-593-15639-1
GARFIELD FAT CAT 3-PACK/ VOL. 24 . . . 978-0-593-15650-6
GARFIELD FAT CAT 3-PACK/ VOL. 25 . . . 978-0-593-87349-6
GARFIELD'S 20TH ANNIVERSARY COLLECTION . . . 978-0-345-42126-5
SEASON'S EATINGS: A VERY MERRY GARFIELD CHRISTMAS . . . 978-0-345-47560-2
GARFIELD'S GUIDE TO EVERYTHING . . . 978-0-345-46461-3
ODIE UNLEASHED! . . . 978-0-345-46464-4
GARFIELD'S BOOK OF CAT NAMES . . . 978-0-345-48516-8
THE GARFIELD JOURNAL . . . 978-0-345-46469-9
LIGHTS, CAMERA, HAIRBALLS!: GARFIELD AT THE MOVIES . . . 978-0-345-49134-3
30 YEARS OF LAUGHS AND LASAGNA . . . 978-0-345-50379-4
GARFIELD MINUS GARFIELD . . . 978-0-345-51387-8
GARFIELD FROM THE TRASH BIN . . . 978-0-345-51881-1
GARFIELD LEFT SPEECHLESS . . . 978-0-345-53058-5
MY LAUGHABLE LIFE WITH GARFIELD . . . 978-0-345-52591-8
GARFIELD'S SUNDAY FINEST . . . 978-0-345-52597-0
AGE HAPPENS: GARFIELD HITS THE BIG 4-0 . . . 978-0-345-52609-0
GARFIELD COMPLETE WORKS: VOLUME ONE: 1978 & 1979 . . . 978-0-425-28712-5
GARFIELD COMPLETE WORKS: VOLUME TWO: 1980 & 1981 . . . 978-0-425-28713-2

✿ **New larger, full-color format!**

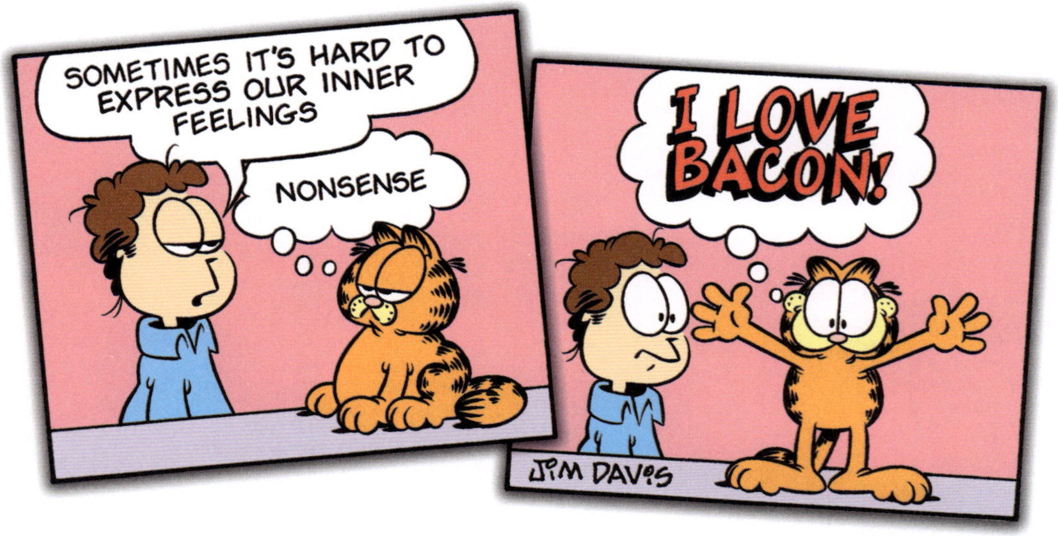
SOMETIMES IT'S HARD TO EXPRESS OUR INNER FEELINGS
NONSENSE
I LOVE BACON!
JIM DAVIS